BUILDING
STRIP-PLANKED BOATS

With Complete Plans and Instructions for
a Dinghy, a Canoe, and a Kayak You Can Build

NICK SCHADE

AUTHOR OF *The Strip-Built Sea Kayak*

Mc
Graw

Camden, Ma..London Madrid
Mexico City...Sydney Toronto

Library of Congress Cataloging-in-Publication Data

Schade, Nick.
    Building strip-planked boats : with complete plans and instructions for a dinghy,
a canoe, and a kayak you can build / Nick Schade.
        p.   cm.
    Includes bibliographical references and index.
    ISBN 0-07-147524-9
    1. Boats and boating—Design and construction.   2. Boatbuilding—Amateurs'
manuals.   I. Title.

VM353.S29   2009
623.82'07—dc22   2008048457

2 3 4 5 6 7 8 9 10 11 12 13 14 15 16   WFR/WFR   1 9 8 7 6 5 4 3 2 1 0

44313624   8/10
ISBN 978-0-07-147524-2
MHID   0-07-147524-9

Photos and illustrations by the author

McGraw-Hill books are available at special quantity discounts to use as premiums and
sales promotions or for use in corporate training programs. To contact a representative,
please e-mail us at bulksales@mcgraw-hill.com.

To my late wife Cathy's mother, Helen.
Without her love and support, I would have a lot less experience
with boatbuilding to put in a book.

Contents

Contents

Acknowledgments

In the twenty-five (or so) years since I first laid strips on a set of forms to build a strip-planked boat, I have learned and benefited from many people in a wide variety of ways. My parents let me and my brother mess around with tools and pound nails into wood, so I always felt like I was a boatbuilder—even when what I built didn't really deserve to be called a boat. My brother, Eric, was there at the first strip boat—it was a canoe he was building for which he recruited my assistance, and that got me started down this road. My late wife, Cathy, encouraged me to quit my real job and move forward with building boats. Michael Vermouth of Newfound Woodworks gave me a place to continue when Cathy passed away. Cathy's mother, Helen Stern, treated me as her son and made it possible for me to keep going when, in other circumstances, I would have had to try something else. Paul Smith of the American Craft Museum encouraged me to try harder. The many participants of my kayak-building bulletin board at KayakForum.com provided all kinds of good ideas and innovations and made me put more thought into what I was trying to do. John Harris at Chesapeake Light Craft took a bet on my business and me that made the time spent working on this book easier to justify. Bob Holtzman, formerly of International Marine/Ragged Mountain Press, got me started working on this book, and Jon Eaton deserves a lot of credit for the patience to let me bring it to completion. Finally, Robin's encouragement, faith, and support were a blessing that made the long months spent working on this book much easier to take.

Part I

The Background

Chapter 1

Introduction

Let's get this clear from the start: it is a waste of time to build your own wooden boat. These days there are far quicker ways to get yourself on the water than going down to a basement shop, fooling around with a bunch of weird tools, making a big mess, and spending time being careful to do it right. You can go out to the local boating store and buy a boat ready to go that will be perfectly serviceable, getting you where you want to go with a lot less fuss and bother.

Instead of wasting your time building a boat you could be at work earning more money, so you can afford the really high-quality glitter on your fiberglass boat, or maybe a hydraulic elevator to lift a plastic barge onto the roof of your car, or something else useful.

There are few reasons to build a wooden boat that make practical sense on a cost-benefit chart, but for some reason lots of people still want to do it. It may be that they just enjoy the process of converting a raw board into a mode of transportation. I think there is more to it than just an excuse to buff the rust off their tool collection. There is some ineffable quality to wood boats that makes them attractive. The quality goes beyond the strict physical appearance because even rather ordinary-looking boats are attractive when built of wood. Wood grain lends an eye-catching complexity to a surface that simply can't be achieved with synthetic materials.

Building a boat is a big project. It takes time, some physical effort, and a lot of concentration and thought. If all you are looking for is a nice boat, there are plenty of other options out there. If you want an inexpensive craft to go fishing in, there are cheaper options available than building one yourself. If all you really want is a pretty wooden vessel, you may be better off getting someone else to build it for you. Don't take on the task if the idea of the project itself does not appeal to you. On the other hand, building a boat is a break from a world of instant gratification and impending deadlines. You will probably end up bleeding or with a painful splinter at some point during the project. It is very possible that the job will cause you to get angry and swear. But it is also a chance to invest time in making something of value with your own hands.

There is something special about boats. Lots of projects can satisfy the bug to build things, but there are few projects accessible to the average do-it-yourself craftsperson that you can travel in. Unlike a bookshelf, a boat isn't just another inanimate object; it is a partner in exploring new territory. Creating this partner with your own hands, deliberately fitting each piece in place, bleeding on it, dripping sweat as you proceed, and agonizing over each detail fills the vessel with value. It is the challenge and time that you put into it that makes the project worth doing.

The Strip-Building Method

Over the thousands of years that humans have been building small vessels for venturing out on the water, people have created hundreds of different methods for constructing those craft. Traditional boatbuilding typically involves creating a frame and a waterproof shell. The frame usually provides the structural strength of the boat while the outer surface is primarily a means of keeping water out so the boat will float. The frame will often consist of some form of backbone, such as a keel, plus ribs supporting the shell. The backbone provides the basis for strength along the length of the boat. The ribs define the shape of the boat and back up the outer shell. The shell may be in the form of planking, or in the case of traditional kayaks it may just be a layer of sealskin.

A more recent technique fastens multiple small wood strips edge to edge and then encapsulates this shell under layers of fabric and glue. This is the *strip-building* or *strip-planking* method. With strip-built construction, the outer shell provides both the structure and the watertight integrity of the boat. This *monocoque* (French for "single shell") structure includes the strength of the ribs and backbone into the waterproof skin of the boat in one integrated, lightweight, and strong piece. In traditionally built small boats, such as a canoe or Adirondack guide boat, the outer surface was ¼-inch-thick (6 mm) cedar supported by a structure of ribs every 4 or 5 inches (10 to 12 cm) held in place with small tacks or screws. In a strip-built boat the strip thickness may still be ¼ inch or less, but the ribs have been replaced with a woven fabric such as fiberglass, Kevlar, or carbon fiber adhered to the wood with epoxy resin.

You may notice that the title of this book refers to strip-planked boats, yet I often use the term *strip-built*. In traditional boatbuilding methods, planks are fairly heavy boards that you fasten to a structure of internal frames, but in the method described in this book, there are no internal frames; the "planks" are very thin strips of wood that, in themselves, represent much of the boat's structure. That's why I use the term *strip-built* most often, but it means the same thing as strip-planked.

Strip-building is simple in concept: bend a bunch of narrow, flexible strips around a set of forms, and cover them with a waterproof reinforcement. And—unlike many seemingly simple concepts—it is actually relatively simple to do. The strip-built method is well suited for mak-

ing small boats with minimal tools. It doesn't require extensive training or skill, and it is tolerant of mistakes. While first-time builders may have trouble building a boat that looks exactly how they want, it is very likely that they will build a boat that performs the way they want. It is the nature of the strip-built method that big mistakes are hard to make, and little ones don't hurt.

Because the wood is encapsulated in fiberglass and epoxy, it is quite certain that the finished boat will not leak, even if elsewhere your craftsmanship is not perfect. The epoxy seals all but the largest holes. The fiberglass also reinforces weak joints, making them much stronger. With the wood under a protective coat of epoxy and fiberglass it will not rot. Because the fiberglass and epoxy are perfectly transparent, the full beauty of the wood shines through.

Some builders of larger boats use a technique, also called strip-planking, in which strips of wood that are the same thickness as traditional boat planks, but narrower from top to bottom, are secured together with glue and maybe some nails, but they don't necessarily sheathe the wood in fabric and resin. This technique works well for larger boats that need thicker planking, but for small, lightweight boats, the fiberglass or other reinforcing fabric saturated with epoxy or other resin is a critical part of the building process. Since this book is tailored toward small, cartoppable boats, it assumes all the wood will be encapsulated in resin and fabric.

This "composite" structure comprising wood, glass, and plastic overcomes a lot of problems with wood boat construction while giving many advantages over standard modern fiberglass construction. The epoxy seals the wood from exposure to moisture, virtually eliminating the possibility of rot. The elimination of fasteners like nails and screws does away with localized stress concentrations that can cause failures. And wood is one of the most structurally efficient materials available. This means that for a given weight of material you will be able to make a stiffer panel from wood than any

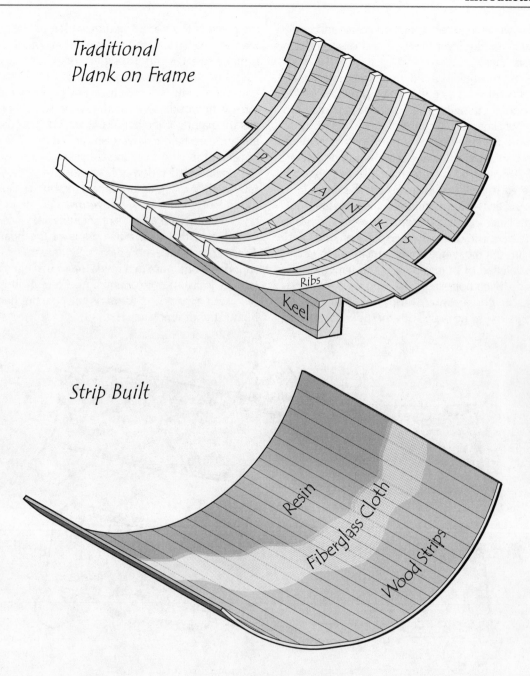

*Traditional
Plank on Frame*

P
L
A
N
K
S

Ribs

Keel

Strip Built

Resin

Fiberglass Cloth

Wood Strips

Figure 1-1. *Traditionally, boats were built with a backbone-like keel with ribs defining the shape. This frame of ribs was then covered with planks to make a watertight hull. The frame provided most of the strength. While the planks provided some strength, without the ribs supporting them, they would split. In strip construction a monocoque shell provides both the strength and the watertight hull. The thin outer planks are reinforced across the grain with fiberglass fabric secured and sealed in place with epoxy resin.*

other material. Although wood is soft and easily scratched, the layer of fabric and resin protects the surface.

Traditional boatbuilding requires high-quality wood. Since the wood provides all the structural strength, poor grain can create serious weaknesses. Because of the way the wood functions in the structure, strip-building is much more tolerant of lower-quality wood and squirrelly grain. The sandwich of fiberglass-wood-fiberglass acts much like a steel I-beam.

In an I-beam primarily the top and bottom flanges carry the load. The vertical web in between just keeps the two flanges separated. As a result the flange on the outside of the bend is stretched or in tension and the flange on the inside is compressed. The web in between is also in compression. Strip-built construction works the same way, with the fiberglass taking

the place of the flanges and the wood acting as the web. Because wood is strongest in compression the result is very strong for its weight.

In brief, the process of strip-building a boat consists of making a building form, covering the form with wood, covering the wood with fiberglass, covering the fiberglass with epoxy, covering the epoxy with varnish, and then finally covering the varnish with scratches as you use the boat. Stated this way it sounds pretty easy. Obviously the details are important, but it helps to think of it in these simple terms.

The forms are a series of sections, like slices of bologna, that define the shape of the boat. These forms are secured to a *strongback*, the supporting structure that holds the forms in their correct location and orientation. Careful setup of the strongback and forms assures the finished boat is the desired shape.

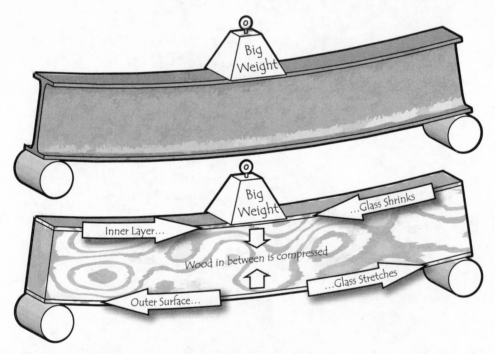

Figure 1-2. *The lightweight strength of the strip-planked shell is achieved in the same way that an I-beam keeps a bridge strong and lightweight. In an I-beam the webs at the top and bottom of the vertical spacer carry most of the force. If these webs were not separated they would bend easily; by spacing them apart, they must either stretch or shrink before the beam bends. On a strip-planked boat, the wood acts as the separator and the fiberglass replaces the web.*

A lightweight softwood such as cedar or pine is generally used. The wood is cut into thin strips about 1 inch (2.5 cm) by ¼ inch (6 mm), or a bit less. This wood is edge-glued together and temporarily secured to the forms with staples. When the forms have been completely covered, the staples are removed and the wood is smoothed with scrapers, planes, and sandpaper.

The lightweight fabric (fiberglass, Kevlar, or carbon) is draped over the prepared wood and trimmed to size. Epoxy resin is then poured and brushed onto the fabric. This bonds the cloth to the wood, and in the case of fiberglass, the fabric becomes completely clear. When the epoxy cures, the shell of the boat is removed from the forms. After smoothing the inside of the boat, the inside is similarly reinforced with fabric and epoxy.

With decked boats like kayaks, the deck and hull are then joined together. More epoxy is added to the outside of the boat to smooth out the fabric texture. This is then sanded smooth. Any outfitting such as seats or gunwales can now be added. Finally, everything receives a protective coat of varnish. Varnish not only enhances the appearance of the boat but also protects the epoxy from sun damage. Every few years you will want to give it a light sanding and reapply the varnish. With a minimum amount of care, you can enjoy your boat for many years.

What You Need to Build a Boat

The tools required to build a strip-built boat are modest. One of my primary tools is an old Swiss Army knife given to me by my grandmother when I was a kid. The only large power tool needed is a table saw to cut the strips. If you don't have one, you will need to borrow a table saw for half a day or so. In addition, you will need some small tools like a block plane, a handsaw, and a sander.

You will need a covered workspace with some control over the temperature. (Remember, the space needs to be a few feet larger than the boat!) You also need a way to get the boat out of the shop. Taking a wrecking bar to the house to extricate a finished boat is more common than people would like to admit, but that doesn't mean it is fun.

Building a boat takes time. You will need some patience. The boat won't be finished tomorrow, but that is part of the beauty of the project. You are putting quality time into making a quality object. You need to be able to resist the urge to take shortcuts. If you want instant gratification, just go out and buy a boat.

Most important, you need a comfy chair in your shop. This is called the "moaning chair." It is there to catch you when you cut your last piece of good wood too short or drill a hole below the waterline. This piece of furniture is a key tool you will use to prevent taking a chainsaw to your project. Remember that almost everything can be fixed if you spend enough time sitting in the moaning chair to come up with a solution. While strip-building is a pretty fault-tolerant means of making a boat, it is inevitable that somewhere along the way you will make use of the moaning chair.

Three Strip-Building Projects

The first ten chapters of this book detail the tasks and methods involved in just about all strip-built boatbuilding projects. The last three chapters describe three boats that you can build using those techniques and demonstrate several design-specific tasks such as installing gunwales and seats.

The Coot, a pram-bowed dinghy, is very easy to build and an excellent first project for anyone the least bit nervous about his or her ability to build a boat. This will make a fine tender for a larger boat.

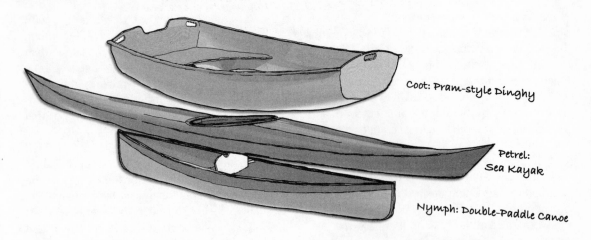

Coot: Pram-style Dinghy

Petrel: Sea Kayak

Nymph: Double-Paddle Canoe

Figure 1-3. *The boats used as examples in this book demonstrate many techniques that are useful for building just about any small boat using the strip-planked method. The Coot is a simple dinghy with transoms at both ends and plywood seats. The Petrel is a sophisticated sea kayak with full deck and coaming. The Nymph is a lightweight double-paddle canoe with a thwart seat.*

The Nymph is a small solo canoe for double paddle with a few features that make it slightly more complicated, and the building as shown involves a few tricks and special materials. Consider it an intermediate-level course in strip-building.

The Petrel is a sea kayak designed for rough waters. As the only fully decked boat of the three, it inherently involves a bit more work, and its cockpit, while highly functional, is also somewhat elaborate. I went all out on the example shown, tricking it out with many optional features—some functional, others cosmetic—to demonstrate how far you can take strip-building if you wish.

Strip-building a boat lets a beginning boatbuilder create a fully functional boat without a lot of skill. It lets a novice builder create a beautiful boat without compromising the performance of the result in any way, and an experienced strip-builder can produce a spectacular work of art that is lightweight, strong, and efficient on the water. There are quicker ways to make your own small boat but few that offer the combination of accessibility for the first-time builder, on-the-water performance potential, and sheer beauty of the finished product.

The goals of this book are to introduce strip-building to beginners, to provide new ideas to novice builders, and to help experienced builders bring their work to the next level. First I describe the general process and then I provide plans and instructions for three different boats. I hope that after reading this book you will have the confidence to tackle building any of the boats I describe, or just about any other small boat using these methods.

Chapter 2

Materials

With all the developments in material science of superstrong substances for aerospace and the military, you would think that wood would be left in the dust. It seems unreasonable that stuff that literally grows in trees could measure up to the performance properties of materials that go into outer space or at Mach speeds. Yet for a lot of purposes wood is actually stronger for its weight than the most exotic modern materials.

Wood

Wood is really what makes this boatbuilding thing all worthwhile. There are a bunch of ways you could go about building a boat that don't involve wood so much, but wood is pretty easy to work with in a home shop, it is lightweight and strong, and it just looks beautiful. What's not to like? It is really hard to go wrong with wood.

People often express surprise when I answer their queries into the weight of my boats. They are under the impression that wood is heavy. I was at a show recently where someone said, "Well, compared to plastic it weighs a lot." I asked him, if he took a chunk of a fiberglass boat and a chunk of wood, which would float? It is true that a big piece of firewood weighs more than a little plastic fork, but if you were to drop both into the water, only the firewood would float. This is because the firewood is less dense than the plastic. If you were to whittle away all the parts of the firewood that didn't look like a fork you would eventually end up with something the same size as the plastic fork. This wooden fork would still float. It would be

lighter than the plastic eating implement, and as a bonus it would be stronger than the plastic version.

If you are interested, there are books out there that will do some fancy calculations to demonstrate that, for its weight, wood is just about the strongest material currently available. Of course someone else may come along with a calculation demonstrating how his or her favorite material is somehow stronger. However, for our purposes it really doesn't matter exactly how strong wood is compared to exotic aerospace materials. Suffice it to say, wood is light and strong. It is a naturally occurring composite of fibers and resins that is hard for synthetic materials to beat. As a result, strip-planked boats are typically lighter and often as strong or stronger than commercially made fiberglass boats, and they are much lighter and stiffer than inexpensive plastic boats.

When selecting a wood, we are looking for the attributes just mentioned. We want something light and easy to work with. Knotty wood will make a fine-looking boat, but it is hard to work with. Lignum vitae, or ironwood, is really strong, but it's heavy enough that a board of it would sink. We could even cut a sheet of plywood into strips, but it would be weird looking. But that still leaves a lot of options.

Strips

This book is about strip-building boats, so for that we will need strips. These are typically produced by running a wood plank through the table saw multiple times, cutting off thin pieces of wood. The result is strips that are the width of the original board's thickness, and for most people, this will be the determining factor for strip width.

Typical strip thicknesses are about ⅛ to ⅜ inch. The strip thickness will depend on the size of the boat, type of wood chosen, and how the boat will be used. Large, heavy boats, those that will carry a lot of weight or will be subjected to high forces, will be better off with thick strips. Small, lightweight boats that will be gently used can get away with thinner material. Heavier woods will often allow the choice of a thinner strip while still maintaining good strength.

There are a lot of variables to consider, but they can be grouped into categories to help you make a judgment: how is it to work with, what does it look like, how will it hold up, and how much will it weigh.

Softwoods. The word *softwood* sounds pretty straightforward, but it really refers to wood that comes from conifers. In other words, the wood may be hard or soft, but the tree has needles and cones. There are some hardwoods that are softer than many softwoods, but in general softwoods are on the softer side. It happens that woods that are soft also tend to be lightweight. Maybe it is really the other way around—that light wood tends to be soft, and it also tends to be easier to shape and less strong. While they may be less strong, many types of softwoods still have good strength relative to their weight.

The standard wood for strip-building is cedar. Atlantic white and northern white cedar are not that easy to find, but they are lightweight and easy to work with. The wood is pale blond, with a little bit of visible grain. These woods are most readily available near where they grow. Atlantic white cedar is sometimes called boat cedar and grows along the eastern seaboard from Mississippi to Maine. Northern white cedar is native to the arboreal forest of Canada and ranges down into the northern United States and south along the Appalachian Mountains. Neither of the white cedars are available in long boards. The trees do not grow that big, but the wood is very nice.

More commonly available is western red cedar, which is often used as siding. Although the trees are native to the Pacific Coast in Oregon, Washington, and British Columbia, its long, clear grain and weather resistance creates demand. It is available in many lumberyards catering to high-end builders and is occasionally found in home centers. The wood varies in color from a pale blond similar to white cedar, through various shades of red and brown, to a deep maroon and rich chocolate. It is sometimes available in long lengths if full-length strips are desired for a longer boat.

Both the white cedars and western red cedar are considered the go-to woods for strip-building. They offer a good combination of strength and weight. They are easy to work with—they cut, plane, and sand easily. While they are naturally rot resistant, this is not really necessary. There are a variety of other trees that are related to these cedars that may provide useful strips.

Cypress grows in the swamps of the southern United States and provides a dark-blond wood with distinctive grain. It is harder, stronger, and heavier than the cedars but may be more readily available to builders who live in its natural range. You may be able to find nice long, knot-free boards at locally operated lumber yards and specialty wood suppliers.

Port Orford and Alaskan yellow cedar are both less common light-colored cedars. They are both at the heavier end of the spectrum but are quite tough. Alaskan yellow cedar is particularly well suited for accent stripes. It is very light in color and often has very little visible grain. While most cedars have quite pleasant smells, Alaskan yellow smells somewhat foul to some people.

Related to the cedars is redwood. This is a fairly brittle wood that is a little heavier than western red cedar. It can have a nice red tone that looks really nice; however, I have had trouble with epoxy bonding to it long term.

The rather intimidating table that follows shows the strength properties of some selected woods suitable for the strip-planked method.

The Specific Gravity column indicates the relative weight of each wood (lower numbers are lighter). The other columns indicate various forms of strength, in terms of bending, taking a hit, or being squeezed, stretched, or otherwise abused. For these, higher numbers are stronger. The nerds among us can get all excited by the different numbers; everyone else can notice that lighter woods are generally weaker, and stronger woods weigh more.

A fairly common cedar you may be able to find is eastern red cedar, also known as aromatic cedar. This is the stuff they make cedar chests from. While the wood is nice looking with distinctive color and grain, it grows in fairly small trees with a lot of branches, so it often has a lot of knots. The knots combined with being somewhat brittle make this wood hard to work with. However, the results may be nice if you have the patience.

If you have trouble finding cedar or need some contrasting colors, most other softwoods work well. Pine is pretty easy to find. You should be able to find clear, knot-free boards at most lumber outlets. Pine is heavier than cedar, has a consistent light yellowish color, and is easy to work with.

Although the spruce 2 by 4 studs available at most home centers are generally pretty poor quality, it is often possible to pick through the pile to find some nice clear specimens that can be milled into good strips. The strips will be heavier than cedar, but the price is right and, as long as the wood is dry, they should work well.

The bottom line is that just about any softwood can be used. Check your local lumber source and see what is available. Outside of North America your selection may be quite different from what is available here, but it is likely that there is something suitable.

Hardwoods. Hardwoods have traditionally been used only for trim on strip-built boats. Stems and gunwales are places where some tougher wood will help protect the boat from wear and tear. But there are reasons to choose hardwood for the strips. Although they tend to

be heavier, that gain in weight is usually offset with a gain in strength. This may allow you to use thinner strips to keep the weight low.

Unfortunately, many of the desirable softwoods are still being harvested from old-growth forests. This raises the ethical issue of whether we should be turning those trees into boats, even if they are pretty. And there is the practical issue that the old-growth wood is getting harder and more expensive to find. Most hardwood, on the other hand, is being harvested from second- and third-growth areas in a pretty sustainable manner. This makes hardwoods an option worth considering.

Being generally harder than softwoods, hardwoods are also harder to work with. Everything from ripping strips to sanding may take a little more effort and time on the harder of the hardwoods. But there are several hardwoods that aren't so hard.

The late boatbuilder and writer Robb White swore by tulip poplar. It is a fast-growing tree that reaches up to the sky straight and tall, showing off its tulip-like blossoms to whoever gets up high enough to see them. The wood is almost as light as cedar and is quite tough. It machines very easily. Although the color may be a little boring—a pale beige with occasional streaks of green that eventually turn muddy brown—poplar is a fairly common hardwood available at home centers at a good price.

Basswood is well known to wood-carvers and model makers as being lightweight and easy to work with. It ranges from white with almost no visible grain to a darker brown. While it is hard to find in long lengths, it makes a good strip material. Like poplar, you may find the color a little boring, but both poplar and basswood take stain well if you want to spice it up a bit.

Sometimes called white walnut, butternut is a low-density wood with a little bit more interesting grain than poplar or basswood. It is a light tan to pinkish or amber color with occasional dark-brown streaks. It machines easily and can be stained, but like basswood, it can be hard to find in long boards.

Mechanical Properties of Selected Woods Suitable for Strip Planking[1]

Species Common Name	Specific Gravity[2] (Dry)	Static Bending			Impact Bending – Height of Drop Causing Complete Failure (mm)	Compression Parallel to Grain – Maximum Crushing Strength	Compression Perpendicular to Grain – Fiber Stress at Proportional Limit	Shear Parallel to Grain – Maximum Shearing Strength	Tension Perpendicular to Grain – Maximum Tensile Strength	Side Hardness – Load Perpendicular to Grain (N)
		Modulus of Rupture (kPa)	Modulus of Elasticity (MPa)	Work to Maximum Load (kJ/m³)		(kPa) ——————————————— (kPa)				N
Hardwood:										
Ash	0.6	103,000	12,000	115	1,090	51,100	8,000	13,200	6,500	5,900
Basswood	0.37	60,000	10,100	50	410	32,600	2,600	6,800	2,400	1,800
Butternut	0.38	56,000	8,100	57	610	36,200	3,200	8,100	3,000	2,200
Cherry	0.5	85,000	10,300	79	740	49,000	4,800	11,700	3,900	4,200
Maple, Silver	0.47	61,000	7,900	57	640	36,000	5,100	10,200	3,400	3,100
Maple, Sugar	0.63	109,000	12,600	114	990	54,000	10,100	16,100	—	6,400
Oak, Red	0.63	99,000	12,500	100	1,090	46,600	7,000	12,300	5,500	5,700
Oak, White	0.68	105,000	12,300	102	940	51,300	7,400	13,800	5,500	6,000
Sassafras	0.46	62,000	7,700	60	—	32,800	5,900	8,500	—	—
Yellow Poplar	0.42	70,000	10,900	61	610	38,200	3,400	8,200	3,700	2,400
Softwood:										
Cedar:										
Atlantic White	0.32	47,000	6,400	28	330	32,400	2,800	5,500	1,500	1,600
Northern White	0.31	45,000	5,500	33	300	27,300	2,100	5,900	1,700	1,400
Port Orford	0.43	88,000	11,700	63	710	43,100	5,000	9,400	2,800	2,800
Western Red	0.32	51,700	7,700	40	430	31,400	3,200	6,800	1,500	1,600
Douglas Fir	0.48	90,000	12,300	72	660	47,600	5,300	9,700	2,700	2,700
Pine:										
Long Leaf	0.59	100,000	13,700	81	860	58,400	6,600	10,400	3,200	3,900
Sugar	0.36	57,000	8,200	38	460	30,800	3,400	7,800	2,400	1,700
Eastern White	0.35	59,000	8,500	47	460	33,100	3,000	6,200	2,100	1,700
Western White	0.38	67,000	10,100	61	580	34,700	3,200	7,200	—	1,900
Redwood	0.35	54,000	7,600	36	380	36,000	3,600	7,600	1,700	1,900
Spruce, White	0.4	68,000	9,200	53	510	37,700	3,200	7,400	2,500	2,100
Spruce, Sitka	0.36	65,000	9,900	65	640	35,700	3,000	6,700	2,600	2,300
Imported:										
Balsa	0.16	21600	3,400	14	—	14,900	—	2,100	—	—
Mahogany, African	0.42	73,800	9,700	57	—	44,500	—	10,300	—	3,700
Mahogany, True	0.45	79,300	10,300	52	—	46,700	—	8,500	—	3,600
Spanish Cedar	0.41	79,300	9,900	65	—	42,800	—	7,600	—	2,700

[1] Extracted from *Wood Handbook: Wood as an Engineering Material*, available online from the USDA Forest Service, Forest Products Laboratory.
[2] Specific gravity is the density relative to water where the specific gravity of water is 1. Lower numbers are lighter.
[3] Specific gravity calculated: volume wet, weight dry.

Figure 2-1. *Use this table to evaluate the strengths and weaknesses of your chosen material for strips.*

Those are some options in lighter-weight, softer hardwoods. They will be the easiest options to work with, but some of the more common harder hardwoods can produce spectacular results. Think of maple with its different figures: curly, tiger, bird's-eye, and so forth. The possibilities for a spectacular-looking boat are exciting. The downside of these figured woods is that they are notoriously hard to work with. However, with patience you should be able to make a strip-built boat out of any wood. Fairly common woods such as walnut, cherry, birch, and oak or less common such as locust, elm, or chestnut are all possible sources of strip material.

These heavier woods will obviously make a heavier boat if you use them at full thickness. At ¼ inch thick most of these woods will be fairly hard to bend. This is fine for a larger boat, but smaller boats have tighter curves that may be hard to conform your strips to. To save weight and to make it easier to fit to the forms, and with more expensive wood to get more strips from a board, you will want to use thinner strips with these woods.

Alternatives. Obviously if we can stray from the standard cedar and other softwoods into the area of domestic hardwoods, we could also go into some of the exotic hardwoods. Many of these woods are harvested from jungles where it may be better they stayed, but they do offer some exciting possibilities. Mahogany is well known for being easy to work with, strong, and beautiful. Spanish cedar is not only used for cigar humidors but also makes nice strips. I even know of a strip-built canoe made of ebony.

Again, due to the weight, strength, and expense of many exotics, thin strips become a good option. Thinner strips do provide less room for error, but presumably, with expensive material you are already being careful not to make mistakes.

You can even avoid wood altogether. All of the techniques described in this book can be adapted to synthetic materials such as foam.

At first blush you may think this is the perfect solution for the lightest boat. After all, foam is lighter than wood. It is usually true that foam is lightweight, but it is not as tough as wood. It tends to dent easily. Because of this, you often need to apply more fiberglass to protect the soft core, which will bring the weight back up. Working carefully, you can make a lightweight boat out of foam strips, but you may be able to make something just as light and even stronger with wood strips.

Plywood. Plywood is often a good choice for parts where a relatively flat, stiff panel is needed. You could make a transom by gluing up a panel of strips and then fiberglassing it, or you could just cut it out of a suitable piece of plywood. While I still like to protect my plywood under a layer of fiberglass and epoxy, using it where a large panel is needed can be a time-saver. Plywood is also useful for making some parts such as the recess around a kayak cockpit that have a simple bend in one direction.

While a layer of fabric on both sides will convert a cheap piece of plywood such as luan "door skin" into something much stronger and more waterproof, marine plywood is still worth considering. The primary difference between marine plywood and the other kinds is that the marine stuff does not have any interior voids or holes in the internal veneers. Voids accumulate humidity, which can lead to rot, and they represent weak spots in the structure.

While you could use fir marine plywood, it tends to have checks or cracks on the surface veneers that are hard to deal with, making it not very nice looking. Under a layer of reinforcing fabric and painted, it would probably be fine. For better-looking results, however, hardwood and mahogany plywoods are a good choice. A common material is okoume. This is available in thickness from 3 mm up to 1 inch. Okoume is a tropical wood related to mahogany. Another source of high-quality material is aircraft plywood and related birch plywoods that are available as thin as 1/32 inch.

Cove-and-Bead Strips. The strip-plank method is strongly associated with cove-and-bead strips. The cove-and-bead is much like a tongue-and-groove, but it can produce a tight joint even when the adjacent strips are oriented at an angle to each other. By milling a radius on one edge (a bead) and a matching hollow on the other edge (a cove), a ball-and-socket-like joint is created. As you strip around the curves of the boat, this joint will be pretty tight without a lot of fussing. The cove-and-bead is made by running each strip through a router, cutting the bead first and then the hollow, more delicate cove.

Notice that I did not say a "perfectly tight" joint. I'll get into that more in a moment, but first, a little background. It would seem to make sense to have the diameter of the cuts match the thickness of the strip: ¼-inch-thick strips suggest a cove that is ¼ inch in diameter. And indeed you can buy bits designed for this purpose.

Notice that a ¼-inch-diameter cove cut full depth into the edge of the strip will be ⅛ inch deep. If you push a ¼-inch-diameter bead ⅛ inch straight into a ¼-inch-diameter cove, and then try to rotate it down a bit, the "wings" at the edges of the cove immediately start push-

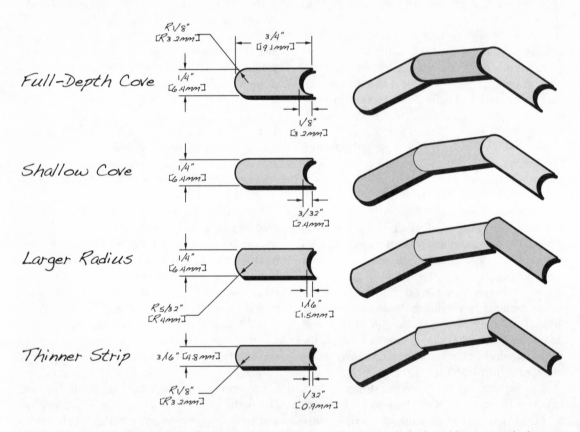

Figure 2-2. *The standard cove-and-bead strip for small boats is about ¼ inch thick and has a ¼-inch-diameter cove or bead on each end. The obvious thought is the cove should be ⅛ inch deep, but this can cause problems. Not only are the feather-edged wings on either side of the cove delicate and weak, but they can also make it hard to seat the bead all the way into the cove when the strips meet at an angle since the wings get in the way. A shallower cove that leaves a tiny square edge on either wing is a little more rugged, and it allows a little more freedom of rotation for easier tight fits on tighter angles. Milling a larger-radius cove-and-bead or using the same bit on a thinner strip also makes tight joints easier but may result in a less smooth surface.*

ing against the side of the strip and don't allow it to rotate without opening up a gap inside the joint. This internal gap will be hard to see as you build, but it may open up during fairing. It also weakens the structure a bit.

The first solution is to leave a little bit of a square edge on each wing. The second is to use a diameter for the cove and bead that is slightly larger than the thickness of the strip. For ¼-inch strips it may be hard to find a ⁵⁄₁₆-inch-diameter bit, so a ¼-inch bit may have to do, but you can also use that same bit on thinner strips.

Using a larger-diameter bit will help eliminate the internal gaps, but I have found that I can actually produce tighter joints by beveling each strip with a hand plane to fit, one at a time. While this method takes longer and requires more technique and skill, it allows for a very snug joint.

Cove-and-bead strips are not necessary to build a good boat. A tight, hand-planed bevel joint will be every bit as strong, and in some cases stronger than cove-and-bead. For very thin (⅛-inch) strips, hand-planed bevel joints are really the only viable option. It takes a lot of work to do the hand beveling, but with practice it becomes pretty routine. Complicated shapes, in fact, may actually be easier to accomplish because the bevel provides a natural stop for maintaining a difficult angle between two adjacent strips.

While cove-and-bead strips can be a time-saver, it depends on the boat how useful they are. It does take time to mill your own cove-and-bead strips accurately and consistently. If you are unable to do a good job with the initial milling, you may be better off just leaving the edges square and then beveling.

Details, Details

So, how thick is thick, how heavy is heavy, and how strong is strong? I was afraid you would ask. It is a complicated set of questions without hard-and-fast answers because it really depends

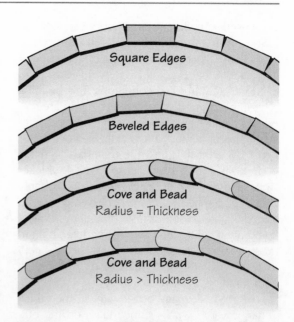

Figure 2-3. *For a quick and dirty boat or a design with lots of flat surfaces, square-edge strips leave some gaps, but epoxy will probably fill them in. However, the surface may be slightly uneven. Carefully hand planing bevels on the edges produces tight joints on the outside of the boat, but it takes a lot of skill to keep the gaps tight on the inside. Again the strips provide no assistance in keeping the surface even, so some additional sanding may be required. Using cove-and-bead strips where the diameter of the cove equals the thickness of the strip produces a smooth surface with initially tight joints, but sanding may open up hidden gaps. Using a larger diameter helps assure tight joints after sanding but may require a little more sanding.*

on what you are trying to accomplish. A dinghy that needs to be tied to a dock, fighting for space with the working skiff of the local lobsterman, probably needs to be stronger than a little canoe that will be used by the little old lady from Pasadena. The answer for one use is not necessarily the best choice in the next.

The baseline of strip-built canoe construction is ¼-inch-thick cedar covered with 6-ounce fiberglass. These scantlings have been used to build thousands of canoes and kayaks that have been used in a wide variety of conditions. Some have broken and failed, but most have survived years of use. If you are building a boat for one or two people that is going to be paddled in calm to moderately abusive conditions, this building schedule is a good starting point. If you are carrying more weight, or powering the boat with an engine, or venturing into extreme conditions, you may want to adjust the materials to make your boat stronger. A denser wood, thicker strips, and/or more or heavier glass are probably called for. Similarly, you may choose to go with thinner, lighter wood or less or lighter fiberglass if you are a lighter than average paddler, plan to race and are willing to shave a margin of safety to achieve better performance, or will restrict your paddling to mild conditions.

I have built many boats with 3/16-inch-thick cedar, covered with 4-ounce glass on the outside and exotic fabrics on the inside, and put them through a lot of abuse. I have successfully broken some, but it took a lot of work. Most boaters are not as willing to put their boat through the abuse I have subjected some of my boats to.

Part of your decision will be based on how you plan to abuse your boat. The forces a boat sees out in deep water in big waves is different from what happens when you run over a submerged stump, and this differs from dragging over rocks. With waves the forces are distributed over large areas; stumps stress small "point" areas; grinding over rocks is more abrasive.

Strength against distributed forces comes through stiffness. This allows the forces to be absorbed over the wide area. Thicker panels are stiffer, suggesting thicker strips. Point loads also benefit from stiffness, so long as the local spot that is subjected to the load is strong enough to survive the concentrated force. A harder wood under the glass can protect against a surface dent, as does a thicker layer of fiberglass. A dent in the surface is the first step toward a failure.

Another way to protect against a structural failure is to make the boat resilient. This is the opposite of stiff and requires thinner strips. A resilient boat will flex gracefully when it hits something. This is a little tricky, because if something is too flexible it won't handle large, distributed loads well. A boat that survives folding in half unharmed is not that useful if it folds in half while you are a mile offshore. But thin strips of a tough wood, with enough glass to hold it all together, could make a resilient boat. As a practical matter it may be pushing the limits of wood to make strip-built boats with thin enough strips to bend resiliently without breaking, but if you are an adventurous builder there are possibilities for building lightweight boats using thin strips.

Abrasion differs from getting hit by waves or running over a stump in that it is more of a surface issue. Abrasion occurs when a sharp object rubs against the boat. This could be the rough surface of barnacles or the sharp point of a hidden rock. The worst case may be a rock sharp enough to slice into the surface. While this kind of abuse may not result in catastrophic failure, over time it can mess up your boat. The best protection against abrasion is a solid layer of reinforcing fabric and epoxy. The wood under the fabric is less important than the protective shell of the resin and cloth.

Resin

One of the most significant downsides of wood is that it really doesn't play well with water. Traditionally built boats are constantly at battle with water. Water makes the wood swell up and get bigger. It then may dry out and get smaller. This opens up seams and loosens fasteners. At the same time little critters and plants find wood a nice place to set up housekeeping. The wood can provide food and shelter for a variety of organisms. All it takes for them to thrive is the presence of a little water and air. As a result wet wood will rot and deteriorate with time. This deterioration is not inevitable; with a little care to keep the wood dry it will last a long, long time.

The question is, how do you keep a boat dry? You don't actually have to keep the boat dry; you just want keep the wood dry. And the answer is—plastics.

Epoxy is a two-part liquid plastic that, when mixed together, becomes a hard, waterproof plastic. By sealing the wood under a plastic layer it is possible to keep the wood dry and free from rot.

Polyester

When most people who know a little bit about fiberglass think of fiberglass they are thinking about a very sticky, stinky liquid resin used to repair cars and large fiberglass boats. This stinky stuff is polyester resin. Polyester is a liquid plastic mixed with solvents that turn into a solid when exposed to a catalyst. It is relatively inexpensive, and you can control how quickly it hardens by adjusting how much catalyst you add. A small amount makes a slow batch; a lot can make a "hot" batch. As the resin hardens, the solvent is driven off, leaving very small holes in the plastic that will slowly absorb water and let it permeate into the wood.

Polyester resin is not a very good adhesive, so it doesn't bond to wood very well, but it can still be used for strip construction if you are trying to save money. I'm not sure it is worth it, but there are some old strip-built boats out there built with polyester resin, so it can't be too bad.

Vinylester

Vinylester is related to polyester resin, but it creates stronger chemical bonds during its curing reaction. It still contains the solvents used in polyester, but it absorbs less water. It has better physical properties than polyester overall, but it is also more expensive. If you are looking for something better than polyester, you might as well go straight to epoxy.

Epoxy

The standard resin used for strip-building boats is epoxy. It is strong, bonds well to wood, and is very resistant to water absorption. Epoxy uses two liquids mixed in precise proportions that fully react with each other to create a hard solid. The two parts of the mixture are typically called resin and hardener. This can be a little confusing because after the two parts are mixed together, the liquid is called resin. Epoxy does not typically contain any solvents, so everything in the two parts stays incorporated into the final product. If the proportions of the resin and hardener are not correct, the mixed resin will not cure completely and may be weak or may remain liquid even after the chemical reaction is complete.

The curing speed depends on the chemistry of the hardener. Most manufacturers formulate several different hardeners to control the speed, making a "fast" and a "slow" hardener. Because the correct proportions must be present in the mix, you cannot adjust the speed by varying the amount of hardener; however, you can use a mix of the fast and slow resins just so long as the total proportion of hardener to resin remains the same overall.

Epoxy bonds very well to wood and other materials, so it is the ideal material for bonding fiberglass to the wood strips. One of epoxy's biggest limitations is that the ultraviolet light in sunlight will cause it to degrade. If the surface of epoxy is left exposed to sunlight for a long time, it starts to deteriorate, becomes cloudy, and eventually just falls apart. This doesn't happen immediately, but any exposed epoxy should be protected with varnish or paint.

You will often come across the term *amine blush*, usually just called blush, associated with epoxy. Blush is a waxy coating that appears on the surface of some freshly cured resin. It is the result of a reaction between the chemicals in the resin and humidity in the air. While there are several brands of epoxy that are said to be blush-free, you should be aware of the possibility even when using these resins. I have found that even ostensibly blush-free epoxies will sometimes blush in really humid weather.

The problem with amine blush is that it interferes with the bonding of additional coats or layers of epoxy. Whenever it occurs, you should clean the surface thoroughly with water. Use fresh, clean water and a clean sponge or scouring pad to clean the whole boat. Dry the whole surface with a clean rag. Be sure the entire boat is dry before applying more epoxy.

Note that sanding off the blush is not as effective as washing. The sanding will clean some off, but it will just smear the rest of it around. The blush will also cause your sandpaper to gum up quickly.

If you think your epoxy has had enough time to cure, yet it still feels sticky, you may have blush. Try pressing your thumbnail into the epoxy; if you cannot easily scratch the surface the epoxy is probably cured and you just need to remove the blush. Take a wet rag, wipe a small patch of the surface, and then wipe it dry. If the surface no longer feels sticky, the problem was blush.

Safety

Whatever variety of resin you use, it is important to remember that they are reactive petrochemicals that you want to be careful handling. Epoxy can cause an allergic reaction and is a skin irritant. Polyester and vinylester resin can damage the respiratory tract and central nervous system. Use them in a shop with good ventilation, wear an organic vapor respirator, and wear protective gloves while handling them.

Despite all that scary stuff, it is possible to use the materials safely. Read the material safety data sheets (MSDS) for the materials you are using. Most epoxies are considered safe for use at home, but you should investigate any chemicals you bring into the house.

Reinforcing Fabrics

This fabric is really the key to the success of the strip-built method. It provides most of the reinforcement required to hold the boat together, and it creates a thick barrier between the rocks and water and the wood core. It is really pretty amazing stuff, and yes, there actually is fabric there over the wood.

It is often hard for first-time observers to wrap their mind around the idea that the outside surface of a strip-built boat is covered with fabric. They see the wood and just think that there is a lot of varnish on it. When they think of fiberglass they visualize the pink stuff in their attic and don't understand how there can be any form of cloth between their hand and the wood.

Fiberglass is not the only reinforcing fabric that can be used on strip-planked boats. It is just the only one that becomes completely transparent when saturated with resin. There are other synthetic materials that are also suitable for reinforcing the boat. We'll address these in the following sections.

Figure 2-4. To help keep the fabric clean and undistorted, make a fabric dispensing rack from 2 by 6 lumber and electrical conduit to hold the rolls. Shown on this rack are black carbon fiber cloth, Kevlar (straw colored), and some different kinds of fiberglass. The plastic keeps dust off the material.

It is the combination of the fabric reinforcement and the plastic resin that makes the system work. Whenever you try to bend something, the outside of the bent material is stretching in tension and the inside is shrinking in compression. Fibers are really good at resisting tension but, as they say, "you can't push a rope," so they need help in compression. The plastic of the resin is good at withstanding this compression. The resin also bonds the fabric to the wood and makes the wood and fabric work together as one integrated composite material.

Fiberglass

Fiberglass comes in several varieties that have different properties. The most common is E-glass, but some people use higher-strength S glass. They are both thin fibers of glass; the difference is in the chemical properties of the glass itself.

Figure 2-5. Reinforcing fabrics are available in a variety of materials. The white fabrics on the left are fiberglass, which becomes clear when saturated with resin. The black carbon fiber (top right) stays black. Woven tapes of different widths (middle right) are available for reinforcing and joining parts. The spool on the lower right contains carbon fiber "tow," an unwoven roll of fibers that can be used to make reinforcing ribs.

E-Glass. E-glass is just standard fiberglass. The only time people will use the term *E-glass* is when they want to differentiate it from S glass. If you go to a supplier and ask for fiberglass, you will generally get E-glass. The "E" stands for electrical, but that doesn't really matter for our purposes, since we don't really care if our boats are good electrical insulators. It is pretty much the same glass used in windows, the kind that looks a little greenish when you look at the edge of a pane. This color isn't really noticeable in the raw fabric, but if you have a piece next to some S glass, the S glass will look marginally whiter.

All fiberglass cloth starts out appearing white. This is due to light reflecting and refracting off all the little individual glass fibers. When it is saturated with epoxy resin, the individual strands no longer disrupt the light and demonstrate that they actually are clear. The glass and the resin have similar light-handling properties, so the glass completely disappears in the resin.

S Glass. The "S" in S glass stands for strength. It is a higher-strength material than electrical glass, with about 40% higher tensile strength and up to 20% higher compression strength. Otherwise the fabric handles just about the same as the standard E-glass. It cuts with the same scissors, and it wets out (fully saturates with resin) in the same way. However, it has slightly different optical properties from E-glass. As a result, while it still becomes completely transparent, it tends to bend the light a little bit in the fiberglass-epoxy layup. This means that it is not completely invisible in the finished boat. Close examination of the surface will reveal a faint weave pattern within the layup.

It is a good option if a high-strength layup is required but you don't want to obscure the wood with an exotic fiber like Kevlar or carbon.

Sizings. Reinforcing fabrics are not merely the base fiber woven into cloth. After the cloth has been woven, it is cleaned and treated. The cloth is then finished with a sizing that helps the resin bond with the material. There are a variety of different finishes that are compatible with different resin systems. Double check with your fiberglass supplier to be sure the cloth you order is compatible with the epoxy. This treatment does degrade with time, exposure to heat and humidity, and rough handling. Cloth is usually fine for a couple of years, but if it is several years old, the cloth should be tested if it is to be used in critical applications.

Weaves. The standard weave pattern for fiberglass is the typical over-under-over-under pattern known as plain weave. This pattern works well for just about all the uses we may have, but there are some other patterns, such as twill, where the yarns go over-over-under-under, or satin weaves, where they go over-under-under-under. The twill is better at conforming to complicated shapes than plain weave, while still holding together pretty well. Satin weaves con-

form even better, but they may get a little loose and distort easily.

Even within a weave style there can be differences. Some cloth has a very tight weave, whereas others are looser. A looser weave generally wets out easily, absorbing resin more readily because resin can get in and air can get out readily. Looser weaves also conform to tight curves better. On the other hand, it is possible to make a lighter boat with tighter weaves because less resin is needed to fill up the spaces between fibers.

Weight. Fabrics such as fiberglass, Kevlar, and carbon fiber are sold by weight per area, typically ounces per square yard. A standard-weight fiberglass for small boats is 6 ounces per square yard, referred to as 6-ounce cloth, and it is available from 24 ounces down to 1 ounce. The practical range for small boats is between 12 ounces and about 4 ounces, but in special situations lighter and heavier weaves may make sense.

Plain Weave   Twill Weave   4H Satin Weave

Figure 2-6. Fabrics are produced in many weave patterns. The "over-under-over-under" weave is called plain weave and is most typical. Keeping the yarns over a few extra times, or going under a few yarns before going over, produces fabrics with slightly different properties. The twill weave goes over two and under two. When made with two different yarns such as carbon and Kevlar, the pattern looks a little like houndstooth, with a distinctive repeating pattern. Because the yarns have few bends, there is less stress on the fibers, making them a little stronger. This is also true of satin weave where the yarns are under for several spots and hop over for one. This relatively loose weave is smooth and conforms easily to complicated shapes.

Exotic Fibers

There are a variety of materials out there beyond fiberglass that are suitable for reinforcing strip-built boats. Essentially, any fabric that can be used in composite layups with epoxy can be applied to wood strips. Unfortunately, none of them are as transparent as fiberglass. Generally those that start out white become somewhat translucent when saturated with resin, but many are essentially opaque. Due to this, they can be somewhat difficult to wet out.

Glass provides obvious feedback when it is completely saturated since it becomes clear. The opaque fabrics usually just become marginally darker when you apply resin, and this does not necessarily indicate they have been fully wet out. The cloth may be saturated, but there may not be enough resin to saturate through to the wood. Cloth that is not adhered to the wood will usually show up as a bubble or ripple in the otherwise smooth surface. Opaque fabrics require careful inspection before you complete the wet-out to assure that it is fully bonded to the wood.

Exotic fabrics are also more expensive. At the time of this writing Kevlar was about two and a half times the price of glass, and carbon fiber cloth was almost eight times the cost. Given the relatively small amounts used in these boats, the cost of the material will still be small compared to the amount of labor you will put into the boat, but you may decide that any benefit is just not worth the expense.

Kevlar. Kevlar is the material famous for being bulletproof. Kevlar is a brand of aramid fiber made by DuPont, but other brands, such as Twaron (from Teijin Aramid), are available. Technically, the bulletproof stuff is a slightly different product (Kevlar 29), but the stuff used on boats (Kevlar 49) is similar.

These fibers are very tough and tenacious. They really don't like to break. The material is also very low density. As a result the fabric suggests the possibility of making a strong, lightweight reinforcement for strip boats.

Unfortunately, it is not as straightforward as it first seems. Kevlar is a low-density material, so for a given volume it weighs less than fiberglass. But if you turn this around, a 6-ounce fabric weighs 6 ounces per square yard regardless of the material, so the low-density Kevlar takes up more volume than the glass. This means it will absorb more epoxy. In the final analysis the exotic cloth may result in a heavier boat unless you use a lighter-weight fabric than you would have used otherwise. While it may seem like an obvious choice to just switch to a lighter-weight fabric, the most commonly available Kevlar is 6-ounce. It is difficult to find lighter-weight versions.

Theoretically it will make the boat stronger. However, as a practical matter, given the resin absorption, you may do as well using a double layer of fiberglass. A hard hit will probably do similar damage to a boat made with one layer of 6-ounce Kevlar as it would to two layers of 6-ounce fiberglass, and the weight will be similar. While Kevlar may have a slight advantage, it has the downside of being hard to work with. It is difficult to cut, requiring special scissors, and is a little more difficult to wet out with epoxy than fiberglass.

Carbon Fiber. Carbon fiber is the miracle fiber of the moment. It is used in everything from hockey sticks to jet fighters. It has a reputation for being lightweight and strong. It also has a striking deep-black color with a distinctive glistening weave texture. The aerospace industry processes it into wings using high-pressure autoclaves to eke the most out of the material.

Because most of us don't have an autoclave kicking around in our basement, we need to lay it up in the same manner as fiberglass. As a result it runs into the same problem as Kevlar; even though carbon fiber itself is light, it absorbs more epoxy than fiberglass, so it is hard to get superlightweight layups by hand. However, it is stronger than fiberglass and results in a stiffer layup, so if you are willing to pay the extra expense to save a couple of pounds you can use a thin carbon fiber cloth to create a lightweight boat.

The downside of carbon fiber is that it is somewhat brittle. It will absorb a lot of energy before breaking, but it tends to fail suddenly when pushed too far. What carbon fiber does effectively is look dramatic. The deep black creates a nice contrast with the wood strips of the rest of the boat.

Carbon fiber is a little hard to work with. While it cuts easily with regular scissors and wets out easily, it is hard to tell when you have completely saturated the fabric.

Like Kevlar, carbon fiber is most commonly available at 6 ounces per square yard. Because of the lower density of the fabric, this can result in a heavier boat than 6-ounce fiberglass used in the same location. Carbon fiber is available in lighter weaves—2-ounce cloth is available—but can be even more expensive than Kevlar.

Hybrids. One way to get the properties of several kinds of fabric is to use a hybrid cloth that combines yarns of different materials. For example, a carbon–S glass cloth may have carbon yarns running the length of the roll, with glass fibers running crosswise. The carbon yarns can be laid across the boat acting as ribs, with the glass running lengthwise for additional reinforcement. Carbon-Kevlar cloth has the stiffness of carbon fiber with the final toughness of Kevlar.

The exotic fabrics have a certain sex appeal and can be used effectively to make a better boat, but the additional performance of these materials is often not proportionate with the added cost and hassle in their use. Use them with the knowledge that they are not going to make a huge difference in the weight, strength, or quality of the finished boat.

Tapes. Just about any type of fabric is available in a narrow tape form. These tapes can be used wherever a narrow piece of cloth is needed to reinforce the boat. Most tapes are woven specifically to be used in tape form and have a selvaged edge where the yarns that cross

the tape turn around and head back the other way. This is useful in that it keeps the edges of the tape from becoming frayed. The downside is the edge tends to be a little thicker than the body. Furthermore, fiberglass tape is available in pretty much one 9-ounce weight, which is a good compromise for a lot of uses but may be thick when used in conjunction with other thinner weights of cloth. The prewoven glass tape also does not seem to wet out as clear as the wider cloths.

It is possible to cut your own tape from wider rolls, just by using your scissors and cutting the width you need. This can be useful where you need long strips but don't need the heavy strength of the prewoven tape. There are also some specialty machine-cut tapes, but they are hard to come by.

One useful form of manually cut tape is bias tape. This is just a fancy name for strips of cloth cut on the bias with the cloth, or at 45 degrees to the weave. If you roll out a square of cloth onto a clean cutting surface and start cutting at one corner heading diagonally across the square toward the opposite corner, you are cutting on the bias. Cut a few strips of the width needed and you now have bias-cut tape.

The benefit of bias tape is that it conforms well to difficult shapes. With the fibers running diagonally across the tape, the fibers can move relative to each other like scissors. They can change angle easily. This allows the tape to get wider or narrower and otherwise distort quite easily. It is this ability to distort that we are looking for. On complicated surfaces or sharp angles the fibers need to adjust to conform, and the bias cut allows them to do so. Because the cloth distorts easily, you need to handle bias-cut cloth gently. Tugging on it will cause it to distort prematurely. Handle bias tape carefully.

Glues

Glue is used in two major ways in strip building. First the strips are glued together edge to edge. Second, after the strips are in place, another form of glue is used to adhere the reinforcing fabric to the wood. The first form of glue just needs to be able to glue wood to wood with a bond that is at least as strong as the wood. The other form is more specialized; it needs to be strong and waterproof and bond to wood as well as glass and other unusual substances.

Notice that I did not say the first form of glue had to be waterproof. Gluing the strips together sounds like something where you would want a waterproof adhesive, but it is not required. The fiberglass and epoxy will coat all the wood, completely encapsulating it in an impermeable layer of reinforced plastic. Even if this protective reinforcement is ruptured, very little water actually gets into the wood. As a result, waterproof glue is not needed between the strips.

Carpenter's Glue

The standard yellow wood glue (available under many trade names, including Elmer's ProBond and Titebond) is polyvinyl acetate (PVA). This is a water-based glue that cleans up with soap and water, dries quickly, and is quite affordable. There are actually waterproof versions of this type of glue on the market, but as stated above they are not required. You may feel that even if waterproof is not required, you might as well use a waterproof PVA if it is the same stuff, but adds an extra degree of safety. While this makes sense, I have not found that the waterproof version is really the same. The standard carpenter's glue has a nice "tack." When you press strips together, the standard glue will grab and hold the new strip quickly, and it will tend to stay in place. If you rub the two pieces together as you are assembling the joint, the seam bonds together very quickly. You still need to clamp or otherwise hold the parts in place for a few minutes longer, but by the time you have the next strip ready, the glue is generally strong enough to remove whatever you have holding the seam tight. I have found that the more waterproof PVA glues do not seem to have this property as much. I also find that some of the

more waterproof PVA glues do not dry as clear as the old standby. Of course, the formulations may change as time goes on, so you may have different results than I did.

PVA is actually a thermoplastic when it is dry. This means that heat will soften it and reactivate the glue. If you make a mistake, it is possible, if difficult, to heat up the wood and pull the joint apart. The downside of this property is, if you do not have tight joints, a boat left out in the sun may have some softening of the joints. This can result in some print-through of the seams to the outer surface, and in the worst case the stress may create a white line in the fiberglass. Striving for nice tight joints between strips can minimize the chance of this.

Cyanoacrylate

The most famous of this type of glue used an advertisement that featured a guy hanging from a hardhat glued to a steel I-beam. Cyanoacrylate (CA) glues like Super Glue cure very quickly and are quite strong, although they can be brittle. While they are expensive enough that I would not recommend them for gluing together a whole boat, their quick-cure capacity makes them a good clamp substitute for hard-to-hold objects. You can purchase spray accelerants that cause the glue to set up almost immediately. I use them in combination with other glues when I want a quick bond. You do not need to deal with the little tubes of glue typical of Super Glue. Several manufacturers sell larger bottles in a variety of different viscosities under trade names including Hot Stuff and Great Planes. I like a somewhat thick CA glue or a gel for most wood gluing.

Epoxy

The same epoxy resin that is used to wet out fiberglass fabric can also be used as glue. The epoxy used in building strip-planked boats is different from the hardware store consumer grade epoxy and 5-minute stuff. Five-minute epoxy has its uses for quick-tacking jobs, but I've switched to CA glue for most of those tasks. The epoxy used to wet out fiberglass and other fabrics is a liquid with a viscosity similar to heavy cream, usually with a mix of 2:1 (resin to hardener) or higher. Many people refer to this epoxy as the West System after the product developed by the Gougeon brothers. I usually use MAS resin, but the West System is a good choice, as is System Three. There are some other, less expensive brands that many people have used with good success. Ask around to get recommendations.

These low-viscosity resins are usually designed to flow into fiberglass and other fabrics to wet it out easily. Lower-viscosity resins do this faster and as a result are easier to use. They will also soak into the wood slightly to promote a strong bond. The mixed resin is used unmodified to seal wood, wet out fabric, and later, fill the weave texture. It can be used straight to glue wood to wood, but this is not really what it is designed for.

Straight epoxy has a fairly low viscosity and does not have much reinforcing ability. This is good when combined with fiberglass. The low viscosity lets it flow into the fabric, and the fabric provides the reinforcement. But used as a glue all by itself it often drains out of the glue joint, leaving a starved bond where there may be gaps or air pockets between the two pieces you are attempting to glue together. This is obviously not going to be as strong as you may wish.

To make a good glue from epoxy, you can add stuff to already mixed resin. Depending on what you are looking for, there are a variety of fillers that will thicken the resin or make it structurally stronger.

Colloidal Silica. A colloid is a dispersion of fine particles in another substance. Colloidal silica, sometimes called fumed silica, is essentially a really, really fine glass powder. You can add it to mixed resin to make it less viscous and harder. The amount you add will depend on how you

are going to use the mixture. A mayonnaise-like consistency works well for gluing wood pieces together, while a peanut-butter-like thickness is good for *fillets*, which are long, coved epoxy structures used to fill in sharp interior angles between two surfaces, such as where a bulkhead meets the inside surface of a hull. The peanut butter consistency is also good for creating wear protection on exposed surfaces such as along a keel line.

Sold under several brand names including Cab-O-Sil and Aerosil, it is a commonly available filler for use with epoxy and other resins. If you need only a little bit, or are looking for a substitute, common baking flour can be used. While the final product is not as hard, wheat flour will thicken resin quite effectively.

Wood Flour. Known to those not in the know as sawdust, wood flour can be used much like colloidal silica. Where the silica makes a whitish mixture, wood flour makes a brown substance that I like to call "dookie schmutz." The color will depend on the wood the dust was made from. A good source is the dust collector of your sander. While the pile under your table saw can be mined for epoxy filler, it will make a coarse, lumpy mix, whereas the sander provides smoother filler. One of the beauties of this filler is if you collect it from your own boat, you will have a filler that closely matches the color of the boat. It will typically be a little darker than the solid wood, but you can adjust the tone by adding some colloidal silica.

I use dookie schmutz where I want a fillet to ease the angle in a sharp inside corner such as the coaming to deck joint of a kayak. Because of the fibers in wood, wood flour adds some structural strength to resin, but the fibers are short enough that it doesn't amount to much.

Chopped Fiberglass. Short strands of chopped fiberglass, sometimes called "kitty hair," will add more strength to resin. This material is commercially available in a variety of lengths. Longer strands create a lumpy mix but are stronger; shorter pieces will mix more smoothly, with some loss of strength. Because mixing forces air into the mix, resin with chopped fiberglass is usually translucent with a milky cast to it. Chopped glass can be added to dookie schmutz where more strength is required or anytime you need a thick structural adhesive.

There are actually a wide variety of chopped fibers that may be added to epoxy resin. Kevlar and carbon fiber are both available in short chopped form. These fillers provide some of the properties of the materials in long fiber form, but with the ability to make a putty or glue.

Graphite Powder. While it sounds like it may be related to graphite cloth or carbon fiber, graphite powder does not have much strength. It is more like a lubricant. This fine black dust may be added to resin to make a coating or paint. The addition of the graphite makes the resin-coated surface quite slippery. If you coat the bottom of your boat with it, the boat will slide easily over rocks with less tendency to scratch. Perhaps obviously, the coating is black, which is usually fine for the bottom of the boat.

Microballoons and Microspheres. There are times when you want a lightweight filler. For example, you might need to fill in an area without adding much weight. What you want to do is add a lot of air to the resin and have it stay in while it cures. Maybe some tiny plastic balloons or itty-bitty glass bubbles? Phenolic microballoons and quartz microspheres are just the thing. You can mix these in the resin to create a low-density putty or filler. The phenolic balloons are reddish brown and the quartz are bright white. They can also be combined with the other fillers noted earlier to create a combination of properties. These lightweight fillers also help make the hardened epoxy easier to sand.

Polyurethane

A recently popular glue on the market is polyurethane based. The most famous of these is Gorilla Glue, but Elmer's and Titebond sell similar products. The glue reacts in the presence of water or humidity, becoming a strong, waterproof adhesive. With a good tight joint this glue works very well. In loose joints, the same chemical reaction turns the glue into a sticky foam that oozes out, sticking to everything. The foam is easy enough to remove, but it can make a mess of your tools and workbench. I have used this on stem laminations, and some people have substituted it for carpenter's glue between strips, but it makes a big mess and is hard to clean up, and I just don't find it worth the cost or effort.

Spray Adhesive

The best way to transfer full-size patterns onto form material is to glue them on. I often use 3M Super 77 that you can obtain from the hardware store, but woodworking suppliers sell a variety of spray adhesives for temporarily attaching patterns to wood. This is a task ideally suited to spray adhesive. Temporary versions are good if you want to be able to peel off the pattern, but I tend to leave the patterns in place. If I don't want the pattern to come off, I will spray both the material and the pattern and press them together.

You can also use some more aggressive spray adhesives such as 3M Hi-Strength 90 to glue foam padding onto seats or backrests.

Hot-Melt Glue

Every crafts shop and scrapbook supply store sells hot-melt glue, which is applied with a heat gun that melts the hard stick of glue. It is not exactly considered a good boatbuilding adhesive, with good reason. It is weak and softens up with heat. But it is fast acting. If you want a quick, temporary clamp, a drop of hot glue often does the trick. I use it instead of staples when I don't want to put holes in the strips. And there are places that will be reinforced with

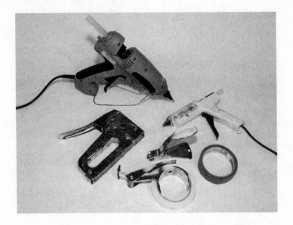

Figure 2-7. The strip planks need to be temporarily secured to the forms. The widely available T-50 utility staple on the lower left is the standard. I like the Bostich heavy-duty staple remover. It does a good job of pulling the staples without damaging the strips. If you prefer, hot-melt glue can be used instead of staples. The glue sticks are strong enough to hold the plank in place but weak enough to break when you are done. Masking tape or strapping tape also provides a good, quick, temporary clamp to hold together adjacent strips.

fiberglass and epoxy where the low strength is not a problem, but the quick set is a benefit.

A variety of formulations of hot glue are on the market, and they seem to change without much notice. I guess the scrapbookers aren't that particular about how their glue works. You should do some testing to make sure that it works the way you expect. Get a high-wattage glue gun that will quickly heat the glue. Some come with a temperature switch that can be useful when you don't need full power.

Tape

Another nontraditional boatbuilding material is tape. Masking tape and packing tape have a variety of uses from acting as temporary clamps to removing excess material when trimming

fiberglass. It is not a material that generally gets left in the boat, but more of a tool that helps in manufacturing.

Masking Tape

Masking tape is useful wherever you want to protect something from getting paint or other glop on it, but it has a lot of other uses as well. It can be used to help create a clean edge on fiberglass, clamp strips in place while glue dries, or protect the boat from sticking to the forms.

I use a lot of the blue painter's tape because it tends to peel off cleanly and can be left in place for a few days without drying out or becoming brittle.

Packing Tape

The fiberglass-reinforced packing tape makes a wonderful clamp when you need to apply more tension or pressure than the masking tape can handle. It can be hard to peel off, but if you fold over the end before sticking it down, it usually pulls up cleanly.

Waxed Paper

Waxed paper comes in amazingly useful in a variety of ways. If you need a slippery surface on the outfeed table of your table saw, a strip of waxed paper works great. If you are making a mess with glue and don't want to gum up your worktable, a strip of waxed paper makes cleanup easy.

Paint and Varnish

While it may not be obvious, the reason for paint and varnish is not to make your boat pretty; that's just a side effect of the real use. Epoxy and wood don't like sunlight. Ultraviolet light is hard on more things than just your skin. It breaks down chemical bonds and causes stuff to fall apart and fade.

Varnish and paint provide a protective layer over the materials that really matter. While the finish may fade, crack, and peel in time, it is better to have it happen to this outer layer than the important structure of the boat.

If you do a good job preparing the surface before applying the first coat of finish, a strip-built boat will not require much work when it comes time to refinish. Unlike traditional wooden boats where you need to sand down to raw wood, you usually only need to scratch up the existing finish a bit before applying more.

Spar Varnish

Spar varnish is the traditional finish for wooden boat parts that are left "bright." It is a clear mix of resins and UV protective additives that bonds to the wood and epoxy to create a protective barrier. This traditional finish is generally fairly straightforward to apply straight out of the can. You usually do not need to mix in any thinners, catalysts, or hardeners; just open the can, pour it through a filter, and brush it on. It can be sprayed if you have the right equipment, but it may need to be thinned down. I use Z-Spar Captain's Varnish from Pettit. I find it easy to use straight from the can, but even varnish from a home center should produce good results. Uncured epoxy can slow down the cure time of the varnish, so if you find your first coat takes a while to dry, don't panic; give it some time.

While not as durable as some of the modern finishes, good old varnish has proved reliable and long-lasting enough for most common uses. A matte or satin varnish looks very nice in some situations, but it is important to note that part of the UV protection of varnish comes from the gloss finish reflecting the harmful radiation away from the boat. The nonglossy varnishes are made dull by the addition of material that also makes it a little softer and less durable.

Polyurethane

Many modern varnishes are partially made of polyurethane, which is harder than traditional oils and resins and increases the longevity of the finish. Some can be used straight out of the can, but others must be mixed with a hardener or catalyst immediately before application. Some of these are quite noxious and should only be applied with professional protective equipment. Regardless of the noxious qualities, you will want to look for formulations with UV protective additives.

Harder finishes are less prone to scratching, but nothing is proof against dragging a boat over rocks. Even the hardest finish available is likely to get scratched up after a year of hard use and may require refinishing even if elsewhere on the boat is still in fine shape. Because harder finishes are more difficult to scratch, they are also more difficult to sand prior to applying the new finish.

Automotive finishes are a good option if you have access to the equipment to apply them. UV protection is a common property of car clear coats. If you know what you are doing, these finishes are a viable option for a boat.

Paint

While you may think it is a shame to cover the beautiful wood with paint, it is actually much better UV protection than any clear finish will ever be. A nice coat of paint on parts of the boat can accent the wood and make the whole boat look better. The primary difference between a marine paint and a good-quality household paint is the level of gloss. Marine paints tend to be shinier, and for that the manufacturers like to charge a lot more. Good-quality exterior household oil-based paint will work very well on a boat and will not be adversely affected by salt water.

Chapter 3

Tools

The tools required for strip-building small boats are modest. A beginner with a limited budget can do a good job with a few basic tools. These tools are common and useful additions to any toolbox if you don't have them already.

Hand Tools

Most of the work of building a strip boat can be done with hand tools, which is nice because they are quiet and generally pleasant to use. Many beginning woodworkers are intimidated by hand tools because they think they are fussy to work with. If there is one trick to making hand tools easier to use it is keeping them sharp. This applies particularly to edge tools like chisels and planes, but any device that is intended to cut even if it is not thought of as an edge tool, such as sandpaper or a rasp, will produce better results when new and sharp.

Students in my boatbuilding classes often have problems making their tools work when the tools are dull. For example, with a plane that isn't cutting, students will fiddle with the adjustments to try to make it work better, but instead they end up with a tool that is all jammed up and now really doesn't work. The solution is to keep your tools sharp.

Sharpening Tools

I cannot emphasize enough the benefits of sharp tools. Many people may have a plane or a jackknife they bought years ago and have never sharpened. Let me tell you right now that it is

dull. Even if you've only ever used it to spread peanut butter, it's dull. It was probably dull the day you bought it, and since then it has gotten duller just sitting in your sock drawer. If you've only used your plane once, that's probably because it was dull. If it had been sharp, you likely would have used it more often.

Counterintuitively, sharp tools are less likely to cause mistakes than dull ones. Sharp tools can be adjusted to remove less material, they are easier to control, and they are less likely to be overpushed, which causes unwanted cuts. This means that for reasons of safety as well as ease, you are better off with a sharp tool than a dull one. Sharp tools are a pleasure to use. Dull tools are endlessly frustrating.

Whole books have been written on sharpening hand tools. It is beyond the scope of this book to try to teach you everything you need to know to get your tools sharp. If you don't know how to sharpen your tools, please do some research to learn how to do it. An Internet search for "sharpening tools" will yield a wealth of information. See also the Bibliography section of this book for books on keeping your tools sharp.

If you are working with softwoods most of the time, your edge tools should stay sharp a long time, but a "long time" is measured in hours of work, not months or years. It is possible (but doubtful) the brand-new plane you bought was sharp when you got it, but after a day of consistent use, resharpen it whether you think it needs it or not.

A well-sharpened edge tool can be used to shave the hair off your arm; however, I don't want to see a bunch of boatbuilders with scarred arms, so I don't recommend you use your body as a calibrated sharpness testing device. Instead, try sliding the sharpened blade along the plastic barrel of a pen. If the blade immediately grabs into the pen it is sharp; if it slides it is not quite as sharp as it could be.

I could get all philosophical with you about how sharpening your tools is the essence of understanding your tools, but what matters is that edge tools cut by being sharp. It is possible today to purchase some very expensive hand tools. They aren't worth a thing if they are dull. The cheapest plane available will work quite well if you learn how to sharpen it. Better tools will not make you a better woodworker, but sharper tools will.

Stones. Try not to get too caught up in the specifics of what kind of stone to use. In the end the principles are the same; you use some sort of abrasive surface to grind away at the steel of the cutting edge until the edge has no radius on it. Then you proceed to finer abrasives until the cutting edge is polished. People use waterstones, oilstones, diamond stones, sandpaper, abrasive powders, files, and grinding wheels (wet and dry). They all work, each has its own benefit, but in the end they are all doing the same thing: grinding away at the steel.

Precision woodwork requires flat grinding surfaces. Softer sharpening stones will tend to "dish" as you use them and will require flattening. The work we are doing building these boats does not require the greatest precision, but a flatter grinding surface will reduce the amount of time spent sharpening.

Honing Guides. Don't be afraid to cheat. Some people may feel that clamping your blade into some fixture to hold it while you are sharpening is a sign of moral turpitude. The goal of sharpening is a good edge on your tool. It is not a path to enlightenment. A honing guide is designed to hold your blade at a consistent angle throughout the sharpening process. It helps assure you only do as much grinding as necessary. This makes sharpening faster and easier. Since the goal is to build a boat, not spend your time with your

Figure 3-1. Sharp tools make just about everything quicker, easier, and more precise. You can do a good job sharpening your tools with sandpaper stuck to a piece of glass, or use waterstones as shown. The little jig that holds the plane blade on the right will shorten the time spent sharpening, or you can use the more sophisticated jigs shown below the stones.

nose literally to the grindstone, anything that speeds up sharpening is a good thing.

There are a wide variety of honing guides available. The most sophisticated help you lock in an angle and create microbevels and all sorts of fun stuff. The cheapest ones just clamp on the blade and roll back and forth and are still very much up to the job.

Knives

When it comes to trimming things, nothing can beat a sharp blade on the end of a handle, commonly known as a knife. Knives can be used to trim strips, sharpen pencils, and remove squeezed-out glue.

Jackknife. My jackknife is probably one of my most used tools. I rough out strip shapes with it, peel up tape, and use the screwdriver blade to pull staples. I like a knife that takes a good sharp edge, has a thin blade, and is comfortable in my hand. I find a modest Swiss Army knife (not one of those with a gazillion blades) works well

Figure 3-2. The tool I use the most fits in my pocket. The little Swiss Army knife shapes most of my strips. The pocketknife below it works almost as well. A replaceable-blade utility knife has a variety of trimming uses but is not as good at shaping strips. A couple of chisels are useful for shaving down high spots.

for me. The thin blade cuts cedar strips without trouble, and the whole thing drops into my pocket easily. Having some other tool blades such as a screwdriver and awl on the knife has often proved handy. While these other blades are not as good as a full-size, dedicated screwdriver or awl, it is often convenient to have something close at hand.

I've tried some bigger folding knives with hefty blades, but I find the small blades work better. Thick blades tend to split strips instead of cutting them. You could probably do well with a fixed-blade whittling knife or some chip-carving knife, but you will want to find a convenient way to protect yourself from the blade while you wander around the boat.

Utility Knife. A retractable-blade utility or box knife is not a replacement for a jackknife or whittling knife, but it does have its uses. It doesn't work well for trimming strips because it is harder to control. Instead I use mine for trimming fiberglass. It does a fine job trimming the edge off fiberglass cloth that has been wet out with epoxy.

I find the retractable-blade utility knives with the reversible, replaceable, trapezoidal blades work better than the snap-off blade box knives, but both will work. Again, sharp is the key to these knives working well. Reverse, replace, or break off the blade when it gets dull. Don't spend time wrestling with a dull blade. By the way, the "safety"-style utility blades with the rounded tips are pretty worthless for most boatbuilding uses.

Planes

Planes are just fancy knives held in a convenient handle and jig. Various parts of this handle help limit the depth of cut, maintain an optimum cutting angle, and get the removed wood out of the way. The best ones have an easy way to adjust the depth of the cut.

Block Plane. A block plane differs from other types by having the blade bevel on the top, but this is not why they are useful for strip-building boats. They are also small, and much of the work you will do with them is likewise small. A block plane fits in the palm of your hand and can easily be used one-handed with the piece you are working on held in your other hand. You can also hold the plane so it cuts pushing away from you or turn it around so you pull it toward you. It is a handy little tool that can do precision work or remove material quickly.

There is a wide range in the quality of block planes available. Big-box stores will have some real abortions but may have one or two that are decent by Stanley or Record. You can find some very nice used planes at tag sales and through used tool dealers; typically these will be by Stanley. Specialty woodworking outlets have some really excellent modern planes by Lie-Nielsen, Veritas, and others.

Look for a plane that has some threaded adjustment for blade depth. There are good planes that require you to tap the blade in and out, but life is easier with a good depth adjustment. On larger block planes, look for

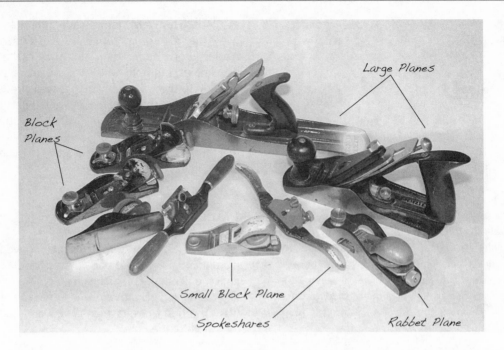

Figure 3-3. *Planes and spokeshaves provide great control for removing small amounts of wood. The little block plane front and center is my favorite. I use it for fitting all my strips, both in tapering strip ends and beveling their edges. It fits easily in one hand and can be pushed or pulled. The two similar block planes shown are also very serviceable; however, new versions of these may need a lot of tuning to get them working well. The larger planes at right don't get used as much, but they are good for creating long, tapered strips or fairly large, flatter surfaces. Also shown is a rabbet plane, with its blade extending all the way to the side of the foot. This allows you to adjust a bevel on a strip already on the forms. The spokeshaves can help fair rounded and concave areas.*

an adjustable throat, which lets you vary the width of the gap that shavings come through. A narrow opening helps control tear-out when working on funky grain. A wider opening allows big hunks of wood to come up easily so you can remove wood quickly. An adjustable throat is less common on the smaller planes.

Hold the plane in the palm of your hand before buying. You want it to fit comfortably without sharp edges cutting into your hand. As would be expected, you will get what you pay for. More expensive planes will generally use thicker, harder steel for the blade and will be machined with more precision.

Unlike furniture making where precision flat surfaces are required, strip-built boatbuild-

ing should not require the intensive tuning-up of a plane recommended by some woodworking magazines. However, you do want to make sure the plane doesn't have places where the shavings will jam up. If the leading edge of the sole has a sharp edge you might want to ease it with a file so it doesn't catch.

Rabbet Plane. A rabbet plane is much like a block plane except the blade comes all the way out to the edge so you can plane right up against a face. This is useful in certain operations, but it is not all that common a need. A shoulder plane or any plane where the blade extends all the way to the edge of the tool would do much the same work as a rabbet plane for our purposes.

Spokeshave. Take a small plane, stick handles out the sides, and you will get something like a spokeshave. They are designed for shaping wagon wheel spokes and offer a lot of control for rounding over long surfaces. They have a short foot, so they also work well getting into concave or hollow areas. They are made with a flat or rounded foot. I find the flat foot to be easier to use. Like block planes, spokeshaves may also be used on a push or pull stroke.

Scraper

A scraper is an edge tool like a knife or chisel, but instead of slicing in along the blade, the blade is dragged perpendicular to the surface. This is an easily controlled way to shave away at hard materials such as glue, epoxy, and wood. They are particularly good at removing drips and high spots without damaging the surrounding surface.

Paint Scraper. Most paint scrapers have a long handle with a blade mounted perpendicularly at the end. You press the blade down on the surface and pull the handle. The blades are typically sharpened at a fairly steep angle of 30 to 45 degrees. I keep a fine file handy to touch up the blade when it needs sharpening. Paint scrapers are commonly available at just about any hardware store or home center, although a woodworking supply store may have higher-quality options.

Cabinet Scraper. Take a small rectangular sheet of thin, high-quality steel, make the edges square and smooth, and then burnish the edge with a hard rod so a tiny little burr is rolled over and you have a cabinet scraper. While it seems like you hold the blade perpendicular to the surface, the actual blade is that itty-bitty little burr on the bottom edge. This slices into the surface and can cut smoothly through the most difficult materials.

    If you choose to take on the task of building a boat from tiger maple, a cabinet scraper can

Figure 3-4. A paint scraper has a variety of uses, from removing glue drips to shaping concave surfaces. My favorite is the one at the top left with the thick handle. This started out with a square blade, but I have ground a variety of different curves at the corners and sides to conform to a variety shapes. I was hoping the wood-handled unit to its right would prove useful since it is preshaped to some good contours, but it was too light. The cheap hardware store version on the top right is much better. The three little ones to the right are useful despite being light. They reach into small spaces well. At the bottom is a cabinet scraper. This does not get much use on softwoods, but it can quickly level off a sag in epoxy. The putty knife to the left can be used as a scraper, as a lever for aligning kayak decks, or even for applying putty.

be used to prepare a beautiful surface. They also work very well for shaving down an uneven coat of epoxy.

Sanding Tools

Most people really don't much like sanding. There are some who claim it is a Zen thing and that they quite enjoy the process, but few have risen to that level of enlightenment. Those of us still seeking the deeper significance of sanding would rather just find a way to get it done in as efficient and timely a manner as possible. Good sandpaper and the appropriate tools can make the whole experience of sanding much more fulfilling. The choice of using power sand-

Figure 3-5. Hand sanding is always a part of strip-planking boats. A good sanding block is essential to fast, efficient work. I use the round unit on the right with "used" disks off my random orbit power sander. The round pad on the left is a soft foam conforming adapter for use with the power sander or hand sanding pad. The standard rubber sanding block at the lower center works very well with sheet sandpaper. I also wrap sheet paper around the chunk of foam to get at inside surfaces. Sandpaper can be glued or stapled to different-shaped blocks of wood to fit curved shapes. Under all the other blocks is a shopmade "long-board" fairing sander. This quickly levels out uneven surfaces.

ers versus hand sanding is going to depend on your experience and your patience. Power tools are usually faster, but this is a mixed blessing. Fast may mean you're messing things up more quickly. I will discuss power sanders later, but sanding by hand is almost always better when it comes to fine detail work. Use power tools when you have large expanses to work on, and hand sand when it is important you don't make a mistake.

Sandpaper. Sandpaper is just a bunch of little edge tools bonded to a piece of paper or cloth. The same need for a sharp edge that applies to knives, planes, and scrapers also applies to sandpaper. If your sandpaper is dull you will be working harder and accomplishing less satisfactory results than when you are using new,

sharp sandpaper. We all have the desire to save money and resources by using sandpaper until it is so worn out that it doesn't do anything at all. We don't want to toss out a sheet until all the sand has been rubbed off.

One key to getting the quick and effective results with sandpaper is to replace it early. Cedar does not wear down sandpaper very fast, but some woods will gum up the paper, and hardwoods can wear it out pretty quickly. Epoxy and fiberglass can be quite hard on the grit, wearing it down quickly. Whatever you are sanding, pay attention to your sanding progress; when it starts to take a while to do what used to take moments, it is time to switch off your sandpaper for a fresh sheet. This may take as little as 5 minutes and rarely more than 10 when using a power sander.

A good-quality stearate-coated aluminum oxide sandpaper will usually work well for wood, epoxy, and varnish. The stearate coating helps prevent gumming up while the aluminum oxide lasts reasonably long.

Sanding Block. It is no good having the best, sharpest, most excellent sandpaper the world has to offer without having something to hold it with. There are times when you just want to hold a bit of folded-up sandpaper in your hand, but for serious material removal, you need a sanding block. Even if you think you are going to do all your sanding with a power sander, you will still want the ability to efficiently sand areas that are hard to reach with power tools.

I wear out a lot of sanding disks in my random orbit sander. But even when they don't cut that efficiently anymore with the power tool, they have some life left for hand sanding. I have a round sanding pad with hook-and-loop material on the bottom that makes good use of those partially spent disks.

I find I do most of my hand sanding with this sanding pad, but for wet sanding a finish, I use a hard rubber block that holds cut sheets. This provides good support behind the sandpaper and doesn't mind getting wet.

Fairing Board. Take a long piece of flexible material, stick some sandpaper to it, and you have a fairing, or long, board. A piece of 3 mm to ¼-inch-thick plywood with handles mounted at each end will do the job. You can use spray adhesive to stick the paper on. I was able to find some hook-and-loop material and long hook-and-loop paper. The long-board quickly knocks off high spots, bridges over low spots, and automatically smoothes the surface to make it more even. It will make a lot of sanding dust pretty quickly.

Vacuum. Clean up that sanding dust with a vacuum cleaner or shop vac. You will be creating a lot of dust in the course of the project and having some way to keep it under control will keep the shop clean and may keep other residents of the house a little happier. You will want to be able to hook the hose directly to your random orbit sander and may also adapt it to collect dust on your table saw and other large tools. Some vacuums intended for wood shops allow you to plug the tool cord directly into the vacuum, and the dust collection will automatically turn on whenever you power up the tool.

Polishing. A fine, dust-free finish on the boat is hard to achieve without a dedicated paint room. If this really matters to you, the best way to remove any dust spots is to buff out the varnished surface.

Most polishing starts with very fine sandpaper, but it is hard to bring the surface to a high gloss the way a polishing compound does. A look at the shelves of an automotive supply store will give you lots of alternatives. You don't want a compound that contains silicone as it can make later refinishing difficult, but most rubbing and polishing compounds will work on boat finishes. Rubbing compounds are slightly coarser than polishing compounds. After sanding you will start with a rubbing compound, then move to a polish. The compounds can be applied and worked by hand, using a bonnet on a random orbit sander, or with a dedicated power buffer.

There are some extremely fine grit sanding products available. These are made with grits of abrasives that are carefully graded to be very uniform. The grits are then adhered to soft foam pads. A complete set of these pads can be used to bring a surface all the way from dust laden to a deep, uniform gloss. They are more expensive than the compounds, but they produce spectacular results.

Finishing Tools

I've heard stories of people so consumed by the process of achieving the perfect varnish coat that they would strip naked before entering the paint room to defend against the introduction of any dust into the sacred space. If you do everything else perfectly, a little bit of dust in the air before your varnish dries will introduce slight imperfections into the glossy finish. It took me years of practice applying varnish before dust made a lick of difference in my finish, and even now a perfect finish rarely stays that way beyond the first time the boat is used.

It is not that hard to get a very nice finish, but getting a perfect finish takes practice and patience. Before getting too caught up in the effort, take stock of what you are going to do with the boat. If you are going to end up dragging it across a beach to put it in the water, it doesn't seem worthwhile to strip naked when applying the finish.

Varnish Brushes. The quality of your finish is dependent on the prep work you do before dipping a brush. The next most important factor is the paint or varnish itself. After that, a good finish requires a good brush. For some people, this means a badger must give up its coat. I've never used a really fine brush. I suspect they are a beautiful thing and do a wonderful job of applying finish to a surface, but I use disposable foam brushes instead.

I have found that I can apply a smooth, even coat with a good-quality foam brush. It may

Figure 3-6. You need brushes and mixing pots to work with epoxy. Yogurt or deli containers work very well, but be sure you clean them out thoroughly before use to avoid contaminating your resin. Plastic party cups or large unwaxed paper cups are a good alternative if you need to buy something. I always keep a variety of small cups around for small batches of resin and for use as "grunge" cups. Disposable roller trays can be used with short paint rollers for applying coats of resin. The cheap bristle "chip" brushes spread epoxy well, and lost bristles disappear in the resin. Cotton swabs are good as small brushes for touch-up work. Foam brushes work very well for applying varnish. Waxed paper comes in handy for protecting your workbench when you need to glue small parts or wet out a piece of fiberglass.

not be as good as an expert can do with a fine natural-bristle brush, but it is still good. It may not seem economically sound to throw away a brush when you could just clean out a bristle brush, but cleaning a brush uses a lot of paint thinner and a fair amount of time, so I figure it is a wash.

The foam brushes I use have fine, open-cell foam. I usually find these at specialty wood-working or marine stores. I have not had good luck with those from big-box stores.

Spraying

If you know how to do it, spraying is an excellent way to get a beautiful finish. If you have the equipment and know how to use it, spraying is probably the quickest and cleanest way to apply a finish. If you don't have the equipment, I don't feel it is worth buying it specifically for a single boatbuilding project. It takes practice to get spraying right and good equipment is expensive, so it may be quite an expense and take a long time before you get the desired finish.

One option that some builders have used successfully is aerosol spray cans. However, you will pay a premium for the same amount of finish, and you may have trouble finding cans of good-quality stuff.

Varnishing Accessories

Beyond brushes there are other tools that will help with successful finishing. You will want rags and need some stirring sticks and containers. Building a strip-planked boat, you will have an almost endless supply of stirring sticks in the form of scrap strips.

Tack Cloth. Dust is a perennial bugaboo of achieving a fine finish. A tack cloth is a useful tool in controlling the dust. The cloth is typically cheesecloth soaked in some sticky stuff. After vacuuming the boat and rinsing it off with water and mineral spirits, wiping the surface with a tack cloth will pick up most of the residual dust.

Tack cloths are used exclusively for oil-based finishes such as varnish. They are not to be used between coats of epoxy. The sticky stuff on the cloth can interfere with proper bonding and curing of subsequent layers of epoxy. Use the tack cloth only before applying varnish or oil-based paint.

Lights. While a brush is an obvious varnishing tool, lights are less expected. The only way to be sure you apply an even coat of varnish without any drips or "holidays," where you missed a spot, is to carefully watch what you are doing. If you cannot see drips and holidays, you will not have much success preventing them. A set of bright lights arranged around your boat as you apply the varnish will make mistakes clear so you can deal with them while the varnish is still wet.

I use a set of halogen shop lights on stands placed at either end of the boat to light my work. Set the lights down at the level of the boat to highlight any mistakes.

Files and Rasps

There are lots of times when a file or rasp comes in handy. They cut well against the grain of wood and can concentrate cutting on a specific spot of epoxy or fiberglass.

Traditional-Cut Files and Rasps. You can spend a lot of money on really fine woodworking files, but I find the most handy to be a 4-in-Hand (or 4-in-1) shoemaker's rasp. This has a flat, coarse rasp and medium file on one side, and rounded versions of the same on the other side. They fit well in a tool apron and come in handy in a wide variety of situations where you need to remove a little material quickly. They tend to work best on hardwoods and epoxy.

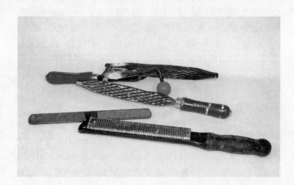

Figure 3-7. Files, rasps, and microplanes can deal with tricky wood that may aggravate a plane. Shinto wood rasps will quickly remove wood or delicately remove epoxy sags. The 4-in-Hand on the left will do the same or soften a sharp edge of fiberglass. The microplane at the bottom has many tiny blades that shape wood easily.

A fine mill-cut metal file is very useful for putting a quick new edge on a paint scraper. Either hold the scraper in your hand or clamp it in a vise and use firm, steady strokes to get your scraper cutting better.

Shinto Wood Rasp. These things are essentially a bunch of bent, two-sided hacksaw blades that are riveted together with a handle attached, and they are wonders of brute force carpentry. They cut in almost every direction and are very resistant to clogging up. I find them particularly useful for removing that big drool of epoxy and fiberglass that somehow ended up in the middle of my deck. A couple quick strokes of this rasp will knock it down to size in an awful hurry. They are also good for removing a lot of wood quickly and surprisingly cleanly.

Microplanes. These are woodworking tools that have migrated into the kitchen to make fine lemon zest for your apple crisp. Time to steal them back out of the chef's drawer and put them to the use they were designed for. They are stainless steel with acid-etched teeth. While they look a lot like a Stanley Surform tool that you may have collecting dust in the back of your woodworking drawer, they work a lot better. These are great tools for fine shaping of wood, and they cut quickly and efficiently. If you have a stem that needs a little sculpting, microplanes do a fine job.

Saws

When you have to cut wood, you are going to need a saw. Like just about everyone else, I have become quite enamored of the Japanese-style saws that cut on the pull stroke. They are laser sharp and cut through cedar like nobody's business.

For basic cutting strips to length, I don't even bother with a saw (see the next section), but for major trimming at the stem or transom, a Japanese pull saw is hard to beat.

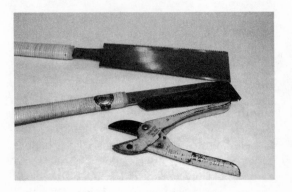

Figure 3-8. *Cutting strips to length can be done with a saw or shrubbery pruners. Shown here are Japanese-style pull saws, which cut on the pull stroke, allowing a very thin blade that cuts very quickly and easily. The top saw has both a ripping blade and a cross-cut blade.*

Figure 3-9. *Fiberglass is usually cut with scissors. They will likely get coated with epoxy, and cutting glass dulls them, so don't go to the sewing kit thinking no one will notice. Second from the right is a battery-powered fabric cutter that may be worth the investment if you do a lot of fiberglass work. If you have a smooth surface to cut on, the rolling cutter on the right works well for cutting strips of cloth.*

Pruners

Here's another reason to raid the spouse's tool kit. A pair of garden pruners makes an excellent tool for lopping strips to approximate length before fine-fitting them in place. I use the kind that has one sharp blade cutting against an anvil instead of two sharp blades that cut past each other like scissors.

Scissors

You will need a pair of scissors to cut fiberglass. A good stout pair will hold up better, but you don't need to buy an expensive pair specifically for fiberglass. They are going to get covered with epoxy, so you most likely won't be able to get away with using the kitchen shears for long, although they would probably work great.

The same scissors that cut fiberglass will work fine for cutting most other fabrics, such as carbon fiber, but they may not be worth a darn for cutting Kevlar. A brand-new pair of high-

quality scissors may cut Kevlar for a while, but as soon as they get dull they will become almost useless for Kevlar. If you get a pair that works, do not cut anything else with them. There are some inexpensive scissors sold for cutting Kevlar that seem to work quite well. Get a pair and paint them gold or something so you know not to use them for cutting apart chickens. Glass can be cut with dull scissors, which is good since it dulls them pretty quick.

Rolling Cutters

If you have the tabletop for them, the rolling cutters sold in fabric stores work quite well for fiberglass. They are especially nice when you need to cut a bunch of bias-cut strips. The downside is you need a smooth tabletop without any scratches or deep gouges. The fibers of glass will get pushed down into the scratch and the roller will fail to cut them. It is most annoying to pull away a length of bias-cut cloth and find that it is attached by one fine strand.

Epoxy Tools

Since epoxy is a glue, it loves to stick to stuff. This means that it has a wonderful way of ruining good tools. While with woodworking tools you can sometimes get away with borrowing something from the kitchen and returning it with the chef being none the wiser; it is much harder to get away with when using epoxy and fiberglass. Your tools will likely get coated with a thin crust of goo, and the glop will not be casually mistaken for a persistent spot of tomato sauce.

Mixing Pots. Despite the obvious convenience, don't use nice Pyrex measuring cups you think are collecting dust in the kitchen. They will be missed. One word: yogurt. If you eat a lot of yogurt you will live to 1,000 and will never be at a loss for containers to mix epoxy. The quart size is perfect. They hold a good amount of epoxy and are deep enough that you won't generally spill much. I also like them for holding varnish. They can often be used multiple times because hardened epoxy pops right out. The smaller, single-serving-size containers are good for small batches. Sour cream containers work as well, but sadly they do not come with fruit at the bottom.

Paper cups also work well, although wax-covered cups may lose a little wax into the epoxy, which can cause issues. I have also used cutoff milk jugs, soda bottles, paint thinner cans, and laundry detergent containers. Whatever you use, make sure it is clean. Leftover detergent or dairy products are not a beneficial addition to epoxy.

Brushes. Most hardware stores carry inexpensive, natural bristle, "chip" brushes. These have wooden handles, metal ferrules, and boar bristles. I buy a box of 2-inch-wide brushes. Chip brushes have a severe tendency to lose bristles. There are a couple of things you can do about it. One, you can glue the bristles into the ferrule with a bead of epoxy or CA glue at the top of the ferrule. This usually restrains most of the bristles. Two, you can wrap your hand with tape, sticky side out, and jam the bristles against the tape to pull all the loose hairs.

For initial glassing it is OK to lose a few bristles; the whitish hairs become almost clear and against the wood they virtually disappear. For the final coats of epoxy, on the other hand, a stray bristle will impede the flow of epoxy, causing a thicker or thinner spot or a drip. This is not the end of the world, but it makes more work in your effort to get a smooth finish.

When I'm doing glassing I usually yank the end of the bristles to remove the loosest and then just live with them pulling out. In the finish coats I spend more effort to minimize the stray hairs.

Rollers. There are two kinds of roller covers that work well with epoxy: foam and short nap. The suitable foam covers have about a $\frac{1}{8}$-inch layer of open-cell foam. These are specialized rollers, not like the ones you may find at a home center. I generally buy them from my epoxy supplier. The short-nap roller covers also have about $\frac{1}{8}$-inch-long upright bristles. You may be able to find these at a home center. The thinness of the foam or nap is important in that it does not soak up a lot of resin but will hold the resin briefly and release it easily without a lot of pressure. I personally prefer the short-nap rollers as they don't seem to pump air into the epoxy the way the cells of the foam rollers can.

Most roller covers come in 7- or 9-inch lengths. I find this is longer than I need, so I cut them in half and slide them onto a short or adjustable-length roller frame. To cut them in half I roll them carefully through a band saw, being sure to clean off all the sawdust debris afterward.

Squeegees. There are various schools of thought on squeegees. Some people like a thick piece of rubber like those used for doing silk screening; other people cut rectangles out of gallon milk jugs. Each person will swear his or her tool is

Figure 3-10. I use plastic applicators or squeegees to spread epoxy and remove excess resin from the cloth. Larger ones get the most use, but small ones are good for small areas. I use the little plastic mixing sticks on the left like a putty knife to smooth small spots or fillets.

Figure 3-11. To temporarily hold the strips in place, you can clamp little U-shaped jigs that fit over the strips to the forms.

the ideal tool for pushing around epoxy. I use the typically yellow plastic squeegees sold at auto parts stores. They are pretty good. They have a nice flex and a good edge. If you leave any residual epoxy on pretty thick it will peel off easily; otherwise, wipe the squeegees clean with a rag for reuse. Eventually their edge gets a little fuzzy from dragging across the fiberglass. A couple swipes with a sharp block plane will renew the edge.

Stirring Sticks. You are building a strip-built boat, so it is very unlikely you will be hard up for stirring sticks. All those strips that came out of the table saw backward at 150 miles per hour because you neglected to use feather boards are probably already sized about right. Any scrap strips are good for stirring epoxy.

Other Tools

Clamps. A boatbuilder can never have too many clamps. Big clamps, little clamps, C-clamps, quick clamps—any kind of clamp you may come across will probably come in handy at some point during the building process. The

clamp I reach for the most is a spring clamp, basically a clothespin on steroids. Spring clamps are quick and powerful, they don't get ruined when handled with hands dripping with epoxy, and they are just plain handy.

Stapler. In strip-planking, a staple can act as another kind of clamp. A 9/16-inch staple shot through a strip into the form will usually stay put until the glue dries. You could use a pneumatic stapler, but they generally shoot the staple in too deep. You want the staple to stand a little proud of the surface. I use a standard T-50 utility stapler. They are affordable, easy to use, and don't require an umbilical to a compressor. There are newer, "easier" varieties of staplers, but I have found that the old-style, heavy-duty one made by Arrow is the most reliable.

If the stapler gets gummed up with glue, you can soak it in hot water for a while to clean off all the glue—assuming you use a water-soluble glue.

Staple Pullers. You can use the screwdriver on your Swiss Army knife to remove staples if it is the closest tool at hand, but it is better to use a tool designed to remove staples. Don't reach for one of those things that look like the jaws of an extinct predator. They will just make scars on the boat. I got a heavy-duty staple remover from the local big-box office supply store. It has a tooth, which slides under the staple, connected to a lever that pries it up. The wide bottom of the tool protects the wood while keeping the strip pressed into place. I modified the tool from the store slightly by sharpening the tooth. The tooth is replaceable if it ever wears out.

Sometimes you will break a staple, in which case it is handy to have a pair of pliers around so that you can grab the end of a broken leg and pull it up.

Measuring and Marking. You won't have to do a lot of measuring, but a tape measure and a combination square with a removable steel ruler will find use. Setting up the spacing of the forms is best done with a tape measure. A combination square helps assure all the forms on the strongback are straight. A simple compass that holds a pencil (like the one you used in school) can be used for transferring shapes and marks.

I never seem to have a pencil when I need one; they all seem to end up on the other side of the boat. Get a big box of pencils and spread them around the shop.

Et cetera. There are going to be other tools you need to complete the boat, but most of them are not really specialized for boatbuilding and are standard to just about any tool kit. For example, you'll need a hammer, screwdrivers (Phillips, flathead, and maybe square-drive), a drill (I recommend a cordless electric drill), and twist drill bits. Also get screwdriver bits for the electric drill, which will save you a lot of time and muscle driving and removing screws. A box of sheetrock screws, although not really a tool, will come in handy for quickly securing forms, holding down a recalcitrant strip, and many other uses.

Power Tools

A dedicated builder who buys precut strips and forms could build the rest of the boat exclusively with human-powered hand tools. A knife, a block plane, a handsaw, a sanding block, and a pile of sandpaper are about all that is needed. But we don't need to be that pure. The right selection of small power tools will make the project go quicker.

Handheld Power Tools

Random Orbit Sanders. A random orbit sander (ROS) has a round head that spins and shakes in an effort to eliminate sanding swirls associated with disk sanders. These sanders have become quite easy to find since I bought my first, with big-box home centers carrying several different brands and European manufacturers offering Pentagon-worthy versions in stylish stacking boxes. I've switched back and forth between

Figure 3-12. Power sanding saves a lot of time. The go-to tool is a random orbit sander, such as the middle unit, the larger one to its left, and the smaller detail sander at lower right. These remove material quickly with a minimum of sanding marks. The largest unit is the most powerful and the fastest, but it's hard to control; the small unit is good for small narrow pieces; and the middle unit is a good compromise. Above the smaller detail sander is a right-angle grinder. With very coarse sanding disks, this tool can remove a lot of material in a hurry. A detail sander is shown lower left, which occasionally is good for getting in tight spots. At top is an automotive polisher for buffing a finish.

a palm-size version and a larger, more powerful right-angle version. The latter is great for doing a lot of damage quickly, if that is what you want to do, but it is heavy and takes two hands to control well. The palm-size unit is easier to control, but it's slower. If you are working on a large, nearly flat surface, the more powerful unit is nice, if dangerous. Most people will do very well with the small, less expensive palm unit.

A good random orbit sander will make quite quick work of turning a roughly stripped boat into a beautiful smooth surface. It will also even out bumpy fiberglass and epoxy. All of this means turning wood or fiberglass into fine dust, so a dust-collection system you can hook up to a shop vacuum cleaner (noted earlier) will make your lungs happy and help keep the fine powder out of the heating system.

The sander also wears out sandpaper very quickly. I find that even the best sandpaper seems to lose its effectiveness after a few minutes rubbing around on the face of an ROS, but it is still pretty good for hand sanding. I use hook-and-loop disks on the ROS and have a little hook-and-loop hand sanding block. Pressure-sensitive adhesive sanding disks are cheaper than the hook-and-loop versions, but they tend to rip when you peel them off the sander and therefore are hard to reuse.

Detail Sander. Most of the fine work of a detail sander can be done by hand. There are few places where there is enough sanding required in a small spot that it is worth the effort of breaking out a small power sander, but then again, part of the fun is collecting tools, and a nice detail sander has a combination of power and precision that is enticing. I'm sure you can find enough work for it to justify the cost. I know I have. You cheapskates who don't want to spend the money are forgiven.

Jigsaw. You could use a handsaw for cutting hatches and cockpits on a kayak or a band saw to cut forms and seats, but a variable-speed jigsaw comes in handy for a variety of uses. I usually have some large coarse blades for cut-

Figure 3-13. Some other useful power tools include routers and jigsaws. The large router in the middle is mounted in a plunge frame that can be used to make some specialty parts. Mounted to a table it can be used to mill cove-and-bead strips with the cutter bits shown below. The trim router on the left is useful for rounding over gunwales. The jigsaw on the right does a good job cutting hatches.

ting forms and some very fine blades for cutting kayak hatches.

Heat Gun. An industrial-strength heat gun is like a hair dryer that can melt solder. You don't need it that hot for anything on a boat, but getting epoxy on the bathroom hair dryer may lead to divorce. A concentrated blast of heat can be used to soften and bend some of the more stubborn strips. You don't need to steam wood to soften it; a little heat can do the job just fine.

Epoxy also becomes less viscous when heated, so a heat gun can be used to help epoxy flow. Heating a spot where you want epoxy to run or soak in well will lower the viscosity of the epoxy, and as the area cools it will draw the epoxy into its pores. If you have an area of epoxy that is full of bubbles, lightly blowing on it with hot air can expand and pop them for a clearer finish.

Router. If you are milling your own strips and want cove-and-bead joints, you will need something to make those coves and beads. As explained in Chapter 2, cove-and-bead is like tongue-and-groove and can help the strips fit together tightly. I can't think of anything in the kitchen that will do the job, so for most people this will be a router. A router is just a motor that spins a cutter really fast. It can be handheld to round over the edge of a piece of plywood or mounted upside down on a router table to mill a cove or bead on a strip.

For milling strips you will want a router table. This will let you safely run strips through the cutters with feather boards in place. See later in the chapter for further discussion of both of these items.

The router requires special bits to be useful. Cove-and-bead strips need a specialized cutter. At this point most major router bit manufacturers make canoe bits, often in matched sets. One bit cuts the cove and the other the bead. These bits cut a round profile with a ¼-inch diameter intended for ¼-inch-thick strips. This diameter may also be used for thinner strips such as ³⁄₁₆ inch. The bits come under a variety of names such as cove and bead, flute and bead, or canoe bits. Lee Valley Tools (leevalley.com) sells both a matched set and a single bit that can be positioned to cut both the cove and the bead.

There are many situations where a router is a good tool. A round-over bit makes quick work of adding a consistent radius to an edge. Straight bits are good for following patterns to make accurate copies of a shape. You can get straight bits with a bearing at one end that will exactly follow a template. This is a great way to make repeatable shapes such as the strongback hole in forms for boats using internal strongbacks.

Stationary Power Tools

With the large power tools you can probably get by with going over to your brother-in-law's for a weekend to get all the work done and bring your production back to your own shop. But what's the fun of that? If you don't have a table saw yet, now is your excuse.

Table Saw. Cutting cedar strips does not take a very powerful saw. It is pretty soft stuff, but if you need to cut 1,000 linear feet of strips, it will mean the saw is running continuously for several hours, so you probably won't be happy with the cheapest out there. Cutting hardwoods takes a little more power, but strip building is not a table saw intensive project, so if you need to justify a really nice saw, take up making cabinets.

The best saw blades I have found for cutting strips are 7¼-inch-diameter blades intended for handheld circular saws. They will work fine in a 10-inch saw. The benefit of these is that they are very thin so they don't waste a lot of wood. They are available with carbide-tipped blades and are very affordable.

You will want a zero-clearance insert for your table saw. This can just be a piece of wood cut to fit your saw that you carefully raise your saw blade up through.

With a more powerful saw you can gang up several blades on the arbor to cut more than one strip at a time, but only do this if you have a power stock feeder.

So now I'm talking about how to feed cattle? Actually, the "stock" in this refers to wood. A stock feeder is a motor with rubber wheels and a gantry system to position the motor over your saw. This is a real luxury and not worth the cost for the casual boatbuilder, but if you are going to cut a lot of strips, it will push your material smoothly and consistently through the saw blades without getting your fingers anywhere near the teeth of the spinning blade.

Instead of a stock feeder, most people use feather boards. These are merely pieces of wood with one end cut at an angle. The angled end is then partially ripped to produce flexible fingers that can be used to press the wood you are milling against the table and fence. They serve to hold the material in its proper place and also prevent the stock from kicking back and getting shot across the room and turned into stirring sticks.

You can make your own feather boards with a band saw. Use either straight-grained

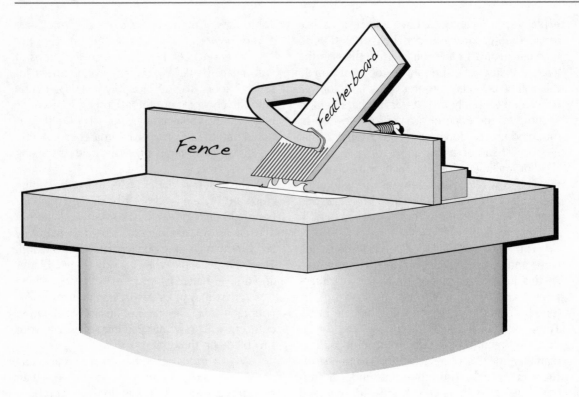

Figure 3-14. *A feather board is just a piece of scrap wood with a comb-like end created by slotting it with a saw. It is used to hold raw material down on the table as you cut strips. Lower the blade below the table, put your board up against the fence, and place the feather board on top so the feathers are slightly bent. Clamp it securely in place. Now remove the board you are about to mill. After turning on the saw, slowly raise the blade up so it cuts into the bottom of the feather board.*

pine or plywood. Cut the end of the pine board at an angle, then cut a series of slices lengthwise into the end of the angle to create a comb-like appearance. This piece can be clamped to the fence or table of your table saw or router table. Adjust the placement so the fingers bend slightly, applying pressure to hold wood you are cutting tight against the table or fence.

A plywood feather board usually is made with a little longer edge and wider fingers. Because the fingers are not as flexible, they need to be placed more precisely.

Band Saw. I am often asked whether it wouldn't be more efficient with wood to use a band saw

to cut the strips. Given the thin kerf of a band saw blade, it would seem to make sense that a band saw would waste less wood than a table saw. I think with careful cutting band saws may work well for this purpose, but the 7¼-inch circular saw blades are very thin and leave a very smooth surface, whereas band saws generally leave a fairly rough surface. But more important, they are not as well suited as a table saw for producing cuts of consistent thickness. The blade has a tendency to wander, and as a result you will probably have to remove more wood to get consistent thickness.

Where the band saw really comes into its own is cutting curves. Band saws make quick and accurate work of cutting out forms and things like inner stems and transoms. You can do all this work with a jigsaw, but a band saw is easier and quicker.

Thickness Planer. One of the keys to a smooth surface on your finished boat is getting all the strips even with one another. The first step toward that end is getting all your strips a consistent thickness. A well-tuned table saw will do an excellent job of this, but a thickness planer will ensure accuracy. The need for consistency is most obvious when you are milling a cove and bead. You want the radius cut exactly in the middle of the strip. If the thickness varies even a little bit the cove will fall out one side. This isn't the end of the world, but you are going to be dealing with the discrepancy later in the building process.

Router Table. A router table isn't a tool all by itself. It is a means of holding a normally hand-held router on an even surface. It allows you to safely mill cove-and-bead strips and follow a template, such as when cutting the strongback hole on the forms of a decked boat such as a kayak.

Safety Equipment

A boatbuilding shop has a wide variety of hazards, from sharp tools and flying debris to loud noises and toxic dust. There are the obviously dangerous things like the spinning blade of a saw, as well as seemingly innocuous dangers like sawdust. Follow the manufacturer's recommended safety instructions for any tools you use. Wear safety glasses whenever you use power tools. If you are sanding or doing something else that makes a lot of noise, wear hearing protection. Most woods have evolved to be at least somewhat distasteful to bugs. What "distasteful" really means is "poisonous." If it is poisonous to bugs, it probably is not so good for humans. In fact, wood dust is considered a potential carcinogen. Wear a dust mask when-

Figure 3-15. Although many of the materials used in strip building may seem benign, there are risks. You should strongly consider wearing hearing and eye protection whenever you run power tools. Wood sawdust is considered carcinogenic; a good dust mask (upper left) will keep it out of your lungs. Even though epoxy does not smell much, an organic vapor respirator (upper right) is highly recommended. You also don't want to get epoxy on your skin, so wear gloves.

ever you are doing a task that may put dust into the air. The little "comfort" masks available at home centers aren't sufficient. Get quality dust filters that go on a professional respirator mask.

Epoxy is a concoction of petrochemicals—while not as full of volatile organic compounds as some other resins, you don't want to mess with it. Wear organic filters on the same respirator mask as you use with the dust filters whenever you are in the room with uncured resin. Wear latex, vinyl, or nitrile exam gloves whenever you are handling wet epoxy, and avoid getting the resin on your skin. Do not handle the epoxy with your bare hands. Even after the epoxy has dried to the touch you should consider wearing gloves when sanding, and always wear a good dust mask when sanding epoxy. Buy a full box of 100 gloves and replace your gloves frequently. The gloves are somewhat delicate and will rip and need to be replaced. There will also be lots of times you need gloves to handle epoxy, then you will need clean hands to handle your roll of cloth, and then need gloves immediately after. If your first pair of gloves are gloppy with epoxy, you don't want to mess up your roll. Take your gloves off and put on a new pair after handling the roll of glass.

It may seem like an inconvenience to pull on an uncomfortable respirator and sweaty gloves every time you handle any little bit of resin, but remember, we build boats because it is fun; there is no compelling reason to take unnecessary risks. No matter how much you would like the boat done by a certain day, it really doesn't need to be. The amount of time expended to be careful and safe is just more time spent enjoying the process of building the boat. And how much time does it really take to put on a pair of gloves anyway?

Chapter 4

Making the Building Form

Strip-planked boats are made on a form based on the cross-sectional lines of the boat. A *table of offsets* is the traditional method of documenting the *lines* of a boat. *Lofting* is the art of converting the table of offsets (which are merely measurements from an arbitrary baseline) back to lines (or, simply put, curved outlines) from which you can then make forms to build a boat. For some people tackling a boatbuilding project, lofting the boat can be one of the most intimidating hurdles. The lofting skills required for a kayak are minimal. The reason for lofting is to get a full-size drawing of the boat. Obviously, for a large sailboat this is quite a stunt. But for most small boats the task does not require clearing out the loft of your workshop. Often you can produce these drawings on large sheets of graph paper or an easel pad from an office supply store.

Offset Tables

The offset tables in this book comprise two or three major sections as shown in the illustration. The upper contains waterline measurements, and the lower one or two contain buttocks measurements for the deck (if any) and hull. There are also small additional sections showing the locations of the gunwale, feature line, and *sheerline* (on a decked boat).

Across the top of the table is a list of form locations (the forms are usually called *sections*, but for our purposes "forms" makes more sense since they will be traced on plywood and cut out, becoming the cross-sectional shapes over which you will form the boat). So what does all this mean?

The Form Offsets

The forms are like slices of bologna cut at intervals from the sausage that is the boat. The slicing typically starts from the front, with the long position being the distance of the form away from the bow of the finished boat. In the Coot table of offsets shown on page 178, for example, the first form is 6 inches from the bow. The second is 1 foot 6 inches from the bow, and each consecutive form is spaced 12 inches apart until the stern of the boat is reached. The forms are created in the shape produced by the intersection of these form planes and the surface of the boat. The buttocks and waterlines are lengthwise slices through the boat; the buttocks are vertical slices and the waterlines are horizontal slices. The intersection of these planes produce contour lines on a map. The 7-inch waterline is a line drawn on the surface of the boat at an elevation of 7 inches above the *datum waterline* or *design waterline* (DWL), and a 3-inch buttocks line is a line drawn 3 inches out from the centerline (CL) of the boat. Looking in three dimensions, the zero point is the extreme bow of the boat on the centerline at the DWL.

The offset tables are created by taking measurements wherever the planes of the waterlines or buttocks slices intersect the contour of the form plane on the boat surface. Every time either a waterline or a buttocks line intersects the surface of the boat at a form location, the position of that intersection is noted. Since the locations of the two intersecting planes are known, the only measurement needed is the third dimension.

It is a little confusing, but in the buttocks sections of the table the numbers are elevations,

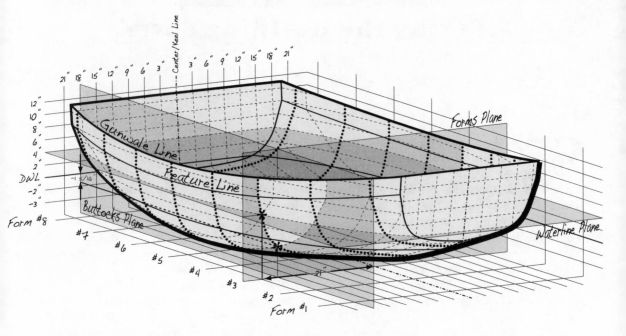

Figure 4-1. Offsets are a means of defining a boat's shape in a table of numbers. The numbers are derived by slicing up the boat along different planes. The horizontal planes are called waterlines because they are parallel to the water. The vertical, lengthwise planes are called buttocks lines for some unknown reason that we probably shouldn't investigate too closely. Finally there is the vertical slice across the boat. These are the numbers we really want because they correspond to the forms used to build the boat. These forms are described by the measurements of where the other two planes intersect the form and the outer surface of the boat. The vertical buttock plane 18 inches from the center of the boat intersects form 3 at 1⁵/₁₆ inches below the datum waterline (DWL), and the waterline plane 4 inches above the DWL intersects the outer surface of the boat exactly 21 inches out from the centerline. Put enough of these points on a piece of paper and you can draw the whole form.

even though a buttocks line is an offset from the centerline. This offset is called a *half-width*, for the simple reason that it is the measurement from the centerline to one side instead of a measurement all the way from one side to the other. The first column of numbers says what the half-width offset is, and all the following columns give the height at which the form intersects the buttocks line. Looking at the buttocks section of the offset table for the Coot, following the 18-inch row out to form 3, you are confronted with the number −1⁵/₁₆. Looking at the figure here you can see that if you measure down 1⁵/₁₆ inches along the 18-inch line starting at the DWL you will get a point on the edge of the

form. Similarly, the 4-inch waterline row of the table yields an offset of 21 at form 3. Measuring 21 inches from the centerline gives another point on the form. Repeating this process for every buttocks and waterline while placing marks on graph paper will eventually produce a series of dots that define the form.

There are two other points that define the shape of form 3; the gunwale and the feature line. The gunwale data puts a mark 9¹⁵/₁₆ inches above the DWL and 21¹¹/₁₆ inches over from the centerline; this marks the top edge of the boat. The feature line describes a corner in the curve defining the form. This corner is located by a height and a half-width. You can now con-

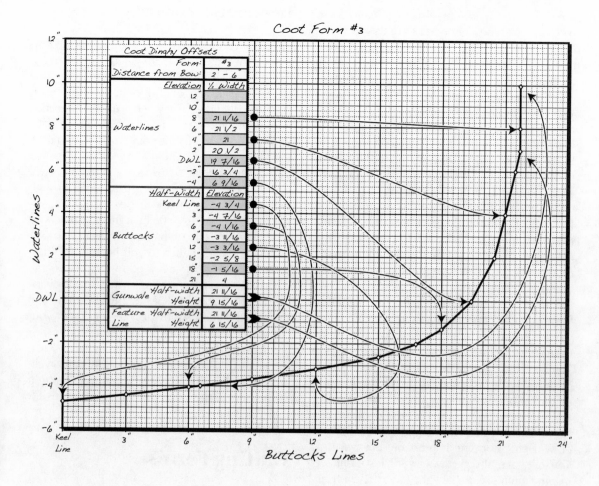

Figure 4-2. *Form 3 shows how the numbers in the offset table correspond to the shape of the form. The numbers in the waterline section indicate the distance out from the center of the boat along the corresponding waterline, so following the horizontal 8-inch line out 21¹¹/₁₆ inches places a point on the curve. The buttocks section includes distances above the DWL along the corresponding vertical line, with negative numbers indicating points below the DWL. Following the 12-inch vertical line down 3³/₁₆ inches produces another point on the edge of the form. The feature line indicates a corner on the edge 21¹¹/₁₆ inches horizontally and 6¹⁵/₁₆ inches vertically. The end of the line is defined by the gunwale, which is also 21¹¹/₁₆ inches over but 9¹⁵/₁₆ inches up. Once you have plotted all the points, connect them together with a smooth curve, except for the feature line point, which should be an angle.*

nect the dots to produce a drawing of the form located at 2 feet 6 inches from the bow of the boat. You can use a French curve or flexible spline to draw a smooth curve from the keel up to the feature line, allow a corner at the

feature line, then continue the line up to the gunwale. On a decked boat like a kayak, you will have data for both the deck and the hull, with a sheerline separating the two, and possibly a feature line or chine, but the process is the same. Symmetrical boats like most canoes are nice because you only need to draw out forms for the front half; the back half are just repeats of the front forms.

The easiest way to do this is on a sheet of graph paper with ¼-inch grids. You don't need to draw both sides right away, so the sheet does not need to be bigger than half the boat width. Near one edge draw a centerline, and several inches up from the bottom mark the datum waterline. You will be less confused if you keep each form on a separate sheet.

A ruler marked in sixteenths of an inch will help you get the data points accurately transferred to the paper. Proceed to mark all the offsets for the form. Mark the sheerline clearly on the drawing. This will come in handy when you start laying strips.

After you have plotted all the points for one form, you must connect them. A naval architect would probably use a French curve or a spline to make sure the connecting lines are smooth. The French curve can be tedious to use; a spline or flexible ruler is easier. A spline can be anything that bends in a nice smooth manner, like a wood batten. Drafting stores sell several different flexible rulers. In the end, all the effort to draw a precision line is probably not worth it. You may actually get away with just connecting the points with straight lines. The offsets are pretty close together. When you are building the boat, the natural tendency of the strips to bend smoothly will hide small problems in your drawing. You can reach a happy medium between straight lines and splined lines by free-handing a curve through each point.

Other Parts

Most boats will have other parts or forms for which the standard offset table is not the best format for documentation, but tables of numbers are still often the most expedient means of presenting the data. Again, you will be plotting the data on graph paper and then connecting the dots.

Drawing the Patterns

Whether you used a pencil and ruler or a computer and printer to plot the data, you will eventually have drawings of all the forms. Include the CL, DWL, diagonal line, and sheerline on the final drawings. They serve as the reference lines when you start building. With open boats, you will need to include some extra material on the forms to elevate them all to the same height off the strongback. With closed boats you will want a hole cut in most of the forms through which the strongback will be strung. Usually this hole is 2 inches wide by 4 inches tall. If you only drew one half of the form, transfer this half-pattern to larger paper so you have both sides. Brown packing paper is a good source of large paper. You will glue the drawings to medium-density fiberboard (MDF) or plywood and cut them into pieces, so if you want a copy of your work, make a duplicate before proceeding.

If this lofting is too much for you, full-size drawings of all the forms and patterns are available from the author. See the Sources section at the end of the book for sources of plans for these boats and others.

Cutting Forms

The forms define the shape of the finished boat. Care and attention to getting the forms right from the start will pay off in faster work in stripping, less time spent sanding, and a better-looking and better-performing finished product. Cutting out the forms is pretty easy. It amounts to nothing more than cutting along a line, but it is worth taking the time to be accurate.

If you have lofted out the forms from the tables in this book, you should end up with a full-size drawing of each form drawn out individually. With a boat like the Coot where each form is quite large, it may not be practical to draw both sides of the boat on one really big sheet of paper. Plans supplied by designers may come full size, drawn with both sides of the boat showing and with each form separate from

Figure 4-3. *Instead of transferring lines from the drawing to your form material, cut out full-size drawings, glue them to the form material with spray adhesive, and cut out around the lines. This way all the reference lines are included on the forms.*

the others, or you may get plans with only half of each form, and possibly drawn all together in one drawing. The most accurate way to transfer the lines to your form material is to glue a full-size copy showing both halves of the boat directly to the material and cut out around the lines.

If you do not have every form drawn individually, you can take the drawings to a copy center to make suitable prints. With designs that are symmetrical bow to stern, you only need to have one pattern for each of the two matching forms in front and back. Look for copy centers that provide services for the architecture and building trades. They will have large-format copiers for dealing with blueprints. These copies may cost a bit, so if you are low on cash you could make careful tracings on newsprint, but some accuracy may be lost. You could also take whatever drawings you have and use a pin to

poke holes through them into your form material and connect the dots with a pencil.

If you are working from a stacked drawing, these plans usually include the front of the boat on one half of the drawing and the back on the other, so you are only seeing half the form. Fold each drawing in half along the centerline of the drawing so that when you carefully cut out along the line on one side, you get an exact copy on the other side. Watch that the fold stays tight so that both sides are symmetrical.

Cut out each form from the surrounding paper, leaving about ½ inch around the outside of each pattern. Distribute these patterns around your form material. The form material may be any sheet stock you have available. I prefer MDF because it is cheap and dimensionally stable, but plywood and particleboard work fine. Half-inch-thick material is thick enough to be stiff and strong but thin enough to be

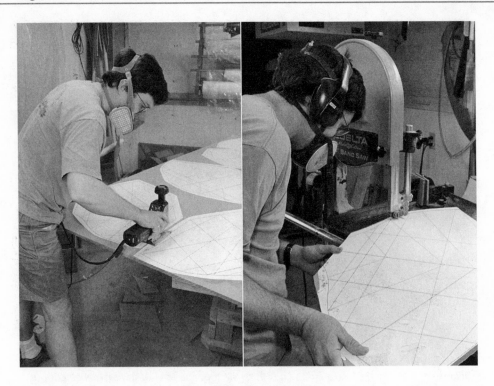

Figure 4-4. *The easiest way to cut out forms is to roughly cut the parts from the panel and then bring them to a band saw. If you don't have a band saw, you may still want to roughly cut before making your close cut with the jigsaw.*

fairly lightweight. The plans in this book assume 1/2-inch-thick forms. For the sectional forms, the thickness is not that relevant, but the end form shape may assume the strips touch the form at a certain width.

I try to lay out the patterns to use the MDF as efficiently as I can. A typical kayak will use less than one 4-foot-by-8-foot sheet. Adhere the patterns to the MDF by flipping the paper over and spraying the back side with spray adhesive. Then lift the pattern and spray under it directly on the MDF. Align the pattern carefully and lay it down into the adhesive. Use the palm of your hand to press down the pattern, working from the center out, to avoid wrinkles. Let the adhesive dry for a while.

I will usually start by roughly cutting out each form from the MDF with a handheld power jigsaw and an aggressive blade. Cut halfway

between the forms, staying well away from the edges initially. This makes the individual forms easier to handle.

If you are building a symmetrical design, cut out another rough area of wood larger than the pattern and tack this together with the chunk containing the pattern so you can cut two copies of the form simultaneously. I will usually nail the two pieces together with finishing nails placed along the centerline at the intersection of any useful reference lines. You will want to remove the nails later, so don't drive them all the way through both pieces, just far enough to hold the pieces securely together. Don't put nails too close to the edge where they might interfere with sawing around the outline.

A band saw is probably one of the best tools for cutting out the forms, but your handheld power jigsaw will do well also. A 1/4-inch wide,

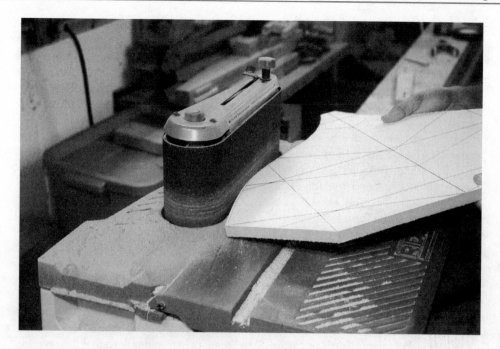

Figure 4-5. If you don't trust your hands to cut out forms exactly on your first try, cut them oversize and then sand down to the line. Here I'm also beveling the edge of the form.

6-tooth-per-inch (TPI) band saw blade will do just fine. On your jigsaw a 10 TPI blade with ground (as opposed to stamped) teeth should work. If you have not changed your blade in a while, now is the time to do it. It is much easier to cut close to a line with a very sharp blade than one where you need to push hard. Don't try to save money on your saw blades by continuing to use the same blade after it gets dull. MDF is quite hard on blades, dulling them quickly, so you may need to replace your jigsaw blade several times.

It is much easier to saw along a line if you can see the line clearly. Have good light on your band saw and try to not cast a shadow on your line. In the end you want the edge of the form right on the line. If you are good, you can probably cut right to the line the first time, but it takes practice. You may want to start by cutting a little *proud* of the line—that is, leaving a small amount outside of the line. Anything you leave, you will eventually need to sand away, so aim to

leave about $1/16$ inch. Uneven edges will make it harder to remove the excess, so try to keep the border consistent. As you get used to cutting you will be able to come closer to the line.

With large forms on the band saw you need to think about whether the form will fit between the cutting blade and side support. I generally cut with the form on the outside of the blade to eliminate any concern, but large pieces of scrap that might interfere should be cut off ahead of time. A band saw will cut off your finger without slowing down. Butchers use band saws to cut through bones when cutting up meat. Set the blade guard down close to the form and control the form as you guide it through the blade while keeping your hands well away from the blade. Push the material through the blade at a smooth, constant rate.

Jigsaws are generally safer. They don't cut as fast and it is hard to get your hand in where you can hurt yourself; however, the blade does poke out the bottom of the material. You don't want to put your hand under the part you are cutting, and you don't want to cut into your worktable. I often put a couple of sticks across the top of a large trash barrel to support my part. The scrap falls right in the trash for my kind of cleanup.

If you want to save some weight on your forms, you can cut holes out where there is excess material. The jigsaw will make quick work; just drill a starter hole and start cutting. Leave at least an inch around the edges and don't allow long, unsupported edges. Leave enough material so that the form is still strong.

The best tool for zeroing in on the final edge of the forms is a table-mounted power sander. I use an oscillating belt sander, but a large disk sander also works. While using a disk sander, make sure you use the half of the disk that pushes your work down on to the table. Coarse, 50- to 80-grit sandpaper is appropriate. With light pressure bring your form up against the moving sandpaper, and rotate the form against the sander. Don't just push and hold it there—you want to keep the piece moving to avoid making a flat spot. Rotate the piece against the direction the sander is moving. If you don't, the sander will be happy to make it move the other way and send a small form spinning across the room.

Work smoothly down to the line. Press the piece against the sander, rotate it, and then pull back. Either hit the same spot again or reset your hands and work down along the edge. Come right to the line. It is more important to be consistent about how you leave the line than to hit the edge or the middle. It is probably easiest to leave the line than to split it in half. I try to draw my patterns with fine lines so there is little doubt of how I am doing. The sander may lift the paper a little bit, obscuring the line. Just press the tattered edge down so you can see the line. Work carefully all the way around the form.

I will sometimes draw up my forms with a bevel indication. This is essentially another form pattern indicating the shape of the face on the smaller side of the form. If the form material is

½-inch thick, this means I determine two form lines ½ inch apart along the length of the boat. I cut the form to the larger line and then hold the form at an angle as I sand it to hit the inner line. This takes some practice and, as I discuss in Chapter 5, is not necessary, but it is an option for those who feel so inclined.

Forms that will be mounted on an internal strongback need an accurately located and shaped hole cut in the middle. The form will be strung on the strongback through this hole, and the hole will serve as the primary reference point for aligning the form. Accurate placement will make accurate alignment easier.

The hole must be placed in the same relative position on each form. I usually use the centerline and waterline as location references, with the hole centered on the centerline and at some constant height relative to the waterline. This height should be based on where you can locate the strongback so that it is as long as possible without interfering with the strips on the outside of the boat.

With the location determined and marked on the form, drill a starter hole near two opposite corners. Use your jigsaw to cut the two edges associated with each starter hole. Again, working over a trash can works well here. You can either cut right to the line if you are confident in your ability, or you can cut a little inside the line and clean it up later.

To clean up the hole after cutting, you will need an accurate jig and a router with a template bit. A template bit is a straight-cutting bit with a bearing at one end of the cutter that is the same diameter as the cutter. This lets you cut a shape the same size as a template. Then you need a template the size of your mounting hole (I use 2 inches by 4 inches). This template needs to be accurate because all your holes are going to match it exactly.

I start making the template by making an accurate rectangle the size of my desired hole. This is easy enough on a table saw. MDF is a good choice for material, but good plywood would work as well. Place this rectangle on top of your template material and trace it. Cut out

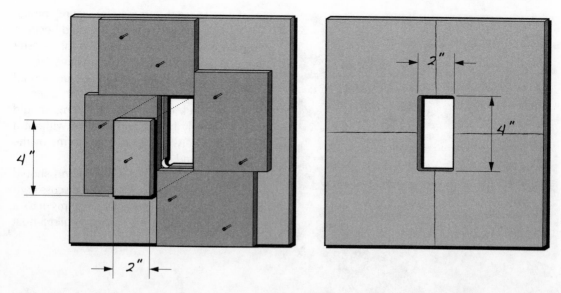

Figure 4-6. *You can cut accurate holes for an internal strongback with a router and a template. The trick is to get your template accurate. I start with an accurately cut 2-inch-by-4-inch rectangle. This is easy to cut with a table saw. Then rough-cut a slightly undersized hole in your template material. Lay the rectangle over the hole, then surround the rectangle with pieces of scrap wood, nailed temporarily in place. Remove the rectangle and use your router to cut the full-sized hole.*

the hole slightly small with a jigsaw. Place the 2-by-4-inch rectangle back on top of the hole and surround it with scraps of material with good straight edges. Nail these down. Pull the rectangle out, revealing the hole. Make sure the hole is fully contained by the scraps and is no bigger. Mount your router in a router table and a ¼-inch-diameter straight template bit with the bearing at the top. Extend the bit so it reaches up through the rough hole, bearing on the scrap bits.

Use the router to remove the excess around the edges of the hole. You should now have a hole exactly the same size as your original rectangle. Remove the scrap bits. The hole will have slightly rounded corners. Mark the center-lines of the hole. Pound a couple of large-head nails such as roofing nails through the template, cut off the ends on the underside about ⅛ inch from the surface, and push them back up flush on the underside so the heads stick up a little on top.

To use the template, line it up on your forms above the pre-roughed-out strongback holes. Use the centerlines to help with the alignment. You can make other marks that correspond to reference lines on your particular forms. Pound the nails flush so they secure the template to the form. Use the template bit on the router table to clean up the holes. Pop the template off and do the next form.

Because of the radius of the bit, this system will leave a rounded corner. Instead of trying to square up all the corners, I generally round over the corners of my strongback with a router. Even the aluminum strongback can be rounded over with a bit intended for wood; it just makes really sharp shavings of aluminum. If you would rather square up the corners of the holes, you can use a rasp or a corner chisel intended for squaring up routed hinge mortises.

I like to make a stack of the forms in the order they will be placed on the strongback, with everything lined up appropriately. This is

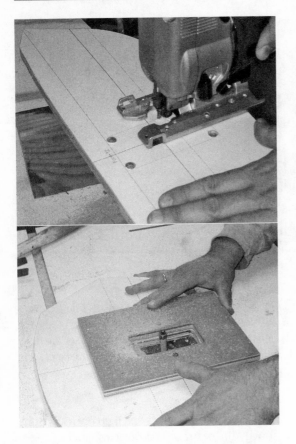

a great way to catch errors before going too far. If the forms are misnumbered it should become quite obvious that the stack of forms doesn't change in a gradual and even manner. If the forms do not have any numbers, you should easily be able to determine the right order by making the stack look good. The forms should get progressively bigger and smaller, without a smaller form between two bigger forms or the other way around.

If everything checks out, your forms should now be done. In Chapter 5 we will discuss converting your cool little stacks of forms into a full-size building jig that is ready to build a boat upon.

Figure 4-7. An accurate internal strongback hole can be made with a router jig. Rough out the hole by drilling holes in the corners, then sawing out the scrap. Tack an accurate jig in place over the hole, and use a straight router bit with a bearing at the end to follow the inside of the jig.

Part II

The Building Process

Chapter 5

Getting Started

I'm sure some builders want to just jump in and start building, without getting too caught up in organizing themselves, but some effort put into preparation now can save time later. There are others who will become so intent on getting everything perfect before they start that they will never actually get around to building a boat. Good preparation will make the project go faster, but there is no substitute for actually getting started for finding out what you really need.

Obviously there are a number of things you have to do before you start assembling the boat, such as cutting strips and forms and setting up the strongback. Other things such as how you organize the strips for easy access are more a matter of convenience but will make a difference as you proceed.

Setting Up Shop

First, you absolutely must have a shop that is about 20 feet by 40 feet, with 10-foot ceilings and radiant floor heating, fully equipped with every power tool imaginable, a dust-collection system, and a great sound system. Internet access is required as well. We can all dream. I build my boats in a small basement with a bulkhead door at one end to get the boat out. I don't really have room to build boats and cut strips at the same time, but I still manage to get a few boats out into daylight every year.

At a minimum, you are going to need a space a few feet bigger than the boat in each direction. For longer boats, you may need to build diagonally across the space to maximize your length. You need room to walk on either side, and unless you like stooping down to get under the boat, you should have enough room to slip around at least one end.

Lots of people have built strippers outside, but it can introduce problems unless you have very consistent weather with moderate temperatures and little rain. The woodworking can be done in a very cold or warm shop, but epoxy and fiberglass work is best done in a climate-controlled space where it is warm enough for the epoxy to cure, but not so warm that it cures before you can get it out of your mixing bucket. It is OK if the shop cools off or warms up when you are not working on the boat, but the ability to have some control over the temperature when you are not around can make many processes more predictable.

You don't want it to rain on the strips before you get a solid coat of epoxy and fiberglass on them, and high humidity will increase the likelihood of the epoxy blushing. In some regions, this may just mean a tarp strung over the work area; in others a fully enclosed shop may prove worthwhile. In an unheated garage, a kerosene or propane heater can usually get the space up to a good working temperature. Liquid epoxy resin is flammable, but the fumes are not a fire hazard. As long as you keep the heater away from drips of wet epoxy, they should be safe. Please read the recommendations of your particular epoxy manufacturer.

For those of us who can't afford the dream shop, a basement or garage will be the best option, although I know of people who have built boats in living rooms and apartment hallways. Making a boat does involve making a bit of a mess. There is dust from sanding and drips of epoxy. While a lot can be done to keep the mess to a minimum, some residual crud will find its way onto the floor and the surrounding environment. If you are building in a cramped apartment it may be wise to factor in your security deposit as part of the cost of building your own boat. Personally, I think it's worth it.

If you are working in a space where you need to protect the floor, a couple of sheets of plywood laid down under your work area should catch most of the mess and survive the whole building process. A little duct tape on the seams will keep epoxy from leaking onto the hardwood floor or carpet.

A good vacuum system and a system for hooking it up to your sander will go a long way to keep the dust from finding its way behind the furnace—or under the sofa—as the case may be.

The easiest system for holding your strongback and boat while you are working on it is a set of sawhorses. If you plan to make a lot of boats, some sort of rolling system may make sense, but a sturdy set of horses is hard to beat.

Milling Strips

Cutting strips is fairly straightforward use of a table saw. I will not attempt to teach you how to use a table saw in this book. There are whole books devoted to that subject. Let me just tell you that there are a lot of experienced woodworkers out there who are missing a few fingers after picking a fight with the spinning blade. A blade that can cut through oak without bogging down will not even burp after chewing off your finger.

Milling strips means turning a beautiful, wide board into a few thin pieces of wood and a lot of sawdust. You want to be as efficient and safe as you can as you do this procedure. For safety you want feather boards or a power stock feeder, and for efficiency you want a thin kerf blade.

Feather boards are pieces of wood cut at an angle at the end and then sliced into a comb. They are used to apply pressure to stock being

moved through power tools and keeping them from moving backward. This allows you to push your boards through the saw while keeping your hands well away from the blade and not worrying about kickback. (See page 44 in Chapter 3.) If you don't know what kickback is, it is related to how the saw may bite off your finger.

At the very least you want a feather board to hold the board down against the table. This usually requires some sort of fence extension to allow a secure mounting point. Set your saw to the thickness of the strips you are cutting. If you are going to plane the strips down to thickness, set the width a little more than the final thickness.

If you are using roughly sawn wood, you will first want to run your material through a thickness planer. Check that all your boards are the same thickness and plane them to consistent thickness as necessary.

With the saw blade lowered all the way down, place your board on the saw, up against the fence. Adjust the feather board so it is slightly flexed and secure it in place. Try sliding the board to be sure it will move. It should move forward easily, but not slide backward at all. Remove the board. Start the saw and slowly raise the blade until it cuts into the bottom of the feather board. With the feather board in place, it should be impossible to get your hands near

Figure 5-1. Applying some wax to the table of the saw will help material slide, making it easier to cut.

the blade while cutting a board because the blade is contained below the feather board.

You will want good support before and after the table. This could be sawhorses or a worktable. I am not a big fan of standard support rollers as they have a tendency to steer the board, making it hard to create a straight cut. I put some waxed paper down on the top of my sawhorses and table to make it easier for the board to slide around.

A straight cut requires constant pressure pushing the board against the fence, while feeding it forward through the saw. This can be hard to maintain with just two hands. Some people use a magnetic feather-board system that can be moved in toward the fence as strips are cut off, making the board narrower. As you get to the end of the board you will need a push stick to guide the board forward on the last bit of the cut. Be careful to keep the board moving straight through the saw.

Note that most saws come with throat inserts with a fairly wide gap where the blade comes through. Thin strips may get caught in this gap. You may want to make or buy a zero-clearance insert. Also, the board will slide much more easily over the table if you wax and buff the tabletop.

Uniform-thickness strips produce the best results, and the best way to get uniform thickness is to apply uniform pressure with a uniform feed rate. This is hard to do by hand, so I purchased an automatic stock feeder. This is like a little motorized car that is anchored to the table so that when you try to make it drive down a board, it pulls the board under it. The

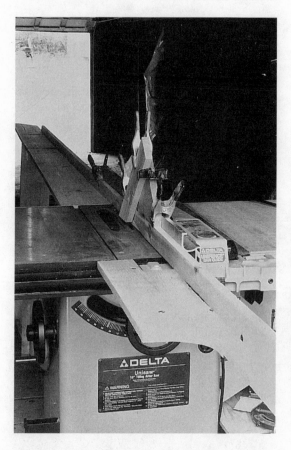

Figure 5-2. Extra-long infeed and outfeed tables on the table saw help control long boards so the resulting strips are more uniform. Extend the fence on the infeed end to assure alignment of long boards. Notice the cutaway on the infeed table so you can grasp the board as it gets narrower.

Figure 5-3. If you are cutting a lot of strips, a power stock feeder is a nice luxury. It feeds the board at a constant rate while holding it down on the table and firmly against the fence all while keeping fingers away from the spinning blade. Notice I am wearing ear, eye, and breathing protection while making all that noise and dust.

Figure 5-4. *You can save some time at the table saw by ganging together several blades on the saw arbor. I use a blade stabilizer as a spacer between the blades. Note that ganging up blades can be very dangerous if you are hand feeding the boards through the saw. I don't recommend this without using a stock feeder.*

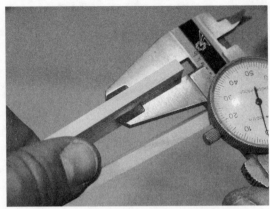

Figure 5-5. *A smooth, fair surface on the boat starts with uniform-thickness strips. Check the strips as they come out of the saw to make sure they are at least as thick as you need after thickness planing. Check a few scraps through your thickness planer before running your strips, and spot-check as you go to make sure nothing moved.*

stock feeder pushes your material at a constant rate while holding it against the fence. This is a luxury item if you are only building one boat, but if you are going to cut a lot of strips, it is a nice addition to your shop. It allows you to cut consistent strips without ever having to get your hands anywhere near the blade.

With the stock feeder and a powerful saw, you can also gang up several blades. Most saws have the ability to place a spacer between two blades so each pass through the saw cuts two strips. This could be quite dangerous to try while hand feeding the stock because it is hard to push the last bit through the two blades. The downside of cutting two strips at a time is you can mess up your wood twice as fast.

As you are cutting your strips, keep an eye on the results. You may find you start getting narrow spots in the strips at one particular part of the board. If you sight down the length of the board along the edge that you are cutting, you will usually find that the edge is no longer straight and this area is cut a little deeper. With careful cutting you may be able to straighten out

the edge a bit, but it is often easier to just flip the board over so you are starting again from the factory-cut edge. If you mess up both edges, you may need to use a hand plane or jointer to true up the edge again.

This can really mess up your life if you wish to do some sort of book-matched pattern. Book matching is a technique that emphasizes wood grain where consecutive slices of wood are opened up adjacent to each other so the grain on either side is a mirror image across the seam. (See the sidebar on page 106 in Chapter 6 for more information.) For a book-matched pattern to work, each strip must come from directly adjacent to the previous strip on the board. Any failure to do this will get into a different grain pattern and disrupt the gradual change expected.

Before cutting a board for book matching you want to make some marks to help you reassemble the order of the board after cutting. You will try to keep the strips in order as you cut, but some diagonal marks drawn across the end of the board will provide a reference if the strips

Figure 5-6. *A lot of wood is turned into dust when cutting strips. Here an 11-inch-wide board (top) is turned into eighty ³⁄₁₆-inch-wide strips (bottom), and 30% of the wood has been converted to sawdust. These strips are destined to be book-matched. The end of the board was marked with a diagonal line. In the cut strips the pencil points to one strip that is upside down.*

Figure 5-7. *Book matching strips requires you to keep the strips in order. Here I've numbered the strips for easy reference. Write the numbers at several locations along the length and on both sides so you can find numbers even when the strips are cut short. I circle the numbers on the back side so I can quickly identify which side should show.*

Figure 5-8. *Every once in a while mistakes happen. This strip broke along the grain. Throwing the strip out would have messed up the book matching pattern. Instead, I used some CA glue to put it back together. Under fiberglass no strength will be lost, and the repair will disappear.*

get shuffled. I use a permanent marker on the end grain and also make some light pencil marks on the face of the board. Using a marker on the face would leave marks on the finished boat.

As you cut the strips for book matching, arrange them on a nearby table in the order they are coming off the board. If you are gang sawing more than one strip at a time, pay attention to the placement of each strip in the arrangement.

After cutting all the strips, it is a good idea to run them all through a thickness planer to assure they are all the same thickness. You only need to finish one side. With careful table saw work, this step is not strictly necessary, but it is one more step that may pay off with less work later on. Most planers will be able to handle several strips at a time, but you don't want to try to feed too many because they can get tangled and make a mess.

Cove-and-Bead

If you are going to make cove-and-bead strips it is particularly important that the strips are of consistent thickness. Because the cove-and-beads need to be centered on the strip, the center needs to be in the same place on all the strips. Set up your router in a router table to cut the bead first. The cove is more delicate, so the less you handle it after milling, the better. You will need some scrap strips to help you set up. These should be just like the strips you will be milling. Start with the fence set so the bit just barely hits the strips. Adjust the bit height so both the top and bottom of the strip are hit equally. Run a few strips through to be sure that they are being milled consistently. When the height is right, adjust the fence so the depth is just sufficient to round over the edge. You don't want to make the strip narrower; if you scribble on the edge with a pencil, the router should just remove the color from the center of the edge.

Set up a feather board to hold the strip down at the router bit and another to hold the strip against the fence. Run another test strip to be sure everything is still running right.

When you're milling the coves and beads you don't want your fingers to come anywhere near the cutter. Feather boards serve to keep your fingers away while holding the strips tight against the cutter. The upper feather board is cut from a piece of plywood and has a board in front of it to help hold it in place with some spring clamps.

Run all the strips through the same way. For example, if you have planed the strips, run all the strips with the planed side down against the table for both the bead and the cove. In this way, any misalignment while centering the bit will be off in a consistent and predictable way. If you are planning on book matching strips you will want to be particularly cognizant of the cove-and-bead location. And depending on your intended stripping pattern you may actually want to have every other strip milled on the opposite side. Think about what you intend to do. Frankly, if I'm going to do complicated stripping patterns, I don't bother with cove and bead at all. My brain cramps up trying to figure it out.

Set up to mill the cove in a similar manner. Replace the bit with the cove-cutting bit. Start with the fence set to make a very light cut centered as close as possible on the thickness of the strip. Flip the strip over and check the height. Adjust the height so it splits any difference. When you think you have it set, adjust the fence until one or both of the top or bottom edges becomes a feather thickness. If one edge becomes finer sooner, the bit is too close to that edge; adjust the height slightly so both edges are the same thickness. When it is right, adjust the fence so the cut is not as deep. You want a slightly square edge on either side of the cove.

Set up your feather boards again, and make sure nothing has shifted. When it all looks good, run your strips again. Again, keep the planed side down or follow whatever rule you chose, but be consistent.

Figure 5-9. *Using a consistent thickness of strips helps produce a smooth surface, but this is particularly important with cove-and-bead strips. It is almost impossible to keep the cove-and-bead centered on the strip if the thickness varies. Running the strips through a thickness planer after they come off the saw solves the problem. Here I'm running five strips through simultaneously.*

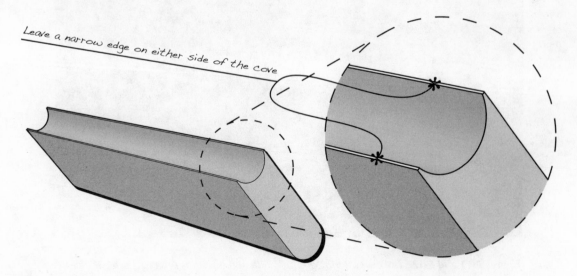

Leave a narrow edge on either side of the cove

Figure 5-10. *The cove side of a cove-and-bead strip can be delicate. If you leave a slightly square edge it will be stronger than a fine feather edge. The strips need to be uniform in thickness to get a uniform edge on both sides.*

Figures 5-11 and 5-12. *The coves and beads are milled on the strips on a router table. Set the router up so the bit is turning opposite of the feed direction of the strip. When the bit height has been adjusted so it cuts down the middle of the strip and the fence has been adjusted so the depth is just deep enough, install feather boards. One board should hold the strip down on the table, with another pressing it against the fence.*

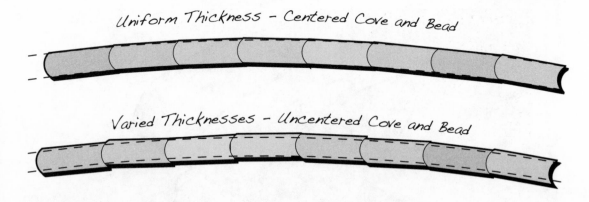

Uniform Thickness - Centered Cove and Bead

Varied Thicknesses - Uncentered Cove and Bead

Figure 5-13. *Carefully milled strips create a smoother finished surface. Sloppy milling requires more sanding, planing, and just plain elbow grease. After all of that work, the remaining wood will be thinner.*

Obviously, the power stock feeder can be used here as well. The consistent feed rate will help produce more uniform strips. Another option if you have the tools is to set up two consecutive routers so the bead and cove are cut in one pass.

Setting Up Forms

The building form is the key to the boat shape. Once the building form is set up, all you really need to do is cover it with strips of wood. While the stripping will even out small errors, an accurate building form is a pretty good guarantee of an accurate boat shape.

The building form consists of two parts: the form or rib shapes, and the spine or strongback that holds them all together. An accurate building form starts out with a straight strongback. A strongback can be just about any reasonably stiff, reasonably straight object that allows you to mount the forms in their appropriate location.

With open boats, the forms are oriented so the boat is built upside down. With deck boats, the forms need to be flipped over during the stripping process. Usually people start with the boat upside down so they work on the hull first. There is no hard-and-fast rule on this, and if you

are using an internal strongback you can start either way. Plans for decked boats that use an external strongback typically assume the builder will start with the boat upside down.

Strongbacks

A strongback can be an old wooden ladder, a plywood box, or an aluminum extrusion. The primary goal is to have a reliable reference so the forms will stay in their proper orientation relative to one another. While I said it should be straight, that is not really a requirement so long as you can establish some straight and true reference lines, mount the forms securely relative to those reference lines, and have confidence that they will stay there throughout the boatbuilding process. When boiled down to its essence, this is not a very high standard. The strongback need not be very sophisticated; it just needs to be reliable.

Strongback Selection. Exactly what you use for a strongback will depend on the style of boat you are building, the material you have on hand, how many boats you are going to build, and what you are comfortable with. There are two basic styles: internal strongbacks, which

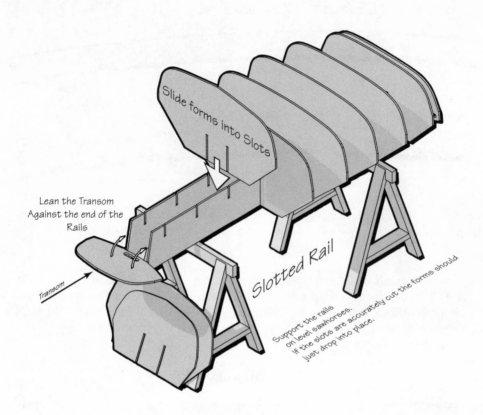

Slide forms into Slots

Lean the Transom
Against the end of the
Rails

Transom

Slotted Rail

Support the rails
on level sawhorses.
If the slots are accurately cut the forms should
just drop into place.

Figure 5-14. *The forms are secured in their appropriate location on a strongback. There are many kinds of strongback, but keeping it simple is always a benefit. The slotted rail is as simple as they come, but may be hard for a first-time builder to produce accurately. Boat kit manufacturers sometimes provide this system. The external strongback is probably the most common. In this example a plywood box beam provides a firm, steady, straight, and stiff base for supporting the forms. The forms are screwed to the box beam via simple wooden cleats. For decked boats like kayaks, an internal strongback is a good option. It can be made of a straight and true 2 by 4 (if you can find one), a small box beam, or if you are building enough boats to justify the cost, an aluminum extrusion. In this case the end forms are screwed in place on the ends of the beam and 11½-inch-long L spacers assure a 12-inch distance between forms. The middle spacer is cut to accept a couple of wedges that tighten up all the spacers along the length of the boat. On a straight strongback this allows the forms to be released and realigned quickly and easily.*

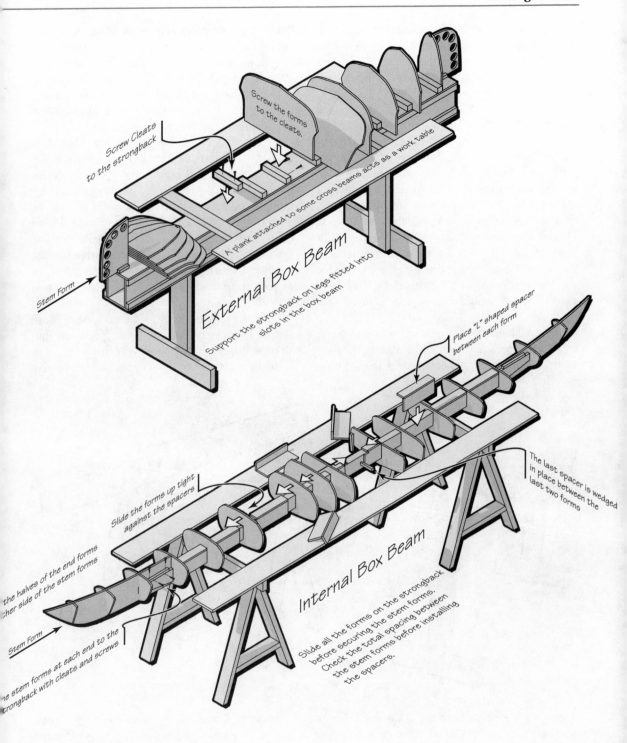

Screw Cleats to the strongback

Screw the forms to the cleats.

A plank attached to some cross beams acts as a work table

Stem Form

External Box Beam

Support the strongback on legs fitted into slots in the box beam

Place "L" shaped spacer between each form

Slide the forms up tight against the spacers

The last spacer is wedged in place between the last two forms

the halves of the end forms ther side of the stem forms

Stem Form

he stem forms at each end to the trongback with cleats and screws

Internal Box Beam

Slide all the forms on the strongback before securing the stem forms. Check the total spacing between the stem forms before installing the spacers.

end up surrounded by the forms, and external strongbacks, which are usually below the forms with the boat built above them.

Most open boats like canoes will be well served with some form of external strongback. Internal strongbacks become an option for closed boats such as kayaks or rowing shells.

An internal strongback offers the ability to flip the boat over at will. This may not seem like a big deal, but it can prove quite handy once you get used to it. In order to strip the deck of a closed boat on an external strongback, you must remove the forms from the strongback. Usually the forms stay attached to the hull after being detached from the external strongback, but it can be convenient to be able to remove the hull while working on the deck, in which case the forms would just fall apart.

Making a Strongback. Back in the day when 2 by 4s were nice and straight, it was pretty easy to make a nice, straight, flat, and true strong-

back using common lumber for studs. A typical strongback would be made like a ladder with two long pieces connected by crosspieces. Whack it together with nails with the spacing between the crosspieces equal to the spacing between the forms, and then you can screw the forms directly to the crosspieces.

Unfortunately, 2 by 4s are not what they used to be, and it may be hard to make the stuff from the local home center into a convenient strongback. The better wood gets used for larger-dimension 2-by material such as 2 by 6s and 2 by 8s. While these still may have a little curve or twist to them, with care you can nail or screw two together into a T form that is quite straight. Unfortunately, as the wood acclimates to your shop space it may shrink or expand and go out of true.

Plywood is easier and dimensionally more stable. If you can cut a sheet of plywood into straight 8-inch-wide panels you should be able to make a straight and accurate box beam. Cut

Figure 5-15. *An external strongback works well for most open boats. A plywood box beam can be made quite precisely with a table saw while the other two styles of external strongback shown here require good straight wood to assure precision. However, you don't need a table saw to make your own. The ladder frame is better for wider boats, and the T-beam is good for smaller, narrower boats.*

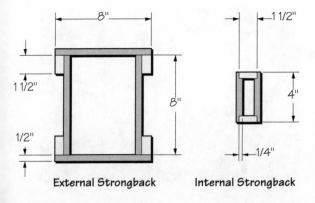

External Strongback   **Internal Strongback**

Figure 5-16. On the left is a typical external strong-back box beam, and on the right an internal one. You can make both from ½-inch-thick plywood. The external uses some ¾-inch-by-1½-inch pine stringers screwed to the side piece of plywood, then the top and bottom are screwed on. The internal is made with plywood sides rabbetted to accept the top and bottom pieces. These can either be plywood or pine lumber.

some strips of 16-foot pine into stringers. With 8-foot plywood it is easy to make a 16-foot strongback. Place two lengths of the 8-inch-by-8-foot plywood end to end. Make sure they are straight. Connect them with two pine stringers along the top and bottom edge nailed in place. Make sure they are straight. Make two of these and tip them up on edge. Place plywood on the top to connect the two sides, and stagger the joints relative to the side pieces. Make sure they are straight. Flip the assembly over. Cut some rectangles of plywood to fit inside the trough. Place several of these rectangles inside and secure them in place. Cover the bottom with more plywood. If you leave some gaps between the bottom piece of plywood you can insert supporting legs and screw them in place. Check again that everything is straight.

I put wheels on the legs so I can roll the whole strongback around the shop. Some people go high-end and mount electrical boxes in the box beam and set themselves up to always have

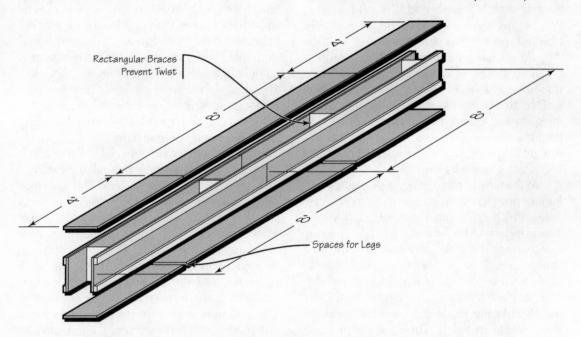

Rectangular Braces
Prevent Twist

Spaces for Legs

Figure 5-17. You don't want all the joints on the box beam to line up. For a 16-foot-long beam, cut two of the top and bottom pieces in half and put the half pieces at the end with the long piece in the middle. With a large external box beam a couple of braces inside the beam help prevent twist. If you leave some open slots in the bottom, you can insert legs into the beam instead of using sawhorses.

an outlet handy. If you really want to go top-shelf you can paint it with flames or dolphins or whatever, but it is really just a workbench that will likely get epoxy dripped all over it before you're done, so don't go overboard. You're trying to build a boat, not high-end strongbacks.

When I started building kayaks I found some really nice straight 2 by 4s that I cherish to this day. I don't much use them anymore, but they still make a decent internal strongback. Just a straight and true 16-foot stick running down through the middle of the forms. Sadly these are not to be found anymore, so I've bought a nice aluminum extrusion. With ⅛-inch walls it is light, and it is perfectly straight, with no twist and exactly 2 inches by 4 inches in dimension. It is really nice, but maybe not the most reasonable for people building just a single boat or two.

A more practical solution is a small plywood box beam described earlier. Just about any plywood will work: CDX is fine, or if you have it available hardwood plywood is nice. You can even use oriented strand board (OSB). I do not recommend particleboard or MDF as they do not have the strength needed. Rabbets cut along the edges of the wide sides will help stabilize the assembly. Try to find a flat, level surface to do the assembly. Glue the whole thing up and clamp it or wrap it with rope to hold it while the glue dries. Make sure that it is straight by getting your eye down near one edge and sighting down its length.

At the time of this writing, new engineered-lumber products were starting to become available, which offer other strongback options. These include 2 by 4s made by finger-jointing together small chunks of wood to form long straight pieces, as well as other 2-by material made from large chips of wood, glued together OSB, or glued laminations of thin veneers. There are also I-beams made of a combination of different wood materials. These newer products offer dimensional stability, straight stock, and the potential of a consistent and true strongback that is hard to obtain in natural lumber.

Figure 5-18. *The slotted strongback is very simple to set up. Two long beams with slots cut in them accept matching slots on the forms. Drop the forms into the slots, make sure they are seated all the way down, and you are good to go.*

I mentioned earlier that I used an aluminum extrusion for most of my kayak strongbacks. Aluminum works well because it can be cut and drilled with woodworking tools. I cut my strongback shorter than needed for most of my boats and then have several solid wood extensions that I insert into the end of the extrusion to compensate when I need a longer strongback. The aluminum strongback works very well with L spacers (described on page 76) because it is rigid, straight, and true, so I don't need to worry about alignment, only spacing.

The last form of strongback I will mention is a bit of a hybrid between internal and external. This is the slotted beam system. This system is most common for kit boats. It uses a piece of wood, typically sheet stock like plywood or particleboard, with slots cut in it. The forms have matching slots. Setting up the forms becomes a simple matter of sliding the forms into their respective slot on the beam. The beam may actually consist of two or more pieces of wood. This system is very simple to manufacture with computer-controlled machinery, but it can also be reproduced at home with simple tools. All that is required is the patience to cut the slots. This type of strongback is most easily adapted to open boats, but some of the ideas can be incorporated in decked boats. For example, end forms and stem forms can be slotted together.

Aligning Forms

Accurately cut holes will help make aligning the forms on an internal strongback easier, especially if you have a nice straight strongback, but you will still want to double-check before you start building. To make it easier to check and to assist you in getting the alignment right, you will need some reference marks on the forms. An accurately marked centerline and some consistent horizontal waterlines are the keys to assuring you get the forms straight.

If your forms do not have reference lines, carefully measure out the centerline and mark it and at least one horizontal line at a constant distance from the bottom or baseline of the form on open-boat forms, or the strongback hole on decked-boat forms.

Mark the strongback with a centerline. Use a piece of string pulled tight down the center of the strongback. While a chalk line does a pretty good job, the act of plucking it to make the mark can throw a bit of a curve in the line. I will often use a piece of fine fishing line tied tight at each end, which I then secure in place with some dots of hot-melt glue at various locations spaced along the length. Be sure not to displace the line as you add the glue drops.

Measure out the form spacing indicated on the plans, and mark the locations on the top of the strongback, allowing enough room on each end for the stem forms. On an external strongback you can screw down cleats next to each

Figure 5-19. *If you don't have reference lines on the forms, you should mark them as necessary. In this case I cut the front and back forms of the Nymph at the same time. One set had the original paper patterns with lines; the other set did not.*

mark now. Use a square to assure the cleats are at right angles to the centerline. With an internal strongback you will need to slide the forms onto the strongback before attaching cleats. A little notch in the forms at the reference lines will provide clearance for the string.

You need to place the forms so the strips touch them right on the reference location of the form. With unbeveled forms, this means that at the front of the boat, where the strips taper in, you want the strips to hit the forms on their front edge, so the front face of the forms should align with the mark on the strongback. Similarly, the strips toward the back of the boat should touch on the back face of the form, so the forms here should be set forward of the line location mark. In other words, the forms are always set to the inside of the form location mark, with the outer face of the form aligned with the location mark.

If you do bevel the edge of the forms, then the reference face of the form becomes the inner face, so the forms should be set to the outside of the location mark.

Beveling the forms allows the edges of the forms to conform to the angle of the strips as they bend around the forms. This means that the edge of the form is at the same angle and parallel to the strips, so the strips lie flush and tight against the forms. I usually do not bother to bevel the forms, but it does create a larger glue area if you are hot-melt gluing the strips to the form. Some designs come with the bevel angle marked on the plans so you can sand in the bevel before installing them on the strong-back. Otherwise you can use a long-board fair-ing sander to knock off the corner of the forms. Align the long-board with the adjacent forms and carefully sand down the high edge (the

Figure 5-20. *Forms are attached to an external strongback with wooden cleats. Mark the strong-back with the appropriate spacing with a centerline marked in place. Screw the cleats in place next to the spacing marks.*

edge closer to the near end of the boat). Keep sanding, checking your angle as you go, until you are almost touching the lower edge.

Set up the end forms at each end of the boat and the middle form at the widest point of the boat. Align these three forms with each other. Use the centerline and horizontal reference lines to check for twist. If you have clamps that will hold the forms, start by clamping them in place. Otherwise run a single screw through the forms into the cleats. It will take a little bit of adjusting to get all the forms lined up. Clamps make it easier to make these adjustments, but screws will be more secure. In the end you will screw all the form in place. Align the centerline of the forms with the centerline marked on the strongback. On a straight strongback without twist, seating the form tight against the strongback should result in a good initial alignment.

Clamp some scrap strips next to the lines on the end forms to extend them so you can sight down from one end to the other to assure that all three forms are in a straight line and at the same orientation. It does not matter if the forms are leaning to one side or the other so long as they all lean the same; however, it is easier to set things up if they are all straight because then you can use a level to help you set them up.

Stretch some fishing line between the scrap strips to help with the alignment. Keep the strings as close to the forms as you can without touching them. Those who are more high tech can use a laser pointer or level to project a line. Tapping on the forms with a hammer or scrap of wood helps make small adjustments. Slide some wedges under the form to make larger adjustments. When the first three forms are aligned well, secure them in place with more

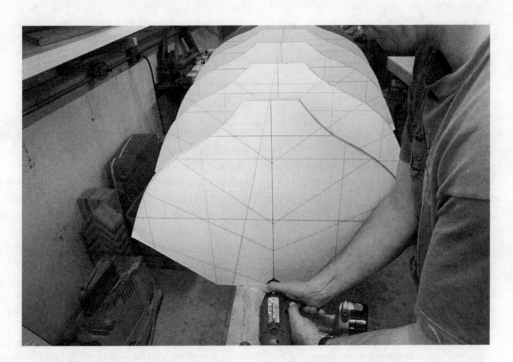

Figure 5-21. *Align the forms along the centerline of the strongback. If your strongback has a flat, untwisted top and the forms are accurately cut, the centerlines at the top of the forms should align naturally. Here I'm pulling a string tightly between the stem forms to check the alignment.*

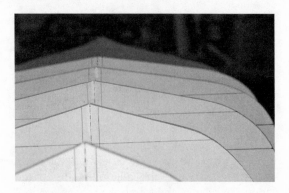

Figure 5-22. *If a piece of string isn't high tech enough for you, a laser can help assure your forms are aligned correctly.*

screws and double-check that they didn't move on you.

You can now use these first three forms as references to aligning the remaining forms. Work from the middle toward the ends. Get your eye down close to the reference lines to check that they are lining up. Work carefully because an uncorrected error in setting up the forms will end up as a funny shape in the finished boat.

When you are done setting up all of the forms, you want to double-check them again. Use some of the strips you will use to make the boat. Lay them against the forms and temporarily secure them in place with a couple of clamps or staples. Get your eye down near the strips and look down their length. Look for sudden change in direction, individual forms that seem to make a high or low spot, or other signs that the forms aren't quite fair. Look at the offending form and try to determine if you somehow set it up wrong. Recheck your reference lines. Maybe there is a drip of glue under the form or it shifted when you screwed it down. Adjust it accordingly.

If the form looks like it is set up correctly, but you just can't make the irregularity go away, you may need to fair the forms. For high spots, this may mean sanding, grinding, or rasping away at the form. Low spots can be filled up with whittled pieces of wood or stacks of cardboard

used as shims so a strip bent around the forms lies smoothly against all of them. If it looks like it will take a lot of futzing to get the forms right, stop and make sure you have the right forms in the right location before doing anything drastic. Some plans will require the forms be set at an uneven spacing to be properly set up. You don't want to mess up your forms only to learn that they were just supposed to be placed an inch farther forward.

Do the trick with the test strips several places around the forms. The strips should not need to run parallel to the final stripping location to stay fair. Except for boats with abrupt surface features such as chines, a strip running in any direction should still run smooth and fair.

Boats with fine ends may have some split forms that are secured on either side of the stem forms. Cut these forms in half, removing the thickness of your stem form from the middle. I use some dots of hot-melt glue to hold these forms on the side of the stem form. Check the location before gluing them in place.

L Spacers

Setup can be much easier if you have a really accurate, straight, and untwisted internal strongback. With my kayaks, my aluminum extrusion allows for some shortcuts that make setup go very quickly. If I cut accurate holes in the forms to give them a tight fit around the extrusion, I do not need to worry about twist. The forms will be aligned correctly just by sliding them in place. All I need to concern myself with is their spacing. For this I use plywood spacers. I glued up a beam out of two pieces of plywood to form an L shape. I cut the beam into lengths equal to the spacing between the forms, minus the thickness of my forms; that is, with a forms spacing of 12 inches using ½-inch-thick forms, I cut the spacers 11½ inches long. My table saw set up with an accurate miter gauge assures a consistent length and square ends.

Accurately measure the distance between the two final forms at each end of the strongback and secure them to the strongback so they cannot slide. Then secure the end or stem forms to these and to the strongback. The following steps will put a lot of pressure on these forms to slide off the ends, so make sure they are well screwed in place. I then drop spacers between the forms and slide them tight toward the end. In the middle I create a spacer that can be secured with wedges. By tapping wedges into the center spacer, all the forms are clamped tightly between the secured end forms and the setup is almost complete. Depending on the design, you may still need to glue on some more end forms to the stem form.

If you have done everything right, this system should not need much attention to get fair, but you should still double- and triple-check it. Sight down the reference lines and lay some test strips over the forms to find any mistakes.

Figure 5-23. With this aluminum strongback, I use L-shaped spacers to hold the forms in place. The end forms are screwed in place, and wedges between the middle forms hold everything tight.

Figure 5-24. These wedges push all the forms tightly against the L spacers and the end forms. If you are gluing the strips to the forms to avoid staples, you can remove the wedges to break the shell free from the forms, then reinsert the wedges to return the forms to their proper location. (Note: Ignore the longitudinal forms shown in this picture; they were not used.)

Figure 5-25. Wrap tape around the edges of the forms to keep glue from sticking. This clear packaging tape will assure nothing sticks at all. Masking tape also works well. It allows the glue to help hold the strips to the forms a little bit, but it still lets the glue break free when needed.

When the forms are all set up and aligned, you want to protect the edges so glue does not stick. I've used masking tape, clear packaging tape, fiber-reinforced strapping tape, a seal coat of shellac, and nothing, leaving the edges alone. I've settled on clear packaging tape as being best for me. Nothing sticks to it, so there is little chance of the boat getting stuck. Some people like a little bit of sticking so the boat doesn't shift around while sanding and fairing. If you are planning on building without staples using the hot-melt glue system, you do want the hot glue to stick a bit. Leaving the edge unsealed

or using masking tape works pretty well in this instance.

Inner Stems and Transoms

The next steps I'll describe could be considered part of actually building the boat, instead of part of the setup prior to building, but because they have a lot in common with setting up the forms, I've included them here. The first part of the boat to go on the forms is the inner stems or the transoms (or one of each), depending

Figure 5-26. *Boats with largely straight bow and stern shapes can use solid wood inner stems. If your plans include the pattern for the inner stem, use the pattern to mark the outer line. Cut to this line, then mark the bevel line. Bevel on both sides as far back as the bevel line. Cut the stem off the piece of wood and tape it onto the inner stem.*

on the boat. An *inner stem* is a reinforcement of the sharp bow or stern. A *transom* is the flat panel on boats that have squared-off ends. The stem is much like a longitudinal form that stays in the boat, and a transom is much like a cross-sectional form that stays in the boat.

An inner stem is not necessary. It is quite possible to just put a sharp leading edge on the bow form and strip over it without gluing any of the strips to the form. This works fine and is a lighter-weight solution that does not lose much strength. The advantage of the inner stem is partly that it makes the building process a little easier. An inner stem allows you to glue the tricky ends of the strips to something solid, and it fills up the really narrow little triangle in the ends of the boat with something so it is easier to fiberglass. The stem does make the bow and stern a little more rugged, but on small boats there probably isn't much need for the added reinforcement.

Inner stems can be made several ways. A solid piece of wood can be cut to shape, or the wood can be bent to fit. You can make a bent stem either by steaming wood or by cutting a stack of thin flexible strips and laminating them together in the appropriate shape.

A bent stem works well when the stem has a distinct curvature. If the plans call for steaming, you can almost always laminate instead, and vice versa.

Laminating the Inner Stem

Cut the laminations thin enough to make the bend. Tighter bends will require thinner laminations. For example, a 2-inch-diameter bend may require ⅛- or ¹⁄₁₆-inch laminations. Thicker stems may suggest fewer, thicker laminations, thus being easier to glue up, but if you make them too thick, they will break. Try some scrap strips before you commit glue to everything.

Drill some holes along the edge of the forms so you can hook on the clamps. Apply glue to both sides of each glue joint. Epoxy or another waterproof glue can be used, but if

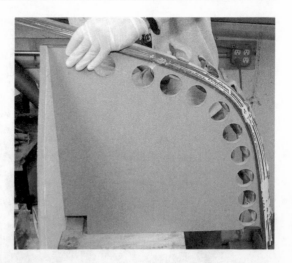

Figure 5-27. *For boats where the stem takes a sharp bend, a bent inner stem works better. This can be laminated or steam bent. With thin enough laminations, the stem will bend easily around the form. The topmost lamination is backed up with fiberglass-reinforced tape to help protect against splitting. This helps the wood bend around a tighter radius with less chance of breaking.*

Figure 5-28. *If the stem laminations are cut too thick they may break. Cut the next set thinner.*

Figure 5-29. *If you don't have a pattern for the bevel angle of the inner stem, you can bevel it while on the forms. Use a strip of wood laid over the forms to look for a tight fit flat against the side of the stem.*

you are glassing over the inner stem, the glue doesn't have to be waterproof; carpenter's glue will work just fine. Start clamping the stack of glued-up strips at one end, and keep adding clamps as you gradually bend the stack around the form. If you are going to add a laminated outer stem later you can glue and bend it at the same time, just be sure to add some waxed paper in between the inner and outer stems so they don't end up glued together.

After the glue has dried, remove the stem and clean up the squeezed-out glue by scraping, sanding, and/or planing. Secure the stem back on the forms and then bevel the sides so that strips bent over the forms lie flush against the side of the stem.

Solid wood stems cut to shape are best suited for fairly straight stems where the wood grain will be parallel to the stem over most of its length. While you can cut it out, secure it to the stem form, and then bevel the edges, it is generally easier to bevel the sides while the stem is still securely attached to the original piece of wood. If the plans indicate the bevel, first cut the outer shape and mark the bevel line, and then plane the bevel before cutting the stem off the board.

The shaped inner stems can be held to the forms with tape or some screws. Be sure to remove them before you cover them with strips.

Steaming Stems

Steaming uses heat to soften wood to the point that it is flexible. This allows you to take a larger, thicker chunk of wood and bend it easily. This works because wood is held together by a natural glue called *lignum* that softens with heat. You don't have to use steam—any heat will do—but steam is by far the easiest. It transfers the heat from your heat source to your wood quickly and efficiently.

Some woods respond to this treatment better than others. Red oak is considered the premier steam-bending stock, but ash also works well. The material should be straight grained, be free of knots, and have no grain running out the edge. Steaming requires much better wood than laminating, which is one of the appeals of lamination.

One of the easiest heat sources is a plug-in electric teakettle. Lee Valley Tools actually sells a kettle specifically for this purpose. Direct the steam into a box just big enough to hold the stems. With your stem stock in the box and supported off the bottom so the heat gets all the way around the wood, plug the ends of the box loosely with rags and start heating your stem stock.

Figure on 1 hour in the steam for each inch of thickness of the wood. Therefore, this means ¼-inch stock should take about 15 minutes. The ¾-inch stock for a boat like the Nymph would take 45 minutes.

Use the same forms as you would for laminated stems. When the time is up on the steam, pull the plug and quickly pull the material from the box (wearing gloves). Secure one end of the stock to the forms, and bend the wood around the forms. Use deliberate speed, but don't rush. Pay attention to how the wood is responding, but don't take so long that the wood cools down. You should be able to bend a stem in less than 30 seconds. Quickly put clamps in place, much as you would with a laminated stem.

Transoms

Transoms are much like forms, but they are located at one or both ends and will stay in the boat. They can be cut in the same manner as the forms. Instead of cheap MDF or plywood, however, you should use good-quality solid wood or marine plywood. Because they will

Figure 5-30. Secure the inner stem with tape and maybe a screw. Make sure the screw is accessible so it can be removed. Remove the tape before stripping over it.

Figure 5-31. Any plywood parts such as transoms that will remain in the boat after stripping should be coated with epoxy to protect the wood from glue drips and other damage.

come off the strongback with the stripped parts of the boat, they should be held in place temporarily. Use clamps, hot-melt glue, or even screws in some discreet location. Before securing transoms in place I like to protect them with a seal coat of epoxy. This will help keep other glue from soaking in and creating a stain later on.

As described above, the strongback has some means of holding the forms in their appropriate locations. Align the transom in the same way you aligned all the forms, using reference marks and test strips to assure it is fair. Hold the transom in place with clamps until it looks right, then secure it more permanently with dots of hot-melt glue or some screws. If you don't want screws through the transom you can temporarily glue cleats to the transom and it screw through the cleats.

This finishes up the preparation work, and you are now ready to get into the meat of the building project. You may want to take a little time to go back and inspect everything to be sure all the forms are straight and aligned correctly. Things can shift and get thrown out of place, and now is your best opportunity to ensure your form is accurate and true.

Chapter 6

Stripping the Hull

In the simplest terms the goal you are seeking to accomplish is to cover the forms with wood. For every boat there will be many ways you could go about achieving this goal, but as you decide exactly how you are going to do it, it is worth reminding yourself that all you are really trying to do is cover the forms with thin strips of wood. This basic principle allows you almost unlimited freedom to get creative by making interesting patterns with the strips of wood, yet reminds you that you don't need to get carried away overthinking what you are trying to accomplish.

What this means from a structural or strength perspective is that there is not too much reason to pick one stripping pattern over another. (It matters, but not that much.) There may be some stripping patterns that are easier to accomplish than others, and one pattern may look better than another, but when you are done, any pattern should function as well as any other so long as the forms are covered with wood and the wood is covered with fiberglass.

Let's talk about open boats versus closed boats. Open boats such as canoes and rowboats are generally built much the same way as closed boats such as a kayak, but they do start out slightly differently because open boats will have some sort of gunwale piece attached at the top edge of the hull whereas closed boats will have a deck attached. The differences are minor, but it is worth distinguishing them because it will change the way you strip your boat.

The First Strips

You have to start stripping the boat somewhere. On most boats this first strip will be the top strip on the hull. I typically call this the *sheer strip* because it defines the sheerline of the boat. On an open boat this is the top of the gunwale. On a closed boat it is typically the transition from the hull to the deck. This is not universally true; there are some applications where you may want to put your first strip somewhere else. Feel free to do so if you have a reason that makes sense to you.

The positioning of your first strip on the forms will go a long way to determining how the rest of the strips will go on and will determine the overall look of the boat to some extent. Since most of the subsequent strips will run parallel to the first one, if the first one is crooked or out of fair, all the strips you put on later will tend to be crooked as well. The run of the strips can also be used to complement the shape of the boat. Strips that create stripes parallel to the waterline tend to emphasize the length of the boat, while strips sweeping up toward the ends—that is, parallel to the sheer or gunwale line—highlight the curvature of the boat.

You may also want to consider how the strips will line up on the forms with an eye toward what will be easiest to accomplish. For example, if there is an area where the cross-sectional shape takes a sharp turn, such as the chine of a kayak where the bottom turns up to the side, it may be worthwhile to position the first strip with some consideration for where later strips will fall near this feature. You will make your work easier by predicting potential trouble areas and laying out your strip pattern to minimize the problems.

Many boats such as canoes and kayaks have a sheer shape that sweeps up suddenly at the end. This curvature may be hard to follow with strips, and instead you may want to let the

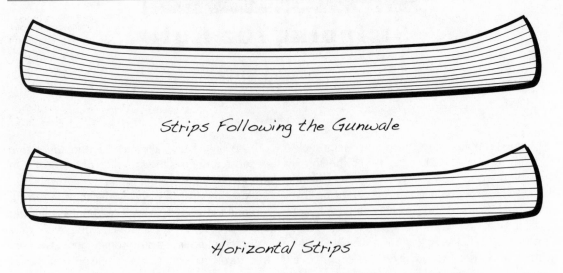

Strips Following the Gunwale

Horizontal Strips

Figure 6-1. *The simple choice of the direction you run the strips will affect the overall look of the boat. Strips following the sheer of the gunwales accentuate the curves, and more horizontal strips make the boat look longer. There is no right choice in this decision, but you may want to take a little time to decide how you want your boat to look.*

strips follow a shape they are more comfortable with and fill in the gaps later.

The strips also don't take too kindly to being twisted a lot in their run down the length of the boat. If there is a chine or sharp turn of the bilge, it may be worthwhile to place the first strips so that as you approach the chine you don't end up with a strip that starts above the chine at one end and below at the other. Make some measurements so you can place the first strip parallel to the chine line so that when you get to the chine, a strip will lie nicely along it and not have to take a sharp (or impossible) twist to cross it.

While it is not a requirement, it is often easiest if the first strip runs the full length of the boat. Even if you did not buy wood that is as long as your boat, you can make a couple of strips that are long enough by scarfing together shorter pieces. A *scarf* is a way to join two pieces by creating a long matching taper in both ends to be joined. I use a little jig on a belt sander. The jig holds the strip at an angle that makes a 1-inch-long taper on the end of the

strip. After sanding in the taper, I glue the two pieces together end to end. If you are not in a rush, use carpenter's glue and clamp the joint until the glue dries. If you want to get going, put a few drops of CA glue on one taper and squirt the other with CA accelerator. Carefully line up the joint and press it together. The CA glue should set up almost immediately. This joint is not superstrong, but after the boat is fiberglassed, it will not matter.

Open Boats

Typically with open boats such as canoes and rowboats, the top edge of the sheer is defined by a gunwale made up of an inwale and outwale. These pieces are mounted after the boat is stripped up and fiberglassed. Because the gunwale provides a finished edge to the sheer, it is less important that you create a nice finished edge with your stripping. You can leave the sheerline ragged and then trim it up after installing the gunwales.

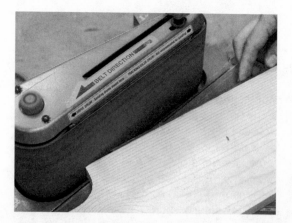

Figure 6-2. You rarely need to make one continuous strip out of two strips that will hold together on their own, but when you do, a scarf is the way to do it. Scarfs are long, tapered joints that supply a lot of glue area; this gradually distributes any load between the two ends. You could plane the taper onto each strip, but a simpler method is to set up a fence against a belt sander. Slide the strip along the fence until you have a sharp end. Repeat for the other strip to make a matching taper.

Figure 6-3. If you have the time, you can use carpenter's glue and a clamp to glue the scarf joint. Be sure the strips are aligned in a straight line; it is easy to have one end go off at a funky angle. For a quick joint, use CA glue. Spread glue on one surface, then spray the other with accelerant. Carefully align the ends and press the pieces together.

Usually the first strip on the boat will be placed at least partially along the sheer. If the sheer has a lot of curvature near the ends, you may want to let the first strip run out straighter and then fill in above to build up to the finished sheerline.

If you choose to follow the sheer all the way to each end with your first strip, remember that the gunwale will usually completely cover over this strip when you finish up the boat. This is not the strip where you use that special piece of rare, exotic, highly figured *poogapooga* wood your grandfather gave you. Save your cherished heirloom accent woods for a couple of strips down where it will actually show.

Because you will have an opportunity to come back later to clean up the top edge of the sheer, you want to be sure you accomplish two things with your first strip: you want to be sure it is fair so that later strips are also fair, and you want to make sure the strip meets or

extends beyond the final sheerline. Place the strip overlapping the design sheerline slightly and secure it.

If you are using cove-and-bead strips, make sure the cove, or hollow edge, is facing up so that it can hold glue. You could plane off the bead edge before securing it in place, or just make sure the rounded part of the strips is beyond what will be the finished edge of the sheer so that it can be planed off later.

Closed Boats

On kayaks and other boats with a closed deck or boats where you do not use a gunwale or rub strip along the sheer, the first strip will usually be the top strip on the sheer for at least part of the length of the boat. As you are stripping along the sheer, the strips you place will end up defining the sheerline. You will generally want to use care stripping along the sheerline because you will not have a lot of opportunity to go back and clean it up later.

For this reason, I typically run one strip all the way along the length of the sheer even if I may not want all my strips to run parallel to this first one.

On a closed boat, the first strip will typically define the transition between the deck and the hull, which usually occurs at the widest part of the form. Because this strip will have more strips added on both sides, it may require a little extra preparation before installation.

With cove-and-bead strips you will want to remove the bead from the side that constitutes the seam joint between deck and hull. Since I typically work on the hull first, this means the edge that abuts the deck should first be made square.

Since the deck and hull often meet at an angle, you may want to put a rolling bevel on this edge. The purpose of the rolling bevel on this sheer strip is to split up the amount of beveling between the first strip on the hull and the first strip on the deck. No bevel on the first strip would require you to make up the entire tight joint with the other strip. This can result in sharp angles that are hard to make and/or thin spots.

Rolling Bevel on the Sheer of a Closed Boat. At some point during the construction of your boat, you will have the need to join the edges of two adjacent strips that meet at a changing angle along the length of the joint. The cove-and-bead edge is the simplest means of assuring a reasonably tight joint between the strips. But there are times when a cove or bead on the edge of a given strip just isn't the best solution. This is when you need a rolling bevel.

A rolling bevel is not a special tool for rolling piecrust to a nonuniform thickness. It is instead a way of forming the seam between two strips so that it is tight along the full length, even when the angle between the strips changes constantly along the length of the boat.

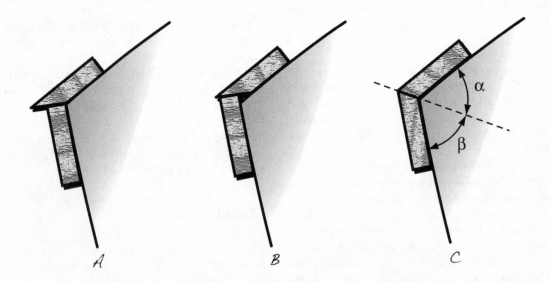

Figure 6-4. *On a decked boat eventually you have to secure the deck to the hull. How you treat the edge of the strips at the seam has consequences for how the joint fits together. If you just leave the edge of the sheer strip of the hull square (A) and align it with the corner of the form, you will need to create a sharp bevel on the deck strip and it will extend out somewhat. You can plane or sand this off later. Or you can raise the hull strip slightly so there is almost no deck overhang (B). This is hard to get right and leaves a thin spot near the seam. The best method is to make a miter joint (C) that bisects the angle of both the deck (α) and hull (β), creating a smooth, tight joint inside and out.*

This bevel is made using a small hand plane to shave the edge of the strip to the appropriate angle. This is simply done by holding the plane at the appropriate angle relative to the strips and cutting away the edge of the strip until the full width of the strip is completely beveled. Very simple. The tricky part is determining what exactly that mystical "appropriate" angle actually is.

The goal of the bevel is to make a tight joint between the strips. Ideally the two strips will fit flush against each other with no gap on the inside or outside of the boat, but for the first strips it is not that important that you make it perfect yet. With later rolling bevels we will want to take a little more care, but this first effort is not that critical.

On a closed boat the forms typically include both the hull (boat bottom) and deck (boat top) in one form. Make a mark, called the *sheer mark*, where the sheer crosses that form. If it is not marked on the plans, it is typically the widest point of the form. This just makes it easier to get the forms out of the stripped deck or hull because it is not trapped by the deck or hull being narrower at the opening than the widest section.

If there is not yet a mark at the widest point of the form, make one now. While you're at it, draw a line that marks an angle halfway between the deck side and the hull side. This will indicate the angle you want to make your rolling bevel at that form. Then take a small scrap of strip material and clamp it to the forms following the indicated angle, with the top edge of the little strip crossing right at the sheer mark. When you have these little strips, or angle sticks, clamped on all the forms, sight down the length of the boat. The strips should progress in a smooth curve down the forms, and the angles should also transition smoothly from one form to the next.

Note that the sheerline is usually not horizontal; it typically starts high at the bow of the boat, curves down toward the middle, and then rises back up again at the stern. If you are using marks on the forms that are all at the same level,

they may be waterline marks or something else. You will want to double-check that you are using the correct marks.

Get your block plane ready: at long last you are now about to start working on your first rolling bevel. Select your desired first strip. If you are uncertain about all this, just select a scrap strip for a trial run. Hold it up in place as you mark the number of each form where the strip crosses the form. This will make it so you can quickly align the strip where it belongs on the boat without having to put the whole thing in place every time.

Starting at one end of the boat, let's say at form 1, place the strip against the angle sticks indicating the sheerline angle. Notice the width of the gap between the outer bottom edge of the

Figure 6-5. The first strip, or sheer strip, of a closed boat such as a kayak is just one situation where you may need to create a rolling bevel. The goal is to create a tight seam on the outside of the hull. Marking each form number onto the strip at the point where they intersect will make it easier to find your spot as you plane the bevel. As you press the strip against the clamped-on scrap, notice the size of the gap between the strip and the scrap. This is how much you need to bevel the strip. If you are fitting against an existing strip, you will again want to note the size of the gap. While you are looking at one form, also look at the forms before and after this one and note the differences in the bevel at each form.

Figure 6-6. *As you prepare to apply the bevel to the strip, make sure you are beveling the correct edge. That is, don't bevel the top edge when you really want the bottom, and don't bevel toward the outside when you need to bevel toward the inside. Place the plane along that edge and tilt the plane so you see a gap the same width as you saw on the boat. You will want to maintain this angle until the bevel in that area is complete. Start planing the edge of the strip near the form number. As you plane toward the other forms adjust your angle to match the differences you noted previously.*

Figure 6-7. *Keep planing until the gap between the strip and the plane just about disappears. Place the strip back on the forms, making sure to align the number with the appropriate form. Check the gap again. Plane some more, matching the new gap as you start, and plane until the gap disappears. Double-check your fit.*

strip and the top of the angle stick. Also take a quick look at the gap at form 2 farther down the boat. Now remove the strip from the side of the forms and hold it horizontally next to you. Bring your block plane up to the strip. With the plane touching the bottom edge of the strip, lean the top of the plane away from the strip until you get a gap between the top edge of the strip and the plane that matches what you saw between the strip and the angle stick on the forms. This is the angle you want to put on your bevel. Hold the strip steady, keep the angle of the plane constant, and start planing away the edge of the strip near the mark that indicates the location of form 1. Use long, smooth strokes. Plane until there is no gap left between the plane and the strip. With a large angle you may need to do six to eight passes with the plane, for small angles,

one or two. Don't plane more than it takes to eliminate the gap between the plane and strip.

Place the strip back up against the forms and down against the angle stick. Check the gap between the strip and the stick. If there is none, great; if there is still a gap, repeat the process using the new gap as your estimated angle. In the beginning you may want to work in on the bevel slowly, but you will soon be able to do it fairly quickly.

When you get the angle right on the first form, go to the next one. Now you will want to blend the angle at this form with the angle you just made. Between the form marks on your strip you will want to roll your wrist as you plane so the angle transitions smoothly from one form to the next.

Some boats will have a lot of change along the length of the strips, where others may hold a fairly consistent angle throughout the length. Theoretically, for those with a consistent sheer angle, you could set up the table saw to cut the bevel, but a hand plane is quick, easy, and safe.

Figure 6-8. *As you move down the length of the boat, check the gap at each form and plane it until it disappears. In between forms, roll your wrist as you plane to gradually transition between the bevels at each form. With a little practice, this whole process will only take a couple of minutes.*

Figure 6-9. *Getting the first strip aligned on the forms to create a smooth, fair curve may require a little finagling. Use some U-shaped jigs to temporarily hold the strip in place while checking the alignment. When you have it right, secure the strip in place with a staple or other fastener.*

It is not critical that you make the angle on the sheer strip perfect. You will be doing a lot to the boat between now and the time you finally bond the deck to the hull. During that time there will be occasions where you mess up your carefully planed bevel and there will be opportunities to fix it up and make it better. The reason to put effort into doing a good job now is really for the practice. If you are using cove-and-bead strips there will only be a couple of occasions where you will need to cut a rolling bevel again, so it is worth getting some practice now when it is not that critical. If you are not using cove-and-bead strips, you will get plenty of practice on the rolling bevel, but a little now may still be welcome.

Installing the First Strip

After you are done thinking about where the first strip goes and have spent the time getting the perfect bevel on it or whatever other procrastination tactics you have employed to delay the inevitable, it is time to stop futzing around and actually start building. Since almost all the subsequent strips will follow the path laid down by the first strip, it is important to get the first one on where you want it. Marks on the forms for the location of the sheerline or gunwale will provide a good starting point.

I usually use a few of the U-clamps (see No Staples later in the chapter) to temporarily hold the first strip in place. You don't need to secure the strip at every form. If your forms are set up well, the strip should bend in a fair curve between the clamps. Since the goal is generally to get a fair curve here, letting the strip find its natural curve is the quickest way to that end.

Align the bottom edge of the strip with the sheerline mark or gunwale location on the form. Slip the U-clamp up from below and hold it in place with a spring clamp. Once you have it loosely located with several clamps along the length, get your eye down near the strip at one end of the forms. Look down the strip and watch for funny wiggles in the strip. These wiggles are most visible with your eye close to

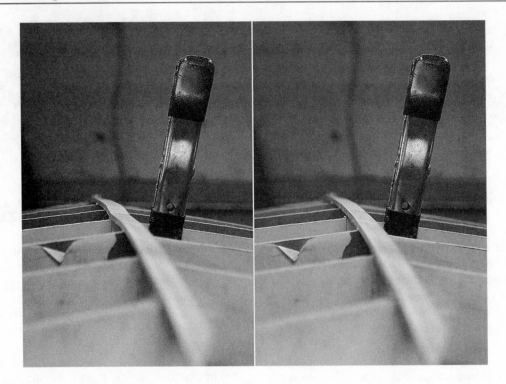

Figure 6-10. Pay attention as you strip new parts of the forms. You may notice some places where the strips make a little wiggle as is visible on the left. In this case the form was a little low. This could be due to a misaligned form or some mistake in cutting. The solution was simply to not force the strip to touch the form. Left to their own devices strips will naturally bend in a smooth, fair curve. Here I just popped the hot-melt glue I was using to hold the strips. With subsequent strips I did not glue them down on this form. If you have a high spot on a form, you can knock it down with a rasp or plane.

the strip, viewing down the length. You want to look for places where the strip bends suddenly, either side to side or up and down. An up-and-down jog usually just requires that you move the clamp up or down a bit. You can remove the clamp completely to see if that makes it better.

Side-to-side jogs indicate a form may be out of alignment or is somehow out of shape. If the jog is just one spot that dips inward, you can remove the clamp from that form and let the strip run free. A bump outward may require moving the form, fairing down the form, or releasing clamps on the forms before and after the bump. Before you get too carried away "fixing" the problem, temporarily put the first strip

on the other side of the boat. If the same form causes a dip on one side and a bump on the other, you probably need to move the form over a bit. Recheck all the alignments on that form after adjustment just to make sure that fixing one problem didn't cause others.

Check the location of the strip relative to the sheer or gunwale marks. If the strip does not come close to the marked location, you may need to add more clamps to get enough bend in the strip. Remember to double-check that the strip remains fair as you move the clamps around.

When you have the strip where you want it, it is time to secure it in place. If you are going staple free, you could just keep using the U-clamps, but they are not all that secure as you put more pressure on them with additional strips. I usually just run a staple through the strip into the form next to the clamp. For staple free building, a small dot of hot-melt glue will work the same. If you have an internal stem that will stay in the boat, you can glue the strip to the stem before stapling or clamping.

Check the strips again to make sure they are still fair. You can pull the staple and readjust as necessary.

The Next Strips

After you have sweated over getting the first strip in place, the next step is to decide where the second strip goes. Whereas the first strip will help determine how all the following strips flow, the second strip will help determine how easily all the subsequent strips will be installed. This strip also contributes to the overall look of the boat.

The obvious choice is to just lay the second strip directly following the first strip down the full length of the boat. This is a perfectly good choice, but there are some reasons why you may not want to do it that way. You may want to have the second strip touching the first strip in the middle and then have it diverge away toward the ends. The primary reason for doing this is to reduce the degree of bend and stress in the strips. Some boats have sheerlines with a lot of sweep up at the ends. It can be hard to make strips take this bend. While you may have been successful with the first strip, you might not want to go through the same effort with any more.

The principle of finding a way that the strips bend onto the boat smoothly and easily and then fitting subsequent strips around them is one to keep in mind. Often there are times when you can make your life easier by letting the strips show you how they best fit instead of forcing them into contortions they would rather not put up with.

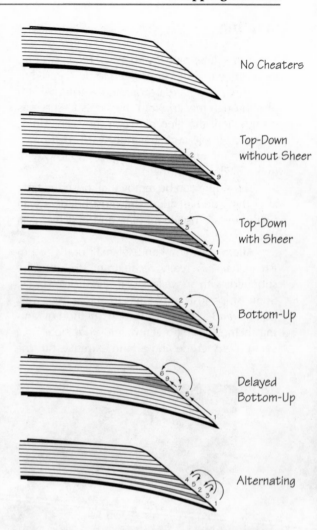

No Cheaters

Top-Down without Sheer

Top-Down with Sheer

Bottom-Up

Delayed Bottom-Up

Alternating

Figure 6-11. Many boat designs have a raised bow and/or stern. You need to cover this rise with strips. You don't need to run all the strips in the same direction; you can install "cheater" strips to fill in the rise. Cheater strips are shorter pieces used to fill in the triangle left between the sheer or gunwale line and the line made if you just let the strips run straight without bending much. Your choice of stripping pattern will affect the overall look of the boat. Generally, longer strips are put in before shorter ones.

Stapling

The forms determine the shape of the boat. But, for this to work, the strips need to be secured to the forms. The standard method is to drive staples through the strip into the forms to serve as clamps until the glue between the strips dries. This is a simple and straightforward method; it can be done quickly and is a pretty solid way of immobilizing the strips.

The staple can be removed almost any time after the glue has dried, but most builders wait until they are done stripping and pull them all out at once.

Alternately, you can use small brads or finishing nails. A really recalcitrant strip can be subdued with a well-placed sheetrock screw. Some strips just don't want to stay where they belong, and a screw is a surefire method of taming them. Zipping a screw into your boat may seem pretty crude and a little extreme, but the

Figure 6-12. Since you will be pulling out the staples eventually, you do not want them pushed in flush with the strip. A little gap between the staple and the wood will provide a starting point for removing the staples later. If you do not bevel the forms, as in this example, you need staples long enough to reach across the gap. You can also align the staples near the close edge.

Figure 6-13. Staples provide by far the easiest and quickest method to temporarily clamp the strips in place while the glue dries. Press the joint close together and shoot a staple through the strip into the form. Rocking cove-and-bead strips a little bit as you press them in place will help seat them and spread the glue inside the joint. Keep stripping up the side until the strips start having to bend the "hard" way, across their width. On the last strip installed on the side, plane off the cove so it will be easier to shape the strips joining it later.

epoxy and fiberglass will seal the hole. If you are going to use the boat hard, a little hole will soon fade into the background of scratches.

Obviously, whether it is a staple, brad, nail, or screw, when you pull it out, you are going to be left with a hole. Again, the epoxy and fiberglass will fill the hole, and it is unlikely that it will leak. The only real downside is aesthetic. There will be a visible mark on the outside of the boat that some people find objectionable.

The staple holes really don't bother me at all. I find them to be barely noticeable from a distance, and up close they are a simple reflection of the hand that built the boat. Like a fingerprint in a hand-thrown pot, they are an acknowledgment that the strips were individually fit, one at a time, by hand and not by a machine.

The role of the staple is as a temporary clamp to hold the strip in place until the glue dries. The beauty of a staple is that it quickly holds the strip in place without getting in the way of adding more strips. There is really no quicker way to get the job done.

With cove-and-bead strips a staple at each form is usually enough. Rock the strip back and forth as you push it into the cove, then press the stapler against the strip and pop in a staple. Work down the length of the strip, adding a staple at each form. By working from the middle of the boat toward the ends, you will move any excess length out of the ends.

With book-matched strips you will often want to align the strips with each other so that the grain lines up from strip to strip. The double lines on the right in Figure 6-15 are marks I made across all the strips while they were on the workbench. By realigning these marks, it is easy to keep track of where the grain will align, even when the details of the grain may not be easy to see.

Square-edged, hand-beveled strips require a little more effort to secure against each other between the forms. You can just pump a couple more staples to hold the unsupported strips to each other. This can go through a lot of staples quickly and does make more of those pesky

Figure 6-14. *On my own boats, I happily pump the strips full of staples. I feel they are an honest side effect of building a boat, and from a distance you just won't see them. A wooden boat will suck up all the perfectionism you can feed it, and you need to pick your battles. Staple holes should not be considered a flaw, but instead an indication of the fact that the boat is made by hand.*

Figure 6-15. *With most boats the sides are relatively flat, so very little beveling is required. Most small boats, however, will have some places where gaps will open up if you are using square-edged strips. These gaps may be eliminated by planing a rolling bevel as described earlier. Notice the double lines on the strips near the right side of the photo. These help align the grain while installing strips cut consecutively from the board.*

Figure 6-16. *A smooth finish in the completed boat starts with a smooth joint between strips. Cove-and-bead strips are pretty much self-aligning but may need some help staying tight between the forms. I've taken to running a length of tape over the strip down onto the previous strips. This is usually enough to pull the joint together, and with square-edged strips the tape will help hold the strips even with each other. Ideally there should be no steps detectable from strip to strip. With standard carpenter's glue the glue sets up quickly enough that the tape may be removed in a few minutes.*

staple holes, but it is as quick as it gets. I've taken to just using some masking tape. This also goes through a lot of tape, but it limits the number of holes. I hook a piece of tape around and behind, pull it over the top of the new strip, then pull down tightly and press it down onto the previous strips, ripping it off two or three strips down.

This tape will need to be peeled off before installing the next strip, but you can do all the fitting with the tape in place, and by the time the new strip is ready, the glue has usually set up enough to hold. If you switch sides of the boat every strip, there will be plenty of time for carpenter's glue to tack up.

No Staples

It is possible to make a strip-built boat without using staples, leaving the strips unscarred, but it takes time, care, and effort. I am going to say up front that I am ambivalent about avoiding staples on strip-built boats. For some builders this extra level of attention to detail may be well worth the effort, but it is worth considering how the boat will be used when it is done. Staples are the quickest, most secure means of securing the strips to the forms. They leave a mark, but that mark is a natural effect of using a perfectly reasonable building technique. They are not something to be ashamed of and hidden. They are there for a reason, and the reason is a sound one. Staples work, are cheap, and are easy to deal with, and the mark they leave is subtle enough that most admirers won't even notice them. If you are going to use the boat hard, the holes will not detract from the practical usefulness of the finished result. You may as well pump the sucker full of staples while you are building and get the boat done sooner, because the aesthetic difference is minor.

But I will admit that boats built without staples can look very nice. On an otherwise well-built boat, the smooth appearance of a deck without the periodic interruption of a line across the boat at each form is very attractive. There will be some people for whom this look is worth any amount of extra work and frustration.

Let's first look at what the staples are for. The staples serve as temporary clamps, which hold the strips in place while the glue between strips dries. Often the staples could be removed as soon as the glue dries. In boats with a lot of shape it may be necessary that these little

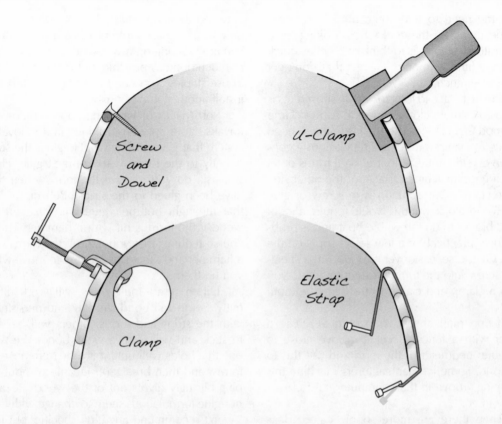

Figure 6-17. *Whether you choose to use staples or not, there may be times when you need a little extra holding power. There are innumerable methods for holding down strips, some of which are shown above. The downside of most of these techniques is that you will not be able to add another strip until the glue has dried. If you don't want to use staples, a little dab of hot-melt glue instead of a staple lets you keep going. You can then use additional clamps for more recalcitrant strips.*

clamps stay in until more strips are attached to hold the strips firmly in their assigned place. But eventually, they will be removed.

Some people try systems like stuffing toothpicks in the staple holes or smearing wood putty over them to hide them when the stripping is complete. Toothpicks rarely match the wood you are using, and the end grain soaks up resin that makes even light-colored toothpicks look dark. With a water-based putty and watercolor paints you can create a good color match, but it takes work. Then once you get the putty in the holes, you need it to stay there while you continue sanding—not as easily done as said. You

can also use a hot, wet rag to attempt to swell up the hole, thus making it smaller. Again the crushed grain around the hole will absorb more resin and appear darker than surrounding wood. These approaches will change the appearance of the holes, and they may be worthwhile in certain contexts, but they rarely make the staple holes disappear. At best they can make the holes marginally less noticeable; at worst they will waste your time and may even result in more visible marks.

If you don't want to see staple marks in your finished boat, there is no substitute for avoiding making the holes in the first place. This eliminates the need to find some miracle solution to hide them. So the goal when looking for a substitute for staples is to think of them as quick and easy little temporary clamps that don't get in the way much.

The first place to look for staple substitutes is clamps. A simple clothespin-style spring clamp is a good first choice. The trick is that you need a place to clamp it to. One side obviously goes on the outside of the strip, but bare forms don't have a good matching surface for the other side of the clamp. One solution is to screw or glue on a wood block, but this would require a lot of wood blocks to do the whole boat and is probably only practical for a few select spots on the boat. Of course, easier yet is to just run a sheet-rock screw into the form adjacent to where you need a clamp and clamp to the screw without a block.

If you plan ahead you could also use a router with a fence to cut a groove close to the outer perimeter of the form and use this to clamp to. Some kit manufacturers machine this clamping groove in their computer-cut forms—ready to go.

Then there are more sophisticated ideas using shock cord or cut-up inner tubes like rubber bands stretched between screws and over the strips to hold them down. This system can provide a lot of pressure on the strips to hold them securely but generally needs some system for adjusting the tension as more strips are added.

Another system that doesn't require much prepositioned modifications to the forms is the use of clamping jigs. These can be little hooks cut out of plywood that slip over the strips so the jigs can then be clamped to the forms. I have a bunch of small rectangles with slots cut into them. These pieces can be positioned over the strips and secured to the forms with a spring clamp. If you have enough of these you can clamp the strips down at every form.

The problem with all these systems is that once you have the clamp, band, or jig in place you cannot put on another strip until the glue

between the strips dries. This is OK if you are only installing a couple of strips a night. But if you are working on a weekend and want to get as much done as possible, but really don't want to use staples, you need a system that lets you install another strip almost immediately.

Rob Macks of Laughing Loon Canoes and Kayaks came up with a unique and innovative system that is very effective. He glues the strips directly to the forms with hot-melt glue. How, you ask, do you remove the forms when they have been glued to the strips? Rob discovered that the right hot-melt glue will flake off the wood if the form is hit with a hammer. This of course requires that you can hit the forms with a hammer and the forms are free to move when you hit them.

Different hot-melt glues will work differently. Some will bond strongly and persistently with the strips and forms; others will be slow to stick and will form a weak bond. We need one that holds well until it is time to remove the forms, and then breaks off cleanly without ripping big ugly divots out of the wood. Because hot-glue formulations seem to change with time, I won't recommend anything specific, but look for glues intended for wood and then experiment with several to see what works best with the wood you are using.

You will need forms set up so they can be released when it is time to remove the boat from the forms. On an external strongback this should be easy enough so long as you place the screws that fasten them to the strongback where you can reach them after the boat is stripped up. With tall forms like those in the middle of a canoe, you can probably break the glue without unscrewing the forms, but it is a good idea to be ready to remove the forms from the strongback if there are problems.

With an internal strongback such as you may use on a kayak, you need a system of securing the forms while you build that can be released when you need to. I came up with the L-spacer system for this purpose. By using wedges in the middle of the boat to clamp all the forms in place from one accessible location, the L spacer can be quickly set up and released when needed.

Even the ideal hot glue will be hard to break free if you use too much. After dry-fitting a strip to be sure it will fit tightly where it needs to be and applying the glue along the strip edge, move down the forms and put a small (about ⅛-inch or 3 mm diameter) dot of hot-melt glue on the form under the strip and press the strip tightly into place, holding it for a few seconds until the hot glue cools and grabs.

The glue only holds the strips at the forms. Between forms you need to be sure the strips are aligned and tight. Some builders use a dot of hot melt bridging between the two strips to hold them in alignment. I use painter's masking tape as temporary clamps, but the result is the same. Press the strips together tightly and give them a little wiggle to help make a tight joint. Be sure the edges are aligned so there is no step from one strip to the next. The joint should feel smooth under your thumb. Press the end of the tape over the back of the strips and pull it tight over the top. Press it down across the joint between the strips and rip it off the roll. It is important to pull the tape tight as you are putting it in place, as this will provide clamping pressure. Place two pieces of tape in each space between forms, dividing the space between the forms in thirds. You may get away with fewer or may find a recalcitrant joint needs more.

While you will obviously need to remove the tape before installing the next strip, typical carpenter's glue grabs fast, and if you work on the other side of the boat, by the time you come back, you should be able to remove the tape.

You should not need to hot glue every strip to every form. If a strip seems to stay where it should be without the glue, don't bother gluing it. If, as you go along, you find some of the strips are lifting slightly, you can always add a little drop of hot-melt glue to secure them back down.

It is important to dry-fit the strips before gluing them in place. You may find that some of the hot glue has squeezed out and interferes

with a tight joint. Just use your knife to cut off the glue.

The hot-melt glue is a surprisingly good staple or clamp substitute, but on some stubborn strips you may need to supplement it with some other clamps. The little U-shaped jigs held in place with spring clamps as mentioned earlier are usually enough to hold a strip in place until you can get another strip added next to it.

After you finish stripping, you will proceed to fairing, sanding, and fiberglassing the outside as normal. The tricky part comes when you need to get the hull off the forms. You have just spent a lot of time gluing the boat to the forms, and now you need to find a way to get it off. If you are using an external strongback, start by unscrewing the forms from the strongback. Hopefully you have planned ahead and have a way to access the screws. With large boats, you have enough flexibility with the forms that you don't need to loosen the forms, but it still helps.

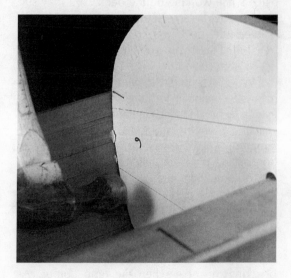

Figure 6-18. If you have not applied too much hot-melt glue during your staple-free construction, you should be able to break the glue free with a sharp rap of a hammer. The forms need to be released from the strongback enough that they can move without breaking.

The forms are freed up by hitting them with a hammer. Do not try to rip them out by pulling the boat away from the forms. This will just rip out chunks of wood. Instead they need to be knocked toward the middle of the boat so the hot-glue bond is broken sideways. Give the forms a sharp knock with a hammer near their edge. The selection of glue will effect how easily this glue bond is broken.

Unfortunately, with an external strongback and a decked boat, freeing up the forms before stripping the deck creates a situation where the forms are not attached to anything. There are two choices in this situation. Either strip the deck before breaking the bond, in which case you must somehow break the glue bond by shoving something in through the sheerline and hammering on the forms with a crowbar, or break the bonds before working on the deck, but lightly secure the forms in place. You could do this by putting a couple of small dots of glue on each form sufficient to hold them in place while working on the deck. You may still need to stick a large screwdriver or crowbar in between the deck and hull to break the forms free, but at least you won't have to break all the bonds at once.

With an internal strongback, you have a means to maintain the alignment of the forms even after breaking the glue bonds. The L-shaped spacer system mentioned previously can be temporarily removed while you break the glue bonds, and then reinstalled without significant loss of form alignment.

Obviously, this idea of hitting your carefully built boat with a hammer is a little scary. It takes a little bit of a leap of faith to glue the whole boat to the forms with the hope that you will be able to break the glue bonds without breaking the boat when the time comes. As mentioned, you will want to experiment with the hot-melt glue to be sure it will work. Keep the dots of glue small; they should hold well enough to clamp the strips but still break when hit to the side.

After you have glassed the outside and removed the shell from the forms, you will need to clean up all those little patches of glue on the inside. A paint scraper will usually do a good job of peeling off small spots. Larger spots may cause the scraper to jump and chatter, causing the scraper to dig in. Instead of trying to scrape these off, it may be better to slide them off using a chisel, plane, or edge of a scraper. Big blobs of glue may be heated with a heat gun and rubbed off with a finger or scraped with a fingernail. After the glue is removed, the rest of the work is the same as if you had stapled.

Let me reiterate that staples are not evil. They are a good, quick, practical manner of securely clamping the strips in place. As a first-time builder you may have aspirations of creating a flawless boat and you may feel that no staple holes is an important part of achieving that objective. I will not try to convince you that perfection is not a worthy goal, but if there is one thing that will make you feel dissatisfied with your finished product, it is a failure to achieve an unrealistic goal. Staple holes are just one small part of what makes a boat look good. I would say that 99% of what it takes to make a really beautiful-looking boat has nothing to do with staples. Unless you are prepared to spend the time and effort to select good wood, arrange that wood in a pleasing manner, assure that the strips fit together very tightly, get the wood very fair and smooth, apply a flawless coat of epoxy and fiberglass, sand it perfectly smooth, apply a really good coat of varnish, and buff it smooth, worrying about staples is a waste of time. You can make a really beautiful boat in about a quarter of the time it takes to make an absolutely perfect boat. And you can be sure that after spending four times as long attempting perfection, there will still be significant flaws that will bother you to no end.

Gluing Strips

It does not take a lot of glue to hold the strips together. Remember that all the strips will eventually be sandwiched between layers of fiberglass and saturated with epoxy resin. All you are trying to do with the glue between the strips is hold the shell together long enough to get one layer of fiberglass on it. If you put too much glue between the strips, it will just drip down the side of the boat and onto the floor. I would also rather have any gaps between strips filled with epoxy than with carpenter's glue. The epoxy will be stronger and less subject to softening when the boat is sitting on the roof of a car in a hot parking lot.

I like to use standard yellow carpenter's glue because it is strong, inexpensive, quite safe, and easy to clean up. Waterproof glues are not needed and not worth the extra effort, price, and hassle.

With cove-and-bead strips you can usually poke the tip of your glue bottle in the cove,

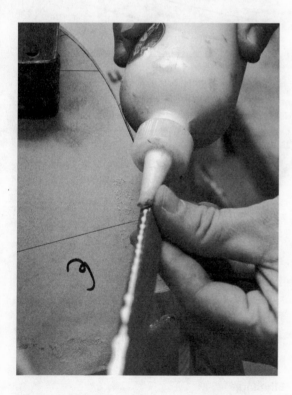

Figure 6-19. Don't apply too much glue. You don't want to make a mess, so just add enough to hold the strips together until the boat is glassed. A ¹⁄₁₆- to ¹⁄₈-inch bead is good. With square-edge strips, use your fingers as a guide to hold the tip of the glue bottle.

give a little squeeze, and slide along the strip as you dispense a bead of glue a little bigger than ¹⁄₁₆ inch in diameter. With square-edged strips you may need to use a finger to guide you as you squeeze out the bead of glue. Don't get carried away; just put enough glue to get a small amount of squeeze-out when you press the strips together.

Yellow carpenter's glue has the handy ability to "grab" pretty quickly. Simply rubbing the new strip on the previous strip will help the glue hold onto the new strip. So long as there are not a lot of forces trying to move the bond, the strip will stay where you put it. Beyond that, the glue tacks up quickly. Two pieces that have been clamped together can often be unclamped in 5 to 10 minutes. Again, the glue joint is not yet at full strength, but it will hold while more strips are added.

Filling In

It is easy to add more strips so long as both ends are hanging off beyond the stems. Eventually, the end of a new strip is going to butt up against the side of an existing strip. Where previously the building tasks have been a matter of assembling pieces, this is the first task you might call woodworking. It involves creating a taper in the end of the new strip that nestles up against the side of the existing strip.

There are a variety of ways you could go about cutting this taper after marking it. The most obvious idea for most people may be to take the strip to a saw or bring a saw to the strip and cut along the line. The first requires trekking all the way over to wherever the saw is, and they both assume the line was marked accurately and that you are going to be able to cut right along the line correctly in one go.

I'm lazy and sloppy and, as a result, I'm not about to walk the five steps across my shop to a saw, and I'm not likely to get the cutting line marked perfectly the first time, and forget about sawing accurately along that line. I'm just not that good.

Instead I try to sneak up on an accurate fit. I mark the taper as best I can and then use a jackknife to make a rough cut. Then I plane down toward the line, checking the fit as I go. I don't even try to do it right all at once. I do it in such a way that I can adjust for mistakes as I go.

Fitting Strip Ends

The fitting taper at the ends is slightly different for beveled strips versus cove-and-bead strips. Because of the cove, you cannot actually see the true end of the taper; it extends out of view up into the cove. It is a little easier with beveled strips, but at least initially, it is not much different either way.

Looking at non-cove-and-bead strips first, before trying to fit the taper, get the bevel along the strip edges roughed out. It need not be perfect initially, but if you just continue the bevel from where you are able to test the fit, you will be in pretty good shape. Mark the taper by holding it in place over its destination, with the end of the new strip aligned with the pointy end of the taper. Hold the beveled edge aligned with the edge of the existing or "side" strip it will lie against. Mark the other edge where it crosses the end strip.

Use a straightedge (a scrap strip works well) and pencil to connect the mark with the tip of the strips. This should approximately define the intended taper on the end of the strip. With a jackknife, whittle off the end of the strip, leaving a little bit of wood above the taper line. With a block plane remove only enough wood to straighten out the taper so that it is parallel to the pencil line. Insert the strip on the boat to check the fit.

Make a note of where the taper binds up first. Usually it will bind at the "toe," or pointy end, or at the "heel," at the other end. (See Figure 6-24 on page 102.) Also pay attention to the gap, noting the width. When you hold your block plane to adjust the fit, you will want to start with it touching the toe or heel as you previously noted and also try to match the gap.

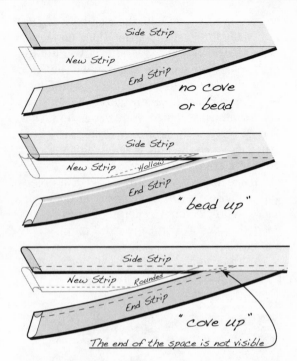

Figure 6-20. *Fitting a strip into the space left between merging strips requires putting a taper on the new strip. This strip runs parallel to what I am calling the side strip, and butts up against the end strip. Without a cove or bead to worry about, this merely requires a simple taper. Cove-and-bead strips complicate the problem. If the end strip has bead showing, you need to create a hollow cove on the new strip. A lot of work with a round file or simply walking over to the router table would make it work. It is easier if all the joints fit into a cove. Rounding over the edges with a plane creates a bead. The only issue remaining is the space that extends beyond the visible gap, so you will need to trim the new strip a little longer.*

While holding this angle, plane the taper until the gap disappears. Try the fit again and repeat until you get a good tight fit all the way along the taper.

If the strip binds at both ends simultaneously, this means the tapered edge needs to be more convex. You will need to take a couple of swipes at each end. If it binds up in the middle, press hard with your plane in the middle.

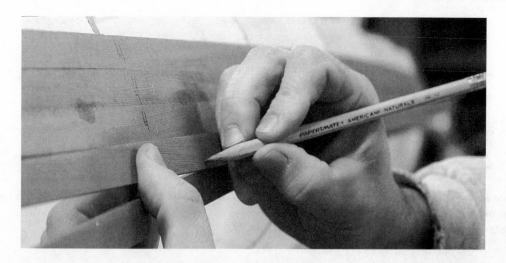

Figure 6-21. *Long tapers such as for the cheater-strip area at the ends of a kayak are fitted in the same manner as other tapers. Hold the strip in place with the end aligned with the end of the tapered gap and mark where the new strip overlaps the gap, then whittle off the excess wood and plane the strip to fit. In these gaps the taper is often not a straight line but follows a curve, so the new strip must be slightly concave along its length. A couple of extra strokes with the plane near the middle of the taper is usually enough to create the curve.*

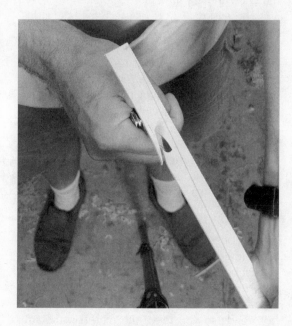

Figure 6-22. *A jackknife quickly removes excess wood as you taper the end of a strip. When you get as close as comfortable with the knife, switch to a block plane.*

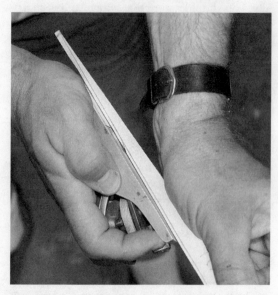

Figure 6-23. *Tapers can be planed into the ends of strips using a push or pull stroke. With a sharp plane you may be able to accurately shape some long tapers without support, but as they get longer you may want to back up the strip with another scrap piece.*

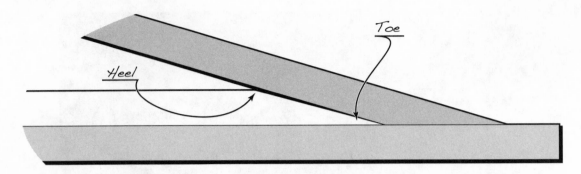

Figure 6-24. *As you fit a new strip it generally binds at the point end (the toe) or the wide end (the heel). Hold the plane so that it touches the same point, and adjust the gap so it matches the gap at the other end. Continue to hold the plane at the same angle as you shave the gap away.*

After you get the fit nice and tight, check the length. If there is still a little bit of square end left at the tip, you will want to use long, uninterrupted strokes down the full length of the taper to form a sharp point.

Really long tapers can be hard to plane because the strip bends away from the plane. First you should assure that your plane is sharp. A sharp plane requires less pressure to cut, so it will not bend the strip as much. But with tapers more than 8 inches long, this may not be enough. I'll use a longer piece of scrap strip to support the strip I am working on. With cove-and-bead strips, just place the strips with edges pressed together and the scrap a little longer than the piece you are working on. With square-edged or beveled strips, it becomes hard to keep the two strips aligned with each other. In this case I will hot-melt-glue a couple of scraps on either side of the support strip to help hold the work piece in place. These retainer strips may get planed away as you use the plane, but they should not interfere with your work.

Really long tapers over 18 inches are best addressed on a workbench. The jackknife still works for hogging away most of the excess, but it is easiest to rest the strip on the workbench while fine-tuning the shape.

Once you have fit one end, it is time to look at the other end. This is easy if the strips just run off the end somewhere. If you are fitting the second end in between two strips just like the first end, the trick is to get both ends fitting perfectly while still keeping the strip long enough. Keeping the length of a long strip accurate while working at making a tight and accurate taper at the end can be a little daunting.

The easiest way is to use two short strips, taper each end, then join them together in the middle. This is particularly useful with really long strips that by their nature are just a pain to deal with. Their length and flexibility means they are constantly poking things, getting caught on things, and generally playing their own games with your head as you try to work carefully on the other end. Two pieces, half as long, are almost always easier to cope with. They don't actually have to be half as long; they can be a third and two-thirds, or a quarter and three-quarters, or any combination that adds up to the full length. Actually, you want them to start out a little longer than the full length so you have room to adjust the length at the joint.

Fit both strips at each end of the space, and then mark the overlap on both strips. Make a little miter box to make repeatable cuts, and cut both ends so you leave the mark on the strip you will use. If the strip ends up a little long, you can plane away the taper on one or the other strip.

Figures 6-25 and 6-26. *For really short cove-and-bead strips where you must fit them at both ends, there may not be enough room to bend and snap them in place. Instead I fit two separate pieces, one at each end, with enough length so they overlap in the middle. Cut an angled end on one piece and use it to mark the length of the second piece while they are dry-fitted in place. Then remove the strips and use the angled end of the cut piece as a guide to cut off the end of the second piece.*

What gets trickier is if you want to use one continuous strip and fit it accurately at both ends. The solution is to cut it a little long and work down until it fits well, but there are some things you can do to help make this task go more quickly. Because long strips can be hard to handle, it gets tiresome to keep refitting the strips as you adjust the length to get a good fit.

After fitting the first end of the strip, dry-fit it in place. Hold it tightly against the existing strips on the forms, working down to the far end. On curved strips, make sure you keep the strip snug with the existing strip and don't let it spring off, as this will make the measurement short. When you get near the unfinished end, make a witness mark across the seam between the new strip

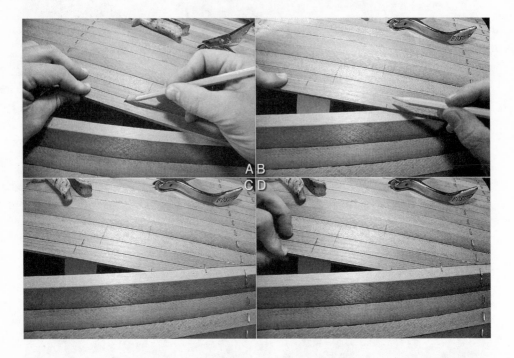

Figure 6-27. *There are times when you need to make the strip fit at a certain point to assure a desired alignment of grain or to fit a strip at both ends. In this case I am using cove-and-bead strips, so I can't see the actual end of the space down inside the cove. If you are trying to fit a strip at both ends, first fit one end well. With that end dry-fitted in place, hold the strip tightly in place down the length until you are near the other end. Create a mark across the new strip onto the existing strips (A), as near to the end as you can fully fit the strip. This will serve as an alignment mark. Next remove the strip from the first end, and back off the strip toward the first end so the taper starts farther down the strip than necessary (B). How far you back off depends on your skill level and the angle of the taper; less skill or more taper requires backing off farther. Cove-and-bead on both existing strips also requires backing off more. Mark the taper based on the backed-off position. Plane in the taper, then dry-fit the strip (C). Note that alignment marks don't quite line up. If the taper doesn't quite fit, adjust it first, then start planing it back until the alignment marks line up (D).*

and the existing one. This mark will be used as a reference to determine when you get the fit right as you work on the new taper. You can now remove the strip and concentrate on just the new end.

Start by laying the strip in place with the marks lined up, then back the strip off a bit toward the already completed end. This will make the strip a little longer when you mark the new end. An offset of about 1 inch is a good starting point. As you get better you may offset it less, and you may want to offset it more for longer tapers. Mark the end of the strip where it crosses the pointy end of the gap and the heel of the taper where the outer edge of the strip enters the gap. Cut the strip to length (a little long) with pruning clippers or a couple of strokes of a handsaw. Shape the taper as done previously, checking the fit as you go.

When the taper fits well, check the length by comparing the witness marks. They will probably not line up initially, but the strip should be overlong at this point. Use long plane strokes along the full length of the taper to shorten the strip. By maintaining even pressure while planing you will shorten the strip without changing the taper. Because of the taper, a thin shaving off the end will have a much larger effect on the length of the strip. Take a cut or two, and then recheck the length. Plane more as needed and keep your eye on the fit of the taper. When the mark between the new strip and the existing strip aligns, stop; you should have a perfect fit along the full length. Dry-fit the strip before gluing it in place to make sure you got it right.

If you mess up anywhere and somehow get the strip too short or find the taper is wrong and you no longer have material to adjust it without making the strip too short, all is not lost, you can just put that strip aside and try again. The piece will likely be usable as the next strip. Of course, if you are trying to book match the strips the order does matter, so you will want to get the fit right on the first try. Note that if you are book matching strips (meaning you want the grain to line up), this same way of marking the

location of the strip may be used at both ends. Align the grain of the strips as needed, then back the strip off so you have room to adjust until you get the fit right at the same time the grain is realigned.

Cove-and-Bead. As I mentioned previously, cove-and-bead strips hide the actual end of the strip up in a hole created by the cove. You want to arrange the strips such that you are fitting the tapered edge into a cove. The reason for this is that it is easy to put a bead on the edge but hard to carve a cove. Because you have coves on both sides of the taper, the point of the strip may extend several inches beyond the visible gap.

Fortunately, the invisible point is generally pretty similar to the visible gap, so you can use it to mark the taper on the first end of the strip. Mark the taper as discussed previously and whittle and plane it. Try the fit with the tapered edge left square until you get a good fit. When the fit is good relative to the visible gap, use your plane to knock the corners off and then round over the tapered edge and try the fit again. This should give a pretty good fit, but you may need to do some more adjustment on the taper and round over the edge again until you get a really tight fit.

It can help to mark the depth of the cove by using a pencil held $1/8$ inch from the edge of the strip with your finger. If you make this mark near the edge of the strip before installing it, it will guide you as you fit strips later. The marks help you see where the true taper lies.

The other end of the strip can be handled in much the same way it is done with square-edged strips, but because of the cove, you will need to back off the strip even farther to account for the invisible length. Dry-fit the first end of the strip and fit the new strip into the cove as far down the strip as possible. Eventually the gap will not allow you to fit the strip into the cove. When that happens, make your mark as close to the end as you can to get a tight fit. Remove the strip and then mark your taper by basing it on the visible taper, backing it off enough to

Book Matching

Imagine dropping some paint between the pages of a blank book, closing it, and then opening it up again. You will end up with two pages facing each other that have the same, but mirror image, pattern on them. You get a similar result when you cut into a piece of wood. The grain on either side of the cut will match when the cut is opened up. As you continue to take more cuts, the grain will gradually change as you progress through the board.

This process can be used to good effect to add a striking appearance to a boat. By carefully installing the strips on the forms based on the order the strips were cut from the board, you can create repeating patterns that change gradually across the surface of the boat.

The downside of attempting this kind of pattern is that any mistake in maintaining the installation order of the strips will stick out like a sore thumb. Even one broken or miscut strip will throw off the whole pattern if the wood has a distinct grain. *This is not a challenge you should consider if you have not strip-built a boat before.* The possibilities to make yourself miserable are many, and while the results are nice, a more random pattern is going to look very nice as well. The effort is only worth it if you are going to make your best effort in everything else in the construction of the boat.

The process starts with carefully cutting the strips. A thick kerf saw blade will result in more wood being removed between the matching faces with a resulting less precise match of grain. Likewise, planing more material off to achieve a uniform thickness will reduce some of the symmetry.

You will want to have a system of keeping track of the order of the strips as they come off the board. I make several witness marks on the original board. Some diagonal lines on the end of the board in permanent pen and across the face in pencil will help you reorder the strips if they should get misordered. As I cut the strips, I spread them out on a worktable in the order they are cut. I move them through the thickness planer, trying to keep them in their original order. When I'm done milling, I reassemble the board and double-check the witness lines

Figure 6-28. *Flipping over every other strip creates an alternating pattern. Since the grain varies across the width of the original board, the grain will vary across the span of the strips.*

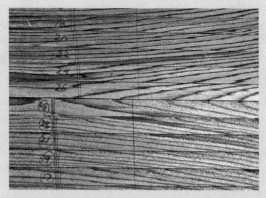

Figure 6-29. *Moving all odd-numbered strips to one side and flipping them over creates a mirror-image pattern.*

to assure the strips are in their proper order and orientation. It is important that no strips are flipped over relative to one another.

When you are certain that they are in the right order, number each strip with a pencil. Turn each strip down the same way so if you are marking the left side of the first strip, you are marking the left side of all the strips. Mark both ends and maybe a couple of places along the length of the strip with a number, just to make it easier to identify each strip as you work.

Once one side is numbered, flip each strip over and number the other side. Do something that will identify this as the "other" side, such as circle the number, underline it, or use a different color pencil. This way you can always easily identify which side you are looking at.

Next, it helps to have some more witness lines on the face of the strips to help in align-

ing the grain on the boat. Line up all the strips on a workbench or sawhorses with all the same sides up. Align all the ends so they are all in the same position relative to one another. Use a pencil to mark some lines going straight across the field of the strips. Make some double lines and others single. In this way you can quickly identify where along the strip you are working.

Book-Matched Stripping Patterns

All the work described thus far is so you can get patterns where the strips match each other in interesting ways. Just laying the strips down in the order they came off the board will make a

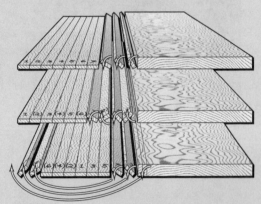

Figure 6-31. Keeping the strips in some kind of order creates interesting patterns. The top pattern progresses slowly across the strips. The middle pattern flips over every other strip, creating an alternating pattern. The mirror-image pattern on the bottom is the result of moving every other strip to the far side and flipping it over.

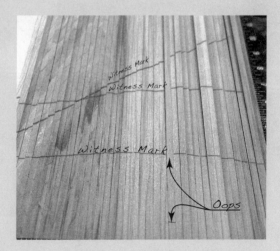

Figure 6-30. Drawing some diagonal lines across the board before you rip it into strips gives you a quick and easy reference to get all the strips back in the correct order. You can then spread the strips out flat and number them.

(Continued)

Book Matching (continued)

pattern where the grain is changing gradually across the field of strips. Or you can flip over every other strip so you see a series of mirror-imaged matching pairs that in turn gradually shift across the field. These mirror images will tend to create arrows and zigzag patterns.

Alternately, you can try for a mirror image around a centerline. In this pattern all the odd-numbered strips go on one side and the even are flipped over and placed on the other side. Check the first pair of strips to be sure they are opened up like a book for the best grain match, and then continue with the others in the same orientation.

As you can see, all of this requires you to pay attention, something that some of us are not good at. One simple mistake can mess up the whole pattern you are attempting to achieve. This all can be quite frustrating when you are trying to figure out the basics of strip-building. I know some readers will insist on attempting this on their first boat and will probably do fine, but I would suggest there are more productive ways to spend your time. Of course, boat building itself is merely a fun waste of time, so if that is what you want to do, go for it.

Figure 6-32. *With cove-and-bead strips where you are fitting both ends of a new strip, the strip ends up being longer than the visible gap because the strip extends down into the cove of the prior strip. Thus you cannot just drop the fitted strip into place; you must snake it in. It can also be very difficult to remove a strip after dry-fitting it. Instead you will want to rely on accurately making the alignment mark described in Figure 6-27. When you have successfully dry-fitted each end separately and the alignment mark lines up perfectly, add glue to the strip, insert it at one end, then bow it up in the middle to shorten it enough that you can slide the second end in place. The strip should then snap into place.*

account for the extra length needed and your ability to accurately produce a tight joint.

Joining Strips

As I said previously, trying to deal with full-length strips that may need to be fitted at both ends is often an unnecessary hassle. Structurally, there is no need to use full-length strips; there is no significant loss in strength incurred by butting two strips together. Working with shorter strips is easier. The primary benefit of a full-length strip is aesthetic, but joining two strips that were cut consecutively off the board will usually result in a virtually invisible joint.

All you really need in most situations is a nice tight joint. A scarf joint is good, in that it will be very tight, but you need to glue up a scarf joint before fitting the strip on the boat. The result is that it is just like using a full-length strip. A butt joint with the ends cut at a simple right-angle joint and pushed tightly together as you build is strong enough, but it does not leave much margin for error. By cutting at a bit of an angle you can quickly make a cut that is easy and will appear tight even if you were not perfectly accurate in making it.

I make a little miter box to make my butt joint cuts. Essentially it is just a block of wood slightly wider than the width of a strip with two plates sticking up on either side. I drop the strip in between the plates and hold my handsaw at an angle as I make the first cut. From then on in, I just use the same slot I made the first time. The angle is not that important, so long as it is consistent. I usually go for about 30 degrees off vertical and about 30 degrees across the width of the strip. Don't measure: just make a cut and use the same slot for all your future joints.

The joints can be assembled on the boat as you strip. Apply a drop of glue on one end. You need not make the joints at a form. I actually find it easier to make the joints between forms where I can get clamps on them. I use a strip of masking tape on either side of the joint to hold it tight.

The Boat Bottom

The sides of the boat are almost always the easiest. When you get to the bottom you will need to start fitting together strips as described above. The same applies to the deck of a boat like a kayak. Within the realm of "cover the forms with wood" lies a wide variety of patterns that will successfully meet that goal. For the typical canoe or kayak shape that is pointy at both ends, you will eventually get to the region known to strip-builders as the "football." This is a lentil- or American-football-shaped space that is pointy at both ends. The transition from the sides to the football may be a little hard to define as you may have some strips that run off the end at one end and need to be fitted together at the other. This transition is very design dependent.

Once you get to the football, you will be fitting strips at both ends of the boat. The goal is to find a pattern that is easy to strip, looks nice, and complements the look of the boat. Some people just keep adding strips, alternating either side so a herringbone pattern is created down the centerline (also called a keel line). For some very flat-bottomed canoes you may be able to strip up a flat panel on a workbench and then carefully cut it to fit the football. On more V-shaped bottom sections, it may work well to completely strip one side of the football with strips that extend beyond the centerline, and then trim it along the centerline before fitting strips in on the other side. Then there are other, more complicated patterns that can enhance the look of the boat. I like a pattern that alternates between strips following the keel and those following the sheer, creating a herringbone pattern in between.

The system of completely stripping one side before trimming along the centerline is nice because it requires a minimum of fitting. The downside is that you need to create a nice, straight trim line following the centerline.

As you strip the first side, be sure that all the strips extend beyond the centerline. Then use a compass to transfer the centerline to the outside of the strips. Hold one leg of the compass

Bottom Patterns

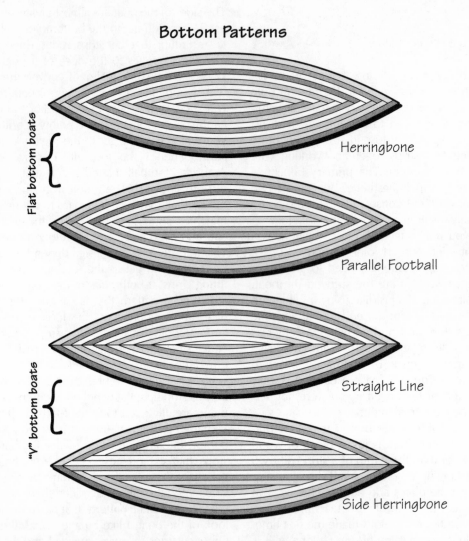

Flat bottom boats

Herringbone

Parallel Football

"V" bottom boats

Straight Line

Side Herringbone

Figure 6-33. *Filling in a large space that tapers toward at least one end means you have to decide how to fill it. On the bottom of a canoe-like boat, this space is called a football. The herringbone pattern continues strips from the sides, alternating each side. The parallel football pattern does the same until a preassembled flat panel of strips is cut to fit. These two patterns work best on flat-bottomed boats that allow the strip ends to fit together smoothly. The straight and side herringbone patterns work on either flat- or V-bottomed boats. Stripping one side, then trimming along the centerline, makes the straight pattern. The side herringbone is like the other herringbone but with strips running parallel to the centerline.*

Figure 6-35. *A rabbet plane can get in tight with the forms, allowing you to clean up the edge well.*

Figure 6-34. *This kayak is being stripped up using the side herringbone pattern using book-matched strips without staples. It takes a lot of U-jigs clamped in place to hold the strips as the hot-melt glue cools. A stubborn strip on the left side is being held down with some tape.*

under the strips, aligned with the centerline, and the upper leg over the strips directly above the centerline. Make a mark at each form and then connect the marks with a straightedge such as a scrap strip. Sight down the line to make sure it is straight before marking it with a pencil. A Japanese pull saw makes quick work of cutting just outside of this line. You can then make fine adjustments with a sharp chisel and rabbet plane.

Relieving Stress

A similar technique can be used when the curvature of the boat makes it too hard to bend the strips in place. On short, wide boats such as Nymph (Chapter 12), if you just try to keep adding strips, eventually some strips may get really twisted up (see figures on next page). At this point you may wish you could start laying strips in some different direction. Try holding a scrap strip up to the boat to see how it would naturally lie with a minimum of twisting and bending. If you find something that looks good, you can add more strips to fill up to this line or trim off in a similar way as described earlier.

Closing

No matter how you address the bottom, you will eventually get to the last strip. On this strip, the techniques that previously worked for determining the needed trim will likely not work.

Figure 6-36. Watch your strips carefully as you install them. Bending them to make them conform to the curves can impose a lot of stress, particularly on short boats like the Nymph. This piece is starting to show some buckling as it turns the corner. Adding more strips probably won't make this go away. It is caused by trying to bend the strip the "hard" way across its width instead of the "easy" way across its thickness. Eventually the strip buckles to transfer the bend to the "easy" way.

Figure 6-37. To eliminate the buckling, lay another strip over the existing strips in such a way that a minimum amount of force is needed to hold it in place, i.e., almost all the bend is the "easy" way. Clamp the strip in place and then trace the edge onto the existing strips.

Figure 6-38. Cut just proud of the line so you can still see all of it. Pull the staples out and remove the strips above the cut. Use a rabbet plane to clean up and straighten this cut. Then resume stripping starting at this new edge.

Most likely, you will have a long gap that is narrower than one strip. At this point you may be able to lay a strip over the gap and reach in from below with a sharp pencil to mark the shape of the gap. Mark the ends from the top where you can see them because the point of the pencil won't reach all the way to the points. Trim off the excess with your jackknife, or if you have a long narrow piece, it may be easier to trim it with a band saw.

Start fitting at one end by planing the piece to a sharp point. Sharpen this point so it can start to fit in the gap on the boat. Mark the strip where it becomes too wide to fit. Start planing behind the mark so you gradually work down the length of the strip until you reach the widest part of the strip, then start working from the other end. Check the length to make sure your strip piece is still long enough, and work back toward the widest point again. Eventually you should end up with a tight press fit. Apply glue to both sides of the strip and push it in place. A couple of strips of tape stretched over it should hold the piece until the glue dries.

As you are getting close to this last strip it is worth putting some scrap strips in place to gauge how big the final strip will be. If it is going to be super narrow, it may be hard to get a good fit. The easiest solution is to make the final strip wider by gluing two strips together and fitting this combined strip in place instead of the one tiny one. Taken to an extreme you can actually fill a large flat bottom by gluing lots of strips together to cover a larger football.

Cove-and-Bead

It is impossible to get the last strip in if you leave the cove on the penultimate strips because the

Figure 6-39. Eventually there will be a last strip. Remember to make the edges of the second to last strip, and maybe the third to last strip, square so you don't need to try to fit the ends down into long holes created by a cove. Place a strip over the hole and reach in underneath to trace the shape of the hole on the underside. Without moving the strip, also mark the ends of the hole on top. Bend a scrap strip over the marks you made to indicate the approximate shape of the hole. Either whittle away most of the excess wood or cut it off with a band saw.

Figure 6-40. Start tapering the strip at one end. Here a piece of scrap protects the boat while allowing me to work right where I need the strip. Test the fit at this end, planing farther along as the tip starts to fit well. Try not to go beyond the previously made marks as this will indicate you are losing some of your margin of error for fitting the other end.

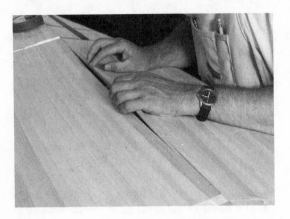

Figure 6-41. As you get toward the middle of the last strip, start fitting the other end. Make some alignment marks so you know where things should line up when it all fits together. As you work back toward the middle again, start working on getting the length right. By carefully checking the fit, noticing where the strip binds up, and gradually planing away at the high spots you should be able to make a snug-fitting strip. By pushing up on the existing strip from underneath you can open up the gap a bit while you press the new strip in place. Check the fit with the strip dry, and then add glue. Strips of strapping tape stretched across the boat will pull the seam tightly together.

gap available is smaller than the space that actually needs to be filled. The solution is to be sure to have square edges all the way around the final gap. The easiest system is to cut the cove off the ends of the next-to-final strips, and then follow the directions above. If you forget to do this and you are left with a gap with a cove around it, you can take a scrap piece of wood and carefully cut the bead off it so you have a piece that is just large enough to fill the cove. This will be small and flexible enough so that you may be able to wiggle it into the gap, or you can fit each end separately and then butt them together in the middle. You should now be left with a gap with square edges that can be filled in the manner previously described.

Remove the Staples

When you have finished covering the whole form with strips you can pull the staples out. On closed boats I usually leave the staples in until both the deck and hull are done, but you can remove them from one side before you are finished with the other. I like a heavy-duty staple remover to pull the staples, but as simple a tool as the screwdriver on your Swiss Army knife can do the trick.

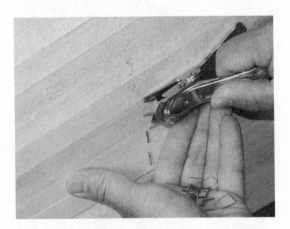

Figure 6-42. A heavy-duty office staple remover makes quick work of pulling the staples. I've filed down the blade a bit to make it easier to shove under the staple, but it easily lifts the staple with minimum damage to the wood.

Chapter 7

Fairing

After you have finished covering the forms with strips and removed the staples, the surface will likely have some glue drips, and unless you have been extraordinarily careful, there will be some uneven spots. It is time to start fairing. For some this is merely a matter of smoothing the surface a bit; for others, you may need to do a little sculpting. Careful work earlier will start to pay off now with less effort required to get a smooth, clean surface.

The initial fairing is something you do to the wood. It entails scraping, planing, and sanding the carefully laid strips to make a smooth surface. After fairing you will be applying fiberglass and epoxy, then scraping and sanding all over again. Care taken at this time will make that later scraping easier. An uneven surface left after this fairing task could cause you to sand through the fiberglass later on.

For the task at hand now, there are two steps, fairing the outside and fairing the inside. Usually you do the outside first, and happily this is easier. Getting the concave contours of the inside surface takes a little more effort, but by selecting the right tools it isn't too bad.

Probably the most useful tool in the fairing process is your hand. It is a very sensitive instrument that can detect tiny defects and irregularities. Make a habit of stroking the boat to feel for spots that need a little work. Also, lights set low beside the boat illuminating it at shallow raking angles can create subtle shadows and highlights which point to surface irregularities.

Scraping

Any glue drips can usually be removed quite quickly with a paint scraper. The scraper is also good at performing an initial smoothing of the surface, knocking down minor high spots quickly and cleanly. A scraper should have a stiff blade and works best if very sharp. Keep a fine metal file available for a quick touchup of the blade.

Hold the scraper firmly with one hand on the handle to pull and your other hand holding the blade, providing downward pressure on the boat surface. Pull the tool quickly with a moderate pressure down on the blade. Keep the handle low down near the surface. A sharp blade should produce long, wrinkled shavings when it is cutting the wood well. The biggest risk with a scraper is it will chatter—skip across the surface while creating a washboard pattern. This skipping can be self-perpetuating. If it starts, change the angle at which you pull the scraper and try again. Switching direction helps as well. Generally you want to pull the tool with the grain. Like petting a dog, if you move your hand from tail to head, pulling the scraper against the rising grain can make the wood fuzz up, and in the worst case you may split out a chunk. A sharp tool will minimize this problem, so if you have squirrelly grain, make sure to keep your scraper sharp.

One of the beauties of scrapers is that they can be easily modified to conform to unusual shapes. You can use either a bench grinder or a file to create an edge that matches the contours of your boat. Most outside, convex surfaces can be handled with a straight blade, but interior, concave surfaces usually need a blade with a convex radius.

Scrape the whole surface of the boat to remove any glue drips. Run the tool down the seams between strips where there is often a little ridge. The goal is not to put a fine finish on the boat but to begin to remove ugliness.

Figure 7-2. *You should scrape or plane in the same manner you would pet a dog—going with the lay of the grain. Unless you like your dog to look like a punk rocker, you go from head to tail. Likewise you don't want the blade to lift up the grain, causing divots. With a sharp blade you can cheat this rule, but it still pays to be aware of the grain direction. Pull the scraper firmly and quickly with a firm hand pushing the blade onto the surface to minimize chatter.*

Figure 7-1. *Although the scraper is really good at removing glue drips, it can also do a lot of fairing pretty quickly. The scraper needs to be held firmly so it does not chatter and skip.*

Figure 7-3. *A sharp scraper will work much better than a dull one. Use a fine metal file to keep a good edge on it. This scraper has been modified with a variety of different radii and a flat section to conform to various shapes. The outside of most boats would probably do well with just a flat edge, but the inside often has some tight turns.*

Outside surfaces are usually pretty easy to deal with. The boat is typically still on the forms, with everything well supported and held in place. After glassing the outside and removing the shell of the boat from the forms, it is lightweight, a little fragile, and not that well supported. Some people will build a set of female forms to hold it securely while working on the inside. I can't say I have ever bothered, although there are times it may have been wise. Instead I just set it on saw horses with a cradle or cushioning on top of the horses and started working on the inside.

Because the shell is not that well supported, it is hard to get the firm pressure between the scraper and surface that prevents chatter. Because the boat is lightweight, it wants to slide around, so you may need to keep one hand on the boat while working with the other. Sometimes you can secure the shell in place with strapping tape or string. To get a firm cutting pressure, you will often have to place one hand on the outside of the shell, opposite the area you are scraping, so the surface doesn't just flex away from the tool. Because one hand is occupied holding and supporting the shell, you may find it easier to choke up on the handle of the scraper a bit. By holding the tool closer to the blade you can control its desire to chatter.

Figure 7-4. *Working on the inside you may need to support the sides to minimize the chatter.*

While working on the inside of the shell, you will quickly get a pile of shavings that can interfere with your ability to work. A little bit of shaving caught under the scraper blade may keep it from cutting. Keep the region you are working on swept clean.

Planing

After scraping, the surface may be ready to go directly to sanding. Wood strips naturally bend in nice fair curves and often do not need any additional fairing, but there are a lot of things that can get in the way of achieving a perfectly fair stripping job. For instance, cove-and-bead strips may not nestle smoothly, you may have not aligned your square-edged strips precisely, some stripping patterns cause a little crease in the surface, or it may just be your first time building and you were a little sloppy. You can try to do better next time, but for now you need to make your boat look good. There is no better tool for smoothing and fairing a wood surface than a sharp plane. The long bottom with a short cutting edge virtually eliminates the possibility of cutting a hollow spot. A plane will neatly shave down any high spots in a controlled and predictable manner. While it is possible to overplane a surface, a sharp plane is easier to control than any other tool.

There is probably no better tool for determining if a surface is smooth and fair than the palm of your hand. As you are working on fairing the surface, run your hand over the wood and pay attention. You will be able to detect high spots, little ripples, dips, and irregularities that don't show up to the eye but will be visible after a few layers of fiberglass and a glossy coat of varnish. A slight bump can often be removed with a couple of strokes of a plane. A sharp plane is much more controlled than sanding, which tends to work in broad strokes over larger areas. When working around fine shapes and details such as feature lines, a plane does a good job of keeping crisp, precise shapes.

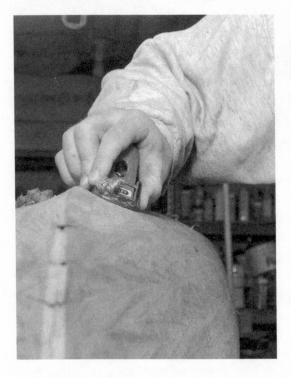

Figure 7-5. This modified block plane has a slightly radiused sole that works well for fairing out sections near the stem.

Figure 7-6. A spokeshave does a very nice job of shaping areas that are concave along their length. The goal is not to remove a lot of wood, but to shave off high spots.

Like the scraper, a plane will work best cutting with the grain. Going against the grain can be a bit like dragging a hoe up a shingled roof, lifting the grain and ripping out little bits. Again, a sharp plane is very important. Setting it for a shallow cut with a narrow opening in front of the blade will reduce the chance of tear-out.

I typically use a block plane because it is lightweight and easy, but for large, mostly flat surfaces, a long bench plane will do a very nice job automatically knocking off high spots. Most planes will not work well with hollow, concave areas. I have modified a small block plane to have a radiused bottom for working in hollow areas, but often it is easier to use a scraper and then sand these areas instead of planing.

For areas that are concave along the boat length but convex across the width, such as the deck at the bow of a kayak, a spokeshave offers a very controlled method for creating fine shapes.

A sharp plane can leave a smooth surface that exhibits the grain of the wood to beautiful effect. With care it may be possible to completely prepare the surface for fiberglassing using only planes, but chances are you will eventually need to sand.

Sanding the Wood

Strip-built boats have a reputation of requiring a lot of sanding, and that reputation has some justification. The trick is to do only as much sanding as is really necessary. With all the fairing steps, your work is made much easier if you are careful with the stripping. The smoother and fairer your initial stripping, the less time you will need to spend sweating over the sanding.

Figure 7-7. *To get a fair, consistent surface you want to sand everything to approximately the same degree. Scribble on the surface with a soft pencil to provide guides for your sanding. Do not press hard, and use the side of the pencil point so you don't create grooves in the wood.*

Figure 7-8. *By working until all the pencil marks are gone you will be sure the whole surface has been sanded and is quite fair. This fairing process can be done with very coarse sandpaper such as 40- or 60-grit. Try to sand with the grain to minimize the scratches.*

If you have a good surface when you start sanding, you may be able to start at a fine grit. However, if you need to do a lot of sanding, a fine grit will only take longer and typically will not produce as good results as starting with a coarser grit.

While "sharp" is not something you usually associate with sandpaper, new sandpaper will do a better job than stuff that has been used. You will get better results and the work will go faster if you switch paper frequently. I will typically change paper on my random orbit sander every 10 minutes. Dull sandpaper will tend to buff the surface instead of cutting. With wood that has distinct annual growth rings, dull paper will not cut through the harder parts of the grain, leaving them slightly above the surrounding wood.

I will start sanding the outside with a long fairing board with 40-grit sandpaper. While this may be a little extreme, it makes quick work of the final leveling after planing. From there I will switch to 60-grit paper on a random orbit sander and work up through finer grits from

there. You want to remove all the scratches from the previous grit before moving on to the next. You can mark up the surface with a soft pencil to help guide your work. Use the side of the pencil point so you are not pressing deep grooves into the wood strips. Scribble over the whole boat so that as you sand you can watch the pencil marks disappear.

The fairing board will not work well on the concave surface of the inside. Instead I will wrap a sheet of coarse paper around a block of wood or foam that nearly matches the shape of the surface. A chunk of firm foam cut with a changing radius will conform to a variety of shapes. Use long, vigorous strokes. Sanding by hand is a whole-body exercise. Avoid short, scrubbing strokes as they will concentrate too much effort on a small area when the goal is to level out and smooth a large area. Short strokes also do not allow the sanding dust to escape from under the block. Have a brush available to move the sanding dust away from the work area, and vacuum up the piles frequently to keep control over the mess.

Figure 7-9. The sharp ends of the boat can be tough to reach to clean up. I glue some sandpaper to a paddle made of plywood to help me reach the tight spots.

Work over the whole boat methodically, removing the pencil marks as you go. If you are using a power random orbit sander, keep the tool moving at all times. I generally work on a 2-foot-wide section extending from the keel or centerline to the gunwale or sheerline. I move the sander side to side across the region, progressing from the centerline down to the sheerline, then work up and down in strokes from sheer to centerline and back, and then move over one foot so the next 2-foot-wide section overlaps the previous area, and repeat the process all the way around the boat. Before switching to the next grit, I will often hand sand the whole boat with the same grit, being sure to work the sanding block parallel to the strips to remove the last signs of sanding scratches. For a fine finish a quick vacuuming of the surface will remove remaining dust and any particulate grit that has fallen off the sandpaper. This grit can add deeper scratches than you would get from the next finer grit.

One potential issue that is most evident with sanding, but occurs while scraping and planing as well, is the creation of slight low spots wherever the form supports the strip. With ¼-inch

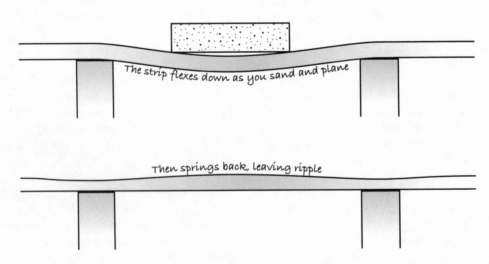

The strip flexes down as you sand and plane

Then springs back, leaving ripple

Figure 7-10. Strips that span forms tend to flex slightly as you sand or plane them. As a result the wood over the forms will tend to get sanded slightly more than the wood between the forms. This may not be easy to notice at first but may show up with a shiny finish. Since thinner strips are more flexible, you may want to use more forms for better support.

strips on 12-inch spaced forms, this problem is minor, but as the strips get thinner without changing the form spacing you may notice that sanding is more effective where the strips are supported by the forms, and between the forms the wood may flex away from the tool as you work. This means the region between the forms gets sanded or planed a little less than where the forms are. This may not be noticeable right away, but when you finish glassing and varnishing the boat you may see a little ripple in the finish where the forms were. This is most noticeable in flat sections of the boat where the shell is more flexible.

To counteract this little ripple, use sharp tools and sandpaper where less pressure is required to accomplish the work. Also, try to pay attention to where you apply pressure. More pressure on the tool while it is between forms will help compensate for the shell flexing away. If you plan ahead, you can create more forms so the span between forms is shorter, allowing less room for flexing.

For most of the wood sanding I will use a soft or flexible backing pad on the random orbit sander. These pads are sometimes called conforming pads. If your sander came with a fairly stiff pad, you can buy adapter pads that go between the tool and the sandpaper. For the first sanding immediately after using the fairing board, I will use the stiff backer pad because it will tend to knock off high spots more efficiently than the soft, conforming pad. As the name implies, the conforming pad will ride up and over irregularities and will not remove high spots as effectively. Again, you must keep the

Figure 7-11. *Hold your random orbital sander flat against the surface and keep it moving. Don't try to concentrate on one stubborn spot by angling the tool or stalling in one place.*

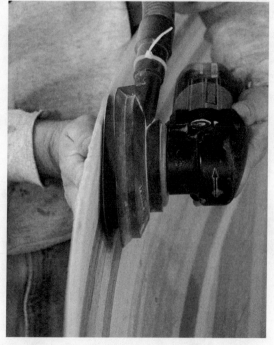

Figure 7-12. *A soft contour pad on the sander helps conform to the surfaces. While working on the inside, support the sides of the boat with your hand as you sand. Hook up the sander to a vacuum cleaner to control the dust.*

Figure 7-13. *A fairing sander does not work well on interior surfaces, but after scraping and planing, you can get a quite fair surface by wrapping sandpaper around a chunk of soft foam or a shaped wooden sanding block with some foam cushion on it.*

Figure 7-14. *Sandpaper leaves a little bit of grit behind that will continue to scratch the boat when you switch to a finer paper. Vacuuming the boat between grits may help you get a better finish. A final vacuuming of any residual sanding dust when you are done will give a cleaner look to the final finish.*

sander moving at all times, as slowing down will tend to make a divot. Keep the pad as flat to the surface as the surface will allow, and avoid the temptation to tip the sander up to concentrate one edge on a difficult spot. If there is a high spot you want to remove, you are better off slicing it down with a plane or the fairing sander. If there is a low spot trapping a dot of glue, you will either need to sand the whole surrounding region down to the lowest level or scrape out the dot of glue and leave a localized, small, low spot to be filled up with epoxy later. Trying to adjust the surface contour with a sander will usually lead to trouble. The contour pad will come in handy on the inside. Use a softer pad to conform to deeper contours.

For most people the finish left by the random orbit sander will be good enough. If you completely remove all the scratches from previous grits with each new grit, you should not see much visible sign of swirling caused by the spinning action of the sander. However, if you can't seem to get rid of the swirls, you may try hand sanding with the same grit after using the random orbit sander. By sanding parallel to the strips and the grain you can make the scratches less visible.

Sharp Corners

A nice crisp, sharp edge along a chine or as a feature line can look classy. Unfortunately, sharp edges are fragile and easily marred. This shows up in the fairing stage. If you don't hold your sander flat to the surrounding surfaces, you will immediately round over the corner and there is no way to put the wood back. Even after the boat is completed and being used, these corners will tend to accumulate more abuse than the surrounding flatter surfaces and will be more prone to damage. They are also stress risers, or places in the boat where the stress and strain of being used accumulates, so they are a potential failure point.

Another problem with sharp corners is that fiberglass cloth does not conform easily to sharp changes in directions. Most glass will not conform to a 90-degree angle. It will need to have the corner rounded over a bit to allow the glass fibers to bend gradually. Rounding corners thus has the dual benefit of easing the application of fiberglass and making the transition stronger.

Because corners sand so quickly, it generally works best to leave the corner sharp until the very end of the fairing and sanding process. When you are nearly done you can carefully ease the corner by hand sanding or with a couple of swipes of a block plane before hand sanding. Six-ounce fiberglass will usually conform to a ⅛-inch radius corner (about the diameter of a pen or pencil) on a 90-degree bend. Lighter-weight glass will conform to smaller radii. While a crisp feature line may look good, you need to balance it with the needs of applying the cloth and strength considerations.

Wetting the Wood

When you think you have just about finished sanding the outside, sponging down the wood with clean water will help raise any scratches and highlight any problem areas. I usually don't bother doing this on the inside, but it does help produce a well-finished surface. First, sweep and vacuum off the sanding dust. Then, with a bucket of clean water, soak a rag or sponge. Wipe down the surface to make it soaking wet. You don't want standing water, but the boat should be able to handle getting completely soaked. Quickly get the whole surface wet, then come back and wipe up the excess with a clean, dry rag or towel.

One thing you will notice immediately is how much better the wet surface looks compared to the dry. The water increases the color saturation and helps make the grain stand out. The epoxy will have the same effect, but with a fine finish it will look even better.

While the surface is still wet, inspect the whole surface. Stray spots of carpenter's glue will show up as whitish spots. Mark these spots with dots of masking tape. Small spots can be cleaned up with a scraper while the glue is still wet. Also look for rough patches where scratches from coarse sandpaper pop up. Mark anything you see with more nibs of tape. Inspect the edges where it is easy to miss spots. Then let the surface dry completely.

After the boat has dried, re-mark the problem spots with a pencil. Again, don't press too

Figure 7-15. *When you think you are about done sanding, wipe the whole surface down with a wet rag. This will help clean the surface of dust, highlight any scratches or raised and compressed grain, help point out any leftover glue, and give you your first indication of what the final finished look of the boat will be.*

Figure 7-16. *If there is any glue left on the surface, it should show up when you wet the boat with water. Carpenter's glue shows up white when it is wet. Other waterproof glues would not show up as easily. You can usually scrape off the glue, let the wood dry, and then give the region a thorough sanding. Mark the area with a flag of tape so you can find the spot again after the wood dries.*

Figure 7-17. With a decked boat you could remove the hull or deck while sanding, staining, or glassing the other half, but often the safest place for it is on the forms. Inserting waxed paper at the sheerline will protect the bottom half as you work on the top.

hard. You don't want to make a deep groove with the pencil. I usually go over the whole surface with the last grit of sandpaper used, paying special attention to the marked areas.

After a final sanding, the surface is ready for fiberglassing. If you are going to stain the wood, do that prior to fiberglassing (see Chapter 8).

After fiberglassing the outside, you will repeat the whole fairing process on the inside of the boat. The procedure is the same. Because most of the surfaces are concave instead of convex, long tools such as the fairing board and a long bench plane will not work as well. Look for tools with a shorter foot or that are rounded. Scrapers are very useful on the inside. A short block plane and a soft pad on your sander will get most of the large areas. I make some specialized sanding tools by gluing sandpaper to plywood with spray adhesive.

You may end up with some glue drips or places where the forms adhered a bit to the strips. Usually a whack with a hammer will break the forms free. A scraper or rasp will remove the drips and glue spots on the inside.

Figure 7-18. The staple holes will often wick a little epoxy onto the forms. This is why the forms have tape on the edges, but sometimes you may need a little persuasion to get the boat off. Some light raps with a hammer usually do the trick.

If you used hot-melt glue instead of staples, you may need to remove patches of glue. Those bits that don't peel away easily with a scraper can be softened up with a heat gun. Because the boat is no longer on the forms it will have a tendency to wander around on your sawhorses. Protect the bottom so it does not get damaged, and if possible secure it in place. Some strapping tape is often all that is needed to keep the boat from moving too much.

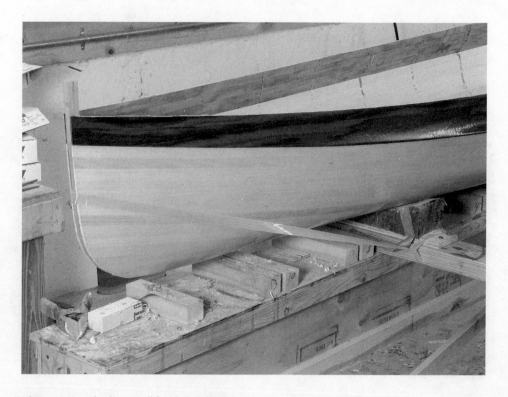

Figure 7-19. *The boat will be very light when you remove it from the forms and start working on the inside. Strategic use of strapping tape keeps it from wandering around as you clean up the interior.*

Chapter 8

Staining

Wood is beautiful as it is; there is no reason you need to go tarting it up with fancy colors, but applying some color with stain can add some pop to the look of the boat. If you ended up with a wide variety of strip tones, a coat of stain can bring the colors closer together. Staining adds another process to mess up, however, so if you are prone to mistakes, you might get better results sticking with the natural color. Just because I included a whole chapter on stain does not imply you need to do it. Feel free to skip this chapter if you like the natural color of your wood.

The first thing to remember when considering staining your strips is that you need to apply fiberglass and epoxy over the stain, and you don't want anything to interfere with the bond between the wood and epoxy. The stain you select should not contain anything that will weaken the bond. Because of this, oil-based stains should be avoided. Second, since you are making a boat, it is presumed that you will bring it outside where, it often happens, the sun shines. Sunlight can make a lot of stains fade. You want to choose a stain that is colorfast and does not fade easily.

Stains come in two basic varieties—pigments and dyes. Pigments have finely ground powders of different colors. Pigmented stain will contain binders that adhere the powders to the surface of the wood. Dyes penetrate into the wood, actually staining the cell structure. As long as the binder does not interfere with the epoxy bond, pigments should work fine; however, dye often allows richer colors without obscuring the grain. Traditional dyes for woodworking such as anilines often are not colorfast, but there are dyes available that hold up to the sun quite well. These are often referred to as non-grainraising

Figure 8-1. *Alcohol- and water-based stains dry quickly. Get your rag very wet with stain, and move it quickly. A dry rag will create a splotching color. If you want a lighter color, follow the stain manufacturers instructions, which typically involve adding a thinner or reducer to dilute the color.*

(NGR) and contain metalized or premetalized dyes. These dyes are mixed with water or alcohol when applied to the wood. I've found these stains work very well with strip-built boats that get a lot of sun exposure.

The downside of using a water- or alcohol-based stain instead of the traditional oil-based is that they dry very quickly. They do not allow you the luxury of applying a little, stepping back, checking it out, and adjusting the results. You need to apply the stain quickly and with assurance and be ready to accept the results.

In addition, the stain or dye will have a tendency to highlight sanding flaws. Scratches will stand out more. Be sure you are happy with your sanding work before you start applying the stain.

Soak a rag with stain and apply it quickly to the boat. Don't stall out, as holding the rag in one place will create dark spots. Keep it moving. As soon as the rag starts to dry out and no longer transfers color to the wood quickly, resoak the rag and keep moving. The wood should look wet with stain. A dry rag will tend to make light spots. Because of the problems involved in getting an even coat, you will probably need to apply several coats. If you want a light color you will need to thin the stain down with a suitable reducer so the desired color is obtained after two or three coats.

It may be possible to even out a splotchy coat of stain by wiping it down with the appropriate solvent. This can lift the stain and redistribute it. You will want to experiment on a panel of scrap wood before you do anything too drastic.

Let the stain dry thoroughly before moving on to applying epoxy and fiberglass. If you are using an alcohol-based stain it is possible the solvent will not interfere with the epoxy, but you run the risk of having the stain run and blotch. After staining, you cannot sand the boat further as you will just burn through the stain. If the surface is a little bit rough because of raised grain, the epoxy and fiberglass will make it smooth.

One downside of staining is that it pretty much forces the boat into a solid color. It is

Figure 8-2. *Staining some of the wood stains all of it. If you want an accent strip, it may be easiest to add it after the wood has been stained. Here the outside of the hull has been stained and fiberglassed. I'm applying a thin strip of wood to the top edge, and then I'll glass the inside. I'll glass the outside when I attach the deck.*

difficult to create a border between two colors. Masking tape does not work reliably because the stain will often wick in under the tape. One thing you can do, however, is create accent stripes. An accent stripe is a contrasting piece of wood that highlights the shape of the boat. With a decked boat like a kayak this can easily be accomplished by applying a thin strip of wood to the top edge of the sheerline after you have glassed the outside.

An accent stripe in the middle of a field of stained wood is more difficult. The one system I found that works reliably is to stain right over the accent stripe and then remove the stain from that piece of wood with a knife. This is easiest when the stripe follows a feature line or crease in the surface. The creased shape of the surface makes it easier to work on the stripe without messing up the surrounding surface. This technique works best with a hardwood accent stripe because the hardwood does not absorb stain deep into the grain, and the harder wood often sticks up a little proud of surrounding softwood after sanding.

The blade of a utility knife makes a good scraper and can be modified to match the width of the stripe. Grind the blade to be slightly narrower than the accent piece. Hold the blade perpendicular to the surface and carefully drag it parallel to the stripe with moderate pressure. Remove the top layer of the wood slowly until the stain color has been removed.

After allowing the stain to dry fully, you are ready to start glassing. If you are worried about the resin bleeding and running, it may be useful to apply a seal coat of epoxy before working with the fiberglass. Information about applying a seal coat is provided in the next chapter.

Chapter 9

Fiberglassing

Many people who are building a boat for the first time come to the project with some woodworking experience and feel comfortable with just about everything we have done so far. For them cutting strips, planing, and sanding are all old hat, but fiberglassing . . . that is scary.

If you are one of the many people who are intimidated by the idea of pouring a sticky liquid over a sort of weird white fabric, the concept to try to lodge in your mind is that you are just making fabric wet. The epoxy is a liquid, which, while thicker and stickier than water, acts much the same way. Fiberglass is just really fine strands of window glass and, even though it starts out white, will become transparent when wet.

While the fiberglassing is a critical step that will affect everything from the strength of the boat to its finished appearance, it is not really that hard. You are taking a liquid, putting it on a fabric, and spreading the liquid around until the fabric is completely saturated. The fiberglass and epoxy are both designed to work in this process and will generally cooperate with you to assure good results.

For most boats the process of fiberglassing will evolve through several steps. After the outside of the boat has been faired, the outer surface is ready to accept epoxy and fiberglass. You may apply a seal coat of epoxy (see Seal Coat later in this chapter), or go directly to laying on the fiberglass fabric and wetting it out with epoxy. After the wet-out coat has cured, a fill coat of epoxy is painted over the body to start filling up the fabric texture. The boat is now usually ready to be removed from the forms, and you can attack the fairing of the inside. When fairing is complete, the inside of the boat

is then fiberglassed in the same manner as the outside. Before proceeding to applying the final finish you may decide to apply more fill coats to the outside.

Using Epoxy

Epoxy is a chemical concoction that when its two parts are mixed together you initially get a liquid. As the chemicals react with each other the liquid turns into a hard solid. For this to happen right it is really important that the chemicals are mixed in the correct proportions and combined thoroughly. The most common mistakes with epoxy are due to using the wrong proportions or not mixing enough.

Epoxies come in two parts—resin and hardener. The word *resin* can be a little confusing because it is used for both the unmixed part and the combined mixture after hardener has been added. Most of the time when I talk about resin in this book it will refer to the result of mixing the initial resin with the hardener. Sorry to be confusing, but I didn't make up these terms. I'm just trying to be consistent with the standard lingo.

So, you take resin and hardener and mix them together to make resin. This mixing is critical. The epoxy manufacturer will tell you the proportions. Read the instructions for your epoxy to find out the appropriate proportions for the mix. Typically the ratio will be 2:1 or 3:1 but may be up to 5:1, with the larger amount being the resin and the smaller amount being the hardener.

Most manufacturers will also have precalibrated pumps available. These pumps should

Figure 9-1. Epoxy suitable for fiberglassing usually comes in large containers with calibrated pumps to help measure out the proper ratio. Keeping the resin warm will reduce the viscosity, allowing it to wet out the cloth more easily.

help you get the mix proportions right. However, it is important that you put the right pump in the right jug. Putting the hardener pump in the resin container is not good. If you make this mistake, pull the pumps out and clean them off thoroughly before replacing them in the appropriate jugs.

Since the pumps are precalibrated you should be able to use one pump of each (resin and hardener) to get the right mix. Again, read the instructions and don't make the mistake of thinking that a 2:1 mix means you use two pumps to one pump if that is not what is intended.

While epoxy is relatively safe stuff to work with, it is possible to develop an allergic sensitivity to contact with uncured epoxy. The best way to prevent this is to prevent contact between the resin and your skin. Besides careful work habits, this means wearing gloves when-

ever you handle uncured epoxy and washing off any spills as quickly as possible. While you are in the throes of wetting out fiberglass, drips of resin can get everywhere and on everything. Not only can this mess up your tools, but drips of epoxy on your tools are potential sources of unplanned skin contact as well. Try to work carefully and keep yourself and your tools clean. Replace your gloves as soon as you detect a rip in a finger. Consider doubling up with two pairs of gloves if you are doing something that will stress the gloves.

Mixing Epoxy

When I use the calibrated pumps to measure the epoxy, I start with one pump of the resin followed by one pump of the hardener and continue with that pattern. This way I always finish with the hardener. If my hand is coming up from the hardener I know I can stop. I'm not very good at keeping count. If I were to do five pumps of resin before doing five pumps of hardener, I'm pretty certain I would lose track somewhere after three pumps.

The pumps are usually just mustard dispensers screwed into the top of your epoxy jug. They can be a little slow when dealing with epoxy. Don't rush them. Wait until each pump has returned fully to the top before pushing out another dosage. Do one pump each of resin and hardener, then let the pump recover.

Your mixing container can be any clean plastic receptacle; I'm partial to used yogurt containers. The quart size is deep enough to hold a decent amount of resin without being so close to the top that it spills easily.

As you are starting out you will be best served by making quite small batches of epoxy. About one cup or less is a good starting point. In a quart yogurt container this will mean there is about 1 inch of resin at the bottom of container. Since different epoxy manufacturers' pumps dispense different amounts, I can't tell you how many pumps this might be.

Hot Epoxy

Epoxy cures via a chemical reaction between the resin and the hardener. This reaction is exothermic, so as the chemicals combine they give off heat. Epoxy also cures faster when it is warm. That means curing epoxy can heat itself up so that it cures even faster. This only happens when the mixed resin is concentrated in an area such as your mixing pot. If you are moving slowly or it is a hot day, you may get a meltdown where the epoxy creates a runaway reaction. The first sign is the mixing cup gets hot. If you feel your epoxy cup is warm, don't spread any more on your boat. Put that cup aside, preferably outside on the driveway. It may start to smoke, and although it is unlikely, it could even catch on fire. It will smell more than usual.

If you put hot epoxy on the boat it will cool down very quickly. As it does so, it will increase in viscosity. This thicker epoxy will not soak into the glass, and the glass will not become clear. Adding more cool, thin epoxy over the top probably won't make it any better. Don't put epoxy that has started to heat up on the boat. It will just make a mess.

However—isn't there always a "however"? —there are times when you actually want your epoxy hot. Because heating the epoxy lowers its viscosity, warming your resin can make it soak into your wood and cloth better. This will help promote a clear layup.

There was one professional builder who said he would heat his shop up over 100°F, then turn off the heat before starting glassing. This served several purposes. It lowered the viscosity of the epoxy, making it flow more easily. It also heated up the air trapped in the grain of the wood, thus expanding it. After the heat is turned off, the temperature of the wood starts to go down, along with the air it contains. All those little air pockets turn into little vacuums as the air contracts. This sucks the resin into the wood and any other gaps or spaces. Furthermore, if there is any air mixed into the epoxy

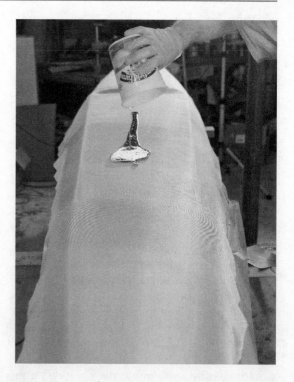

Figure 9-2. *Once the epoxy is mixed, the chemicals start doing their thing. The longer they are in a concentrated mass the faster they will react. Dumping your mixing pot onto the boat quickly will slow down the reaction, giving you more time to work.*

or trapped in the weave of the cloth, this air will also contract as it cools, with the result of making bubbles shrink and disappear. Even if you don't want to burn the fuel to heat up your workshop to 100°, you should do most of your epoxy work during a time when temperatures are either constant or dropping.

You should also note that doing the opposite—heating up the boat while applying epoxy—will force air out of the wood and expand any trapped air. There have been a lot of people who thought they would speed up the cure by putting their boat out in the sun or by cranking up the heat. Unfortunately, they would return to find their boats covered with large bubbles and foamlike places where expanding air bubbled through the resin. Again, you should avoid doing epoxy work while the temperature is rising. Small temperature changes are not a big deal, but don't start your epoxy work on a cool morning in the shade when you know the sun will be hitting your work area an hour later.

If a rising-temperature building situation is really unavoidable, be sure to apply a seal coat before glassing, as this will limit the effect of air temperature on the wood.

Seal Coat

A seal coat is a layer of epoxy applied to the boat before laying down the fiberglass to limit the absorption of epoxy when wetting out the glass later, as well as to limit the effect of temperature on the wood as mentioned above. The seal coat is first painted on with a brush, then spread out with a roller. (Just using the brush would typically result in too thick a layer.) You could apply the epoxy directly from a roller tray, but some places are easier to reach with a brush, so I save the roller tray and load the brush with epoxy from the mixing tub.

Just apply one coat of epoxy to the bare wood. You may notice that some spots stay glossy and wet looking, where others look dark and more dry. This is normal. The wood absorbs resin at varying rates due to grain orientation differences. This tendency is the reason for applying a fill coat, and as long as you have successfully applied one complete coat, it will do the job. Don't try to add more epoxy in an effort to achieve an even appearing coat.

If you are staining the boat, apply the stain prior to applying the seal coat. You will probably want to add a seal coat over the stain. The seal coat often assists in making the stain coat appear more uniform.

The seal coat provides more control over the fiberglass layup. Without a seal coat, the wood will absorb epoxy until the grain is filled up, its source of epoxy dries up, or the epoxy

Figure 9-3. *A seal coat limits how much epoxy is absorbed later when applying fiberglass. Brush on a little epoxy, then spread it around with a roller. There should be no need to thin the epoxy. The seal coat is not a requirement, but it does make the later coats that wet out the fiberglass a little bit easier to accomplish.*

cures. With a seal coat, the grain is capped off so later epoxy will not get absorbed and air has a harder time getting in and out of the wood.

If you don't apply a seal coat, you may end up with some starved spots in the fiberglass where the wood sucked the epoxy out of the weave. This is not that hard to deal with. If you babysit the boat, you can continue to apply more epoxy until the wood absorbs its fill. This is a good idea regardless of whether you use a seal coat, but it may not be how you want to spend your time. Because the seal coat seals the wood, it is a means to keep the weight of the finished boat at a minimum. Less absorbed epoxy means a lighter boat. Allowing more absorption will result in a stronger bond for a tougher boat, but this is one of the constant trade-offs between strength and weight.

There are good reasons you may not want to apply a seal coat. For example, it adds another step and probably another day to the project. If you apply the seal coat you must let it cure. This also means that the wet-out coat, when you apply the fabric, will be bonding to at least partially cured epoxy. If you can't get back to

Figure 9-4. *Wood will absorb the seal coat at different rates depending on grain orientation and other factors. Don't worry that some spots look dry (dull) and others wet (shiny). This is OK. Once the epoxy has cured it will seal the wood from absorbing more resin.*

Figure 9-5. *Gaps less than $\frac{1}{16}$ inch wide between strips will fill with epoxy when you glass, but larger gaps should be filled. You can fill them with colored wood putty or epoxy mixed with sanding dust. Apply masking tape completely around the gap to prevent staining the wood. Press the filler in between the tape, then remove the tape. After the filler dries, sand the area lightly.*

the project for a while, you will need to sand the seal coat to help promote a strong bond, and if the seal coat epoxy should blush, you will need to clean off the blush by scrubbing the boat with water and then drying it with a rag. Without the seal coat, the wet-out coat is bonding directly to the wood, which is probably the strongest option.

Whether or not you apply a seal coat should depend on your building schedule, how much control you have over the temperature, and whether you will be able to check in on the boat as the wet-out coat cures. If it is your first experience with using fiberglass and epoxy, a seal coat does give you more control and will probably make the process easier.

Preparation

Once you put epoxy over the wood there is very little you can do to make the wood look better, so be sure you are happy with what you have. The wood should be sanded smooth and either swept clean of dust or vacuumed. Inspect the

surface for anything you want to fix. If you see rough spots, sanding marks, glue spots, and so forth, fix them now, and resand as necessary.

If you see gaps between strips, you need to decide if they are worth filling. Narrow gaps (less than $\frac{1}{16}$ inch) will probably get filled with epoxy as you apply the seal coat or the wet-out coat and will not cause structural problems. Wider gaps should probably be filled, and if you are really worried about appearances you may choose to fill even the smaller gaps.

If you saved your sanding dust when sanding the boat, you can use the dust mixed with epoxy to make filler. Even though this dust may have come from the same wood as the strips, it will still appear darker than the surrounding wood. Add a little bit of lighter color material such as colloidal silica to help match the color. Remember that the application of epoxy will darken the wood, so attempt to match the color of the wood when it is wet. Place masking tape around the gap such that all you see is the gap itself. Press the filler into the gap with a putty knife and scrape off the excess. The tape will protect the surrounding wood from getting stained with the filler. Peel off the tape right away.

You can either roll the glass out over the wet filler or let it dry and give it a light sanding to knock down any material above the strips.

Instead of epoxy and sanding dust you may also use water-based wood putties. These may come precolored, or you can add a little bit of artist's watercolors to match the tone of the surrounding wood.

Inspect the area around the boat, looking for sharp corners or other objects that may snag the glass. It doesn't take much to create a deformed spot in the glass by rubbing it across a rough drip of epoxy or a bit of wire. These snags aren't a catastrophe, but they do weaken the layup slightly and make it harder to get a smooth finish.

Cutting the Glass

Presumably sometime before you reached this point you decided exactly what layup you intend to use with your glass. For instance, you have chosen 6-ounce E-glass versus 4-ounce S glass; fiberglass on the inside or some exotic such as carbon fiber; one layer versus two, and so forth. Now you need to figure out exactly how you are going to put that material in its place.

Are you going to roll out one continuous piece of cloth, or will you piece it together, overlapping at the joints?

There are several considerations when making these decisions: ease, efficiency, speed, appearance, and strength. One piece of continuous, unbroken cloth is almost always going to be stronger and will look better than piecing several smaller pieces together. But putting smaller pieces together may use the cloth more efficiently. If the cloth is expensive, like carbon fiber, wasted cloth is not welcome. Fitting small pieces around complex shapes is often easier

and quicker than trying to make a large piece conform against its will. Finally, some boats are just too big to cover with one piece.

I will generally try to cover large external areas with one piece for appearance's sake, but I am more willing to piece together several on the inside.

The easiest way to get the cloth the right size is to roll it out onto the boat and trim it in place. If you have a partner, have your partner stand at one end holding the end of the cloth while you hold the roll and walk down toward the other end, unrolling as you go. Try to hold the cloth up above the boat so that it doesn't snag on anything. Carefully check the alignment before draping the cloth down over the boat. Make sure you have enough length at both ends and that it will cover all the way from gunwale to gunwale.

On the outside of the boat, a large perimeter of excess cloth will help absorb excess resin dripping off the sides before it falls to the floor, but if you don't want to waste too much cloth as

Figure 9-6. *It does help to have an assistant when rolling out the fiberglass. Working alone it is easy to snag something, and even the pressure of rolling the cloth on the boat surface can distort the fabric a little bit. But with care and a pair of scissors in your pocket before you start, you should be able to handle the task alone. Note that the waxed paper is still in place between the deck and the hull.*

a resin trap, you can trim it a couple of inches below the edge.

On the inside of the boat, excess cloth will weigh down the top edge of fabric, causing it to pull away from the boat a bit. Make sure you have enough fabric to cover the whole inside before trimming, and then clip off the excess an inch or two above the top edge.

Use sharp scissors to trim the cloth. If you are going to use the trimmings, treat them gently as you cut them free and avoid letting them drop onto a dirty floor. Large pieces may be rolled back onto the original roll. Smaller scraps can be kept in a loose pile. Try not to fold or compress the scraps, as creases in the cloth can be hard to eliminate if you use the pieces later.

Figure 9-8. *A little fiberglass hanging below the boat absorbs drips and keeps them off the floor, but this can also waste some perfectly good cloth. I trim the edge several inches below the sheer/gunwale.*

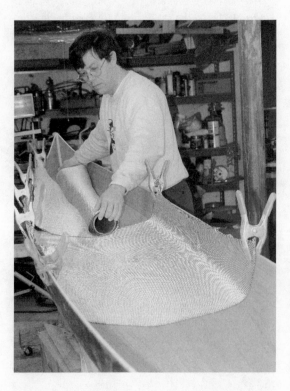

Figure 9-7. *The most efficient way to cut the cloth is to lay it across the boat, overlapping adjacent pieces by about 1 inch. This is not as desirable on the outside because the overlaps create bumps running across the boat, but on the inside it works very well with minimum waste of fabric.*

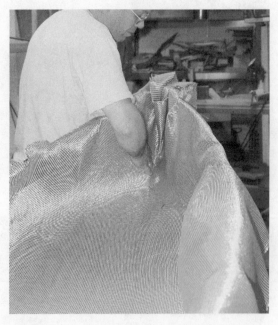

Figure 9-9. *On the inside of this canoe I did not want any seams to disrupt the pattern of the carbon-Kevlar cloth, so I draped in the cloth in one piece and carefully trimmed near the stem. I initially left a little extra fabric around the stem area, and then cut it back to fit right up next to the stem. The top edge around the gunwale gets trimmed off about 1 inch above the edge.*

137

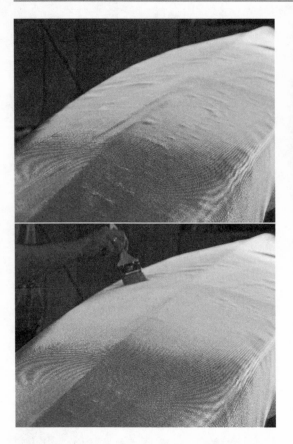

Figure 9-11. All the fabrics used for reinforcing strip-built boats are subject to some distortion from rough handling, but a visible weave like this carbon-Kevlar hybrid cloth will show the pulls most distinctly. Try to align the cloth carefully on the boat so all parts can be smoothly covered with a minimum of tugging and pushing.

Figure 9-10. After draping the glass onto the boat you will have small wrinkles and bubbles. You want to try to get the cloth as tight to the boat surface as possible before applying resin. Do not run your hand over the surface in an attempt to smooth the fabric. This will tend to cause creases and snags. Instead, use a chip brush to smooth the surface. Start in the middle and work out to the sides and ends.

Smoothing the Cloth

A smooth coat of fiberglass starts with making sure the cloth lies smoothly on the boat when it is dry. While wetting out the cloth will help it conform, if you have big wrinkles in the dry cloth, you will probably have to struggle removing those wrinkles when it is saturated with epoxy.

If you have lightly sanded your seal coat or you did not do a seal coat, the glass will usually move fairly easily. Don't use the palm of your hand to smooth out the cloth. This just presses the fabric against the surface and increases the friction. The cloth will also stick to your hand a bit. As a result you will likely just create creases in the cloth. Instead, use a brush. The same chip brush you will later use for spreading epoxy will work well when dry. Any light brush with soft bristles will work. If you have an old drafting brush, that will work great. Starting in the middle of the boat, sweep down the length, pushing excess fabric off the edge and toward the ends.

On the inside of the boat, your natural inclination will be to use your hand to push the cloth down into the low spots. *Avoid this inclination.* It will cause snags as the fabric drags against the top edges. Instead, lift the edges of the cloth up and let gravity drop the cloth down into the boat. In deep spots such as the ends of a canoe or kayak, you may need to help the cloth in with your hands, but again, lift the sides so the fabric does not drag over the edges of the boat and snag. Use a dry brush to smooth out any wrinkles, working from the middle toward the sides and ends of the boat.

Wetting Out the Cloth

Wetting out the cloth means pretty much what it sounds like. It means making the cloth wet, but in this case it means making it wet with epoxy. This is not brain surgery; it is just making fabric wet, something any baby can do from day one. However, there is a need to be a little more systematic than your average infant. We want the fiberglass (or whatever fabric we choose) to be completely saturated with epoxy, but ideally, the cloth should not contain any excess beyond the minimum required to fully saturate.

For reference, a good layup done by hand using the techniques described next will end up approximately 50% glass and 50% epoxy by weight. I don't expect you to weigh your materials, as that is not practical for most builders, but do understand from this that if you are leaving behind big areas with a lot of epoxy on them relative to the amount of fiberglass, you are using too much epoxy.

While you are wetting out the cloth you want to be doing one of three things at all times: making dry cloth wet, smoothing out the cloth, or removing excess resin. If you are fussing with your layup but not accomplishing one of these three things, you are at best wasting your time and at worst making the layup worse.

It is obvious when fiberglass cloth is saturated; what was white is now clear. When the fabric has the right amount of resin, it has a matte finish with the texture of the weave clearly evident. If the cloth is shiny, it has more resin than required. If it is a bit gray with flecks of white, the cloth is starved and needs a little more resin.

For most boats it is easiest to start wetting out the cloth in the center of the boat and move systematically out toward the ends, moving down both sides simultaneously. To limit the number of wrinkles, you want to move in a continuous front instead of working in unconnected patches. Dry patches surrounded by wet cloth tend to trap wrinkles, making it harder to get a smooth coat of glass. However, you don't need to get all the cloth thoroughly saturated in the first pass. It is often better to make a fairly quick initial pass over the whole boat, leaving the occasional partially wet-out spots, coming back later to touch up the spots you missed.

The epoxy I typically use allows me to work fairly slowly in a 65° to 70°F basement shop. A small batch can stay in the mixing pot for 10 to 15 minutes, and once it is spread in a thin layer it stays workable for up to 45 minutes. However, these times will vary with temperature. The same epoxy in 85° weather may only give you a few minutes of pot life and require quick work while spreading on the boat. The working time is also dependent on the epoxy formulation. Most epoxy manufacturers offer "fast" and "slow" mixes suitable for use in different temperatures to control how much time you have to work. Usually the jugs of epoxy will include information on pot life and working time.

Start working by mixing up small batches until you have a good feel for how quickly the epoxy starts curing. If you ever feel the cup of mixed epoxy start to heat up, throw that batch out. It will not soak into wood or fabric as it is supposed to. As you get more accustomed to the reaction rate of the epoxy you may want to mix up larger batches, but remember that the exothermic reaction of epoxy means that larger batches have a shorter pot life.

Dump and Spread

I generally try to slightly oversaturate the cloth initially, and then remove the excess resin later. With low-viscosity resins this allows air bubbles

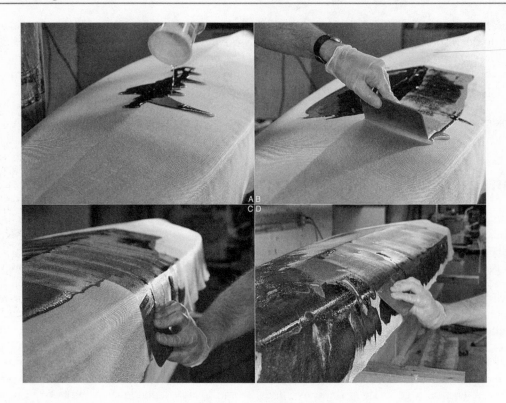

Figure 9-12. *When applying epoxy, start in the middle and move down to the sides and out toward the ends. This way you do not trap wrinkles between two wet-out regions. Dump the mix of resin near the middle (A), and then quickly spread the epoxy around with a squeegee (B). Hold the squeegee at about a 45-degree angle to move large amounts of resin over a distance. Do not use much pressure on the squeegee. Pull resin down over the side (C), decreasing the squeegee angle as you approach the edge to deposit it in place instead of dumping it on the floor. Spread the resin quickly even if it causes occasional dry spots in your first attempt. As you proceed, squeegee wet and shiny spots toward white spots (D), and dab on a little extra epoxy as needed. Don't try to pour epoxy onto sloping or vertical surfaces. When you can no longer make a pool of resin on a nearly level surface, use a brush to add resin where you need it.*

to rise to the surface where they can pop or get scraped off.

I start by mixing up a relatively small batch of epoxy resin (6 to 10 ounces), mixing it thoroughly. A deep mixing container allows you to mix easily without worrying about spilling any. This batch of resin is then dumped in a thick line about 12 inches long along the centerline of the boat near the middle of its length.

Move quickly so you don't just get a river flowing onto the floor. Use a squeegee to spread the puddle around. Pull the puddle a little bit lengthwise and then start pulling it toward the edges.

Use the edge of the squeegee to move the epoxy around. Hold it at about a 45-degree angle with the edge pressed against the cloth. Starting in a wet area, use moderate pressure,

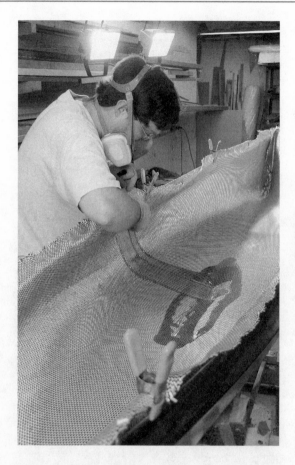

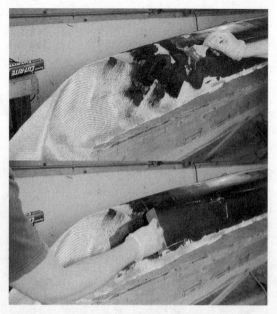

Figure 9-14. The most common mistake with fiberglass and epoxy is to add too much epoxy, resulting in a heavy boat with little added strength. This is often because novice builders keep brushing on more epoxy until the fabric is clear, and continue hunting down white spots with a fresh brush full of epoxy when there is already plenty of resin available on the boat. Instead, brush a little epoxy at one edge of a dry spot and use the squeegee to spread it across the whole area.

Figure 9-13. On the inside, start by dumping epoxy in a nice puddle in the middle of the boat, then pull resin up the sides with a squeegee.

pulling the squeegee with the edge dragging behind. This will raise a bead of epoxy under the squeegee blade. When you get to a dry spot, tip the squeegee down so the face is sliding over the cloth, unloading the epoxy into dry cloth.

As you pull resin from the more level areas in the middle toward the more vertical sides, roll your wrist to maintain the squeegee at the same angle relative to the surface. Before you slide off the side, press the squeegee flat down onto the surface of the boat to unload the blob of resin onto the boat instead of onto the floor.

Listen to the cloth as you use your squeegee. When you are successfully moving epoxy, the squeegee will not make much noise. If you start hearing a dry scratching sound, you need to add more epoxy. Don't keep working the epoxy and cloth if you see that your efforts are not making any difference. Mix more epoxy and move on.

Add the new epoxy at the wet edge of the saturated cloth, using your squeegee to pull it into the dry areas. On flat level surfaces, dumping on more resin continues to work well. On the sides where gravity will just dump a puddle on the floor, use a wet brush to dab on more resin. Do not keep brushing on more epoxy until the cloth is clear. This will apply much more resin than is required. Instead, dab on a few spots and then squeegee it around. See how far the resin goes and then dab on more as necessary. Attempting to wet out the whole boat with a wet brush is slow and will waste epoxy as it generally results in more epoxy on the boat than needed to wet out at the "ideal" 50-50 ratio of resin to cloth.

Again, try to get most of the boat wet out in one quick pass. Don't worry initially about the occasional unsaturated spot, so long as it is smooth and wrinkle-free. Come back later and dab on more epoxy as needed, squeegeeing as you go.

While doing the initial wet-out on the interior of the boat you will often get bubbles caused by bridging (see the Bridging section later in the chapter). Do not try taming every single one of these every time they pop up. Working in one place will often make a bridge pop up somewhere else. If you keep going back every time a little flaw appears, you will end up running around in circles. Instead, move deliberately down the length of the boat, dealing with egregious problems as they appear, but leaving the minor, recurring problems for the second pass. By moving quickly it will actually be easier to deal with problems because the epoxy will have less time to stiffen up and the fabric will still slide easily.

Moving Cloth

At some point in your fiberglassing career you are going to have to deal with places where the glass doesn't lay flat. This can happen for a variety of reasons, but they all really boil down to two different, but related problems: too much cloth or too little. Too much cloth is the most common, but generally the easiest to deal with. Not enough cloth in an area is less common, but can be perplexing to deal with.

With either situation, too much or too little cloth, the way to deal with it is to move cloth in or out of the problem area. By this I do not mean cut out a section or patch in a piece, although that is the last resort. Instead I am referring to sliding the fabric along the surface of the boat until you get the right amount of cloth where you need it.

Epoxy serves as a good lubricant for this process. Dry cloth can snag on small surface irregularities. Cloth that was wet out for a long time may start to get sticky. It is easier to work with fiberglass and epoxy if you work quickly and efficiently. Delaying in one place too long to resolve an issue can make it harder to deal with future issues; therefore, it is good practice to move along quickly, not spending time to get every spot perfect before moving on to the next. Work on getting the initial wet-out of the fabric done quickly and then come back to resolve minor issues later.

Fiberglass and other reinforcement fabrics move along the axes of threads in the weave. By applying pressure along the length of the threads, it is possible to move the fabric around to flatten wrinkles and fill in bubbles.

You can get the cloth to move by wiping or dabbing with a brush, scraping or wiping with a squeegee, or stroking and pushing with a gloved hand.

Wrinkles. Wrinkles occur when there is more cloth than can lie flat in one area. If the wrinkle makes a flap that folds over when you squeegee over it, there is no amount of pressing it and poking at it that will make it go away. You may be able to make it disappear temporarily by wiping over it with a squeegee, but chances are very good that it will pop right back up when you move on to another spot. Don't waste your time poking at the thing: you need to get to the root of the problem and remove the excess cloth to a place where it doesn't create a wrinkle.

To get rid of the wrinkle, you need to move the excess cloth out of the area to a place where the excess fabric can release itself. This means, off the edge of the part or into dry cloth. Wrinkles want to move in a direction perpendicular to the direction of the ridge. For example, if

You can either use your squeegee to carefully push the wrinkle along the grain of the cloth until it reaches that spot, or you can gently grab the cloth in that spot to pull the fibers and straighten out the bent fibers in the wrinkle.

Sometimes the wrinkle is a long distance from a potential escape point. A wrinkle across the back deck of a kayak behind the cockpit may be pulled out by gently tugging on the cloth back near the stern of the boat. As you pull, watch where the cloth moves, shifting from side to side until you find the strands of fiber that cross the wrinkle and gently pull it flat.

Excess fabric tends to accumulate in patches of dry cloth. For this reason try to wet out the cloth in a solid front without allowing intermittent patches of dry cloth between spots where it has been wet out.

If you have a wrinkle that does not seem to be moving well when you wipe the squeegee over it, you may be able to loosen up the cloth a bit by brushing on a little more epoxy as lubricant.

Bridging. On concave surfaces, pulling on the cloth will often lift the fibers off the surface. The result is a bridge where the fibers span the low spot creating a bubble under the cloth. In other words, the fibers are not long enough to fit down into the low spot. Feeding more cloth into the low spot eliminates bridges.

Since bridges usually appear in concave areas, you can expect to deal with them while glassing the inside of the boat. Bridges typically occur along the inside keel line, especially inside the deeply V-shaped areas at the bow and stern of some boats. They also show up on the inside along chine lines where there is a sharp corner that allows the fabric to lift up easily.

Like wrinkles, no amount of poking and prodding down the bridge will eliminate it. Painting on extra epoxy will appear to fill in the bubbles under them for a while, but usually the thick puddle of resin will eventually drain away, leaving a bubble and an excess of resin somewhere else. The solution is feeding more cloth into the bridge area.

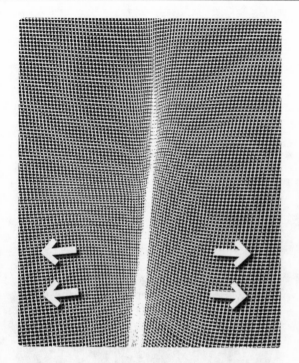

Figure 9-15. *Wrinkles occur when there is more glass on a region than there is area to contain it. They are removed by sliding the glass to a region where there is room, or off the boat. Observe the yarns of the cloth running across the wrinkle and note where they go. Look for the side of the wrinkle where the yarns run off the edge closest to the wrinkle. Use your squeegee or brush to pull the cloth away from the wrinkle toward the closest edge. You may also use your hands to pull on the cloth from the edge, pulling out the excess cloth.*

a wrinkle is vertical on the side of the boat, it needs to be pushed down the length of the boat.

Typically, wrinkles align themselves with the weave of the cloth and must be moved along the fibers. If you look carefully at the grain or fiber orientation of the cloth you can see where you need to go to eliminate the wrinkle. There are two places you can go: off the boat or into dry cloth. Follow the fibers that cross the wrinkle and determine whether the edge of the boat or dry cloth is the shortest distance.

Like wrinkles, the extra fabric must feed in along the fibers that are creating the bridge, or those that cross perpendicularly over the low spot being bridged. This usually means pushing the fabric down the side of the boat into the low spot. A somewhat dry brush dabbed down the side is often enough to slide in a little extra cloth, thus nestling the fibers back down onto the surface. Sometime it just requires a little light squeegeeing. Another great tool is attached at the end of your wrist. Use a gloved hand to stroke the surface of the cloth to slide the fibers toward the bridge.

On boats with a sharp keel line as well as chines, bridges may occur in both areas at the same time. Attempts to lower the bridging in one often raises a bridge in the other. In this case, work from the center out to the sides.

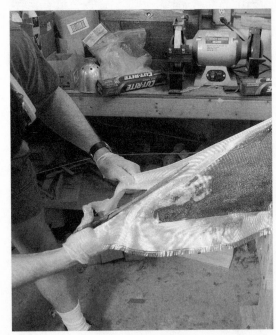

Figure 9-16. While working on the inside of the boat you will often pull the glass in a manner that raises a bubble or bridge (top) between the glass and the strips. This is especially common in a chine or keel line where there is a sharp angle. Your instinct will be to put your squeegee in the middle of the bubble and push down, or get a big blob of epoxy on your brush and try to fill it in. Don't bother. That may make the bubble disappear briefly, but it will usually reappear. Instead, you need to feed fabric into the bridge so there is enough cloth to lie flat against the wood. Use your brush to gently push fabric down the side toward the bridge (bottom). Slowly feed fabric in until the bubble disappears.

Figure 9-17. Most wrinkles need to be moved toward the ends of the boat. Depending on the shape of stem, you may need to trim the glass at the ends. While it is possible to wrap the trimmed glass around either side, I find it easier to let it come off straight and then trim it off later.

Feed cloth in toward the centerline, and then push more down the side into the chine.

Snipping. There may be times when the contours of the boat are just more than the cloth can conform to. It is amazing how complex a surface the fabric will adapt to, but as a last resort you may need to cut a gore into the cloth or cut completely across a strip of fabric. Only do this if there is no way to slide the excess cloth out of a wrinkle or there is no more fabric to feed into a bridge.

With a wrinkle, the excess fabric ends up as two ends overlapping each other. Wet these flaps out, and smooth them down. Cutting a bridge of lifted glass creates a gap that needs a patch of fabric laid over the hole. Ideally any overlap should be at least 1 inch wide.

You can use scissors to cut fiberglass cloth even when the fabric is wet, although it may end up gluing your scissors together when the epoxy cures. You can also use a sharp utility knife to slice the cloth if you can cut against a surface that is not going to show.

Missed Spots

After the first pass, getting the fabric mostly wet out, you should start back in the middle looking for dry and starved areas where the cloth is white or grayish. The most common places to miss are right along the edge where epoxy from the middle didn't quite reach all the way. Dab on a small amount of epoxy and spread it over the area with the squeegee. Avoid using an aggressive brushing motion when applying the resin. The brush will tend to move the cloth, which can cause wrinkles or raise bridges. Instead, load up your brush, swat the inside of your mixing cup a few times to shake off the excess, and then press the brush onto the surface of the fabric without dragging it over the surface. Then use the squeegee to move the epoxy around to cover the rest of the dry spot.

If the cloth is fully saturated, there should be no reason to touch it with a loaded brush.

Inspect the whole thing again to be sure everywhere is saturated, then step away from the boat.

Conforming to Shapes

Some shapes are so complicated that fiberglass cloth does not like to lie smooth. The cloth does not like to bend around sharp angles. Most cloth will not bend over a sharp 90-degree angle. And compound curves can confound most fiberglass. For the cloth to conform, the yarns must be flexible enough to bend, and they need the ability to move around relative to each other. This is where bias-cut cloth comes into use. Bias-cut cloth likes to distort.

Cut a piece of cloth with the weave running diagonally to the axis of the feature you need to cover. Because bias-cut cloth distorts easily, it must be handled gently. Carefully lay it into place, pushing it down gently, without stroking it. Use a fairly goopy brush to dab it down onto the surface. Stroking along the bias will tend to further distort the cloth, so do most of your work with dabbing motions that just push the cloth down onto the shape. Once the cloth starts to become secured in place with resin, you can start stroking the resin around with a light touch of the brush or with a squeegee.

Lightweight cloth is much better at conforming to complex shapes than thicker, heavier cloth. If you have a particularly complicated shape such as a kayak coaming, bias-cut 4-ounce cloth may be what you need. It is amazingly malleable and can conform to some complex shapes.

Scraping the Excess

At this point it is very likely the fabric is saturated with more epoxy than it really needs. It is time to scrape off the excess into a grunge cup. A grunge cup is typically a paper cup with a slit cut in the lip. A plastic cup will work, but they tend to rip as you use them. While it doesn't

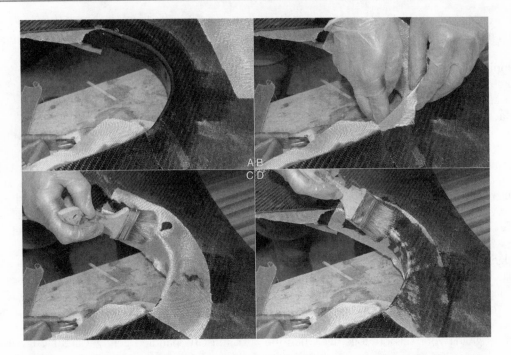

Figure 9-18. *Sharp corners may not allow a typical piece of glass to lie down smoothly. Cutting the cloth diagonally, on the bias, so the fibers run at a 45-degree angle over the corner reduces the stress on the glass, which allows the cloth to distort very easily. While this is good, the piece must be handled gently. First apply some resin to the destination area (A). Then carefully stick the cloth to that resin (B). Push the cloth down by dabbing (not stroking) with your brush (C). Keep dabbing with more resin to completely wet out the cloth (D).*

seem right that a paper cup is less likely to rip than a plastic one, that is the case. I use a pair of scissors, diagonal wire cutters, or a utility knife to cut a slit in the part of the paper cup at the seam where the paper is doubled up.

Again, starting in the middle of the boat and working toward the ends, use your squeegee to scrape the surface of the cloth to remove any resin in excess of the minimum required to wet out the fabric. Hold the squeegee at a 45-degree angle relative to the surface. Starting at the centerline, draw the squeegee toward the side of the boat. Use moderate pressure, just enough to press the cloth down onto the boat surface but not so much that you leave the fabric looking white or gray behind the squeegee. Pull all the way to the edge, rolling your wrist down over the side so the squeegee maintains a

constant angle relative to the boat surface. Right at the edge, increase the angle to 90 degrees as you lift the small worm of epoxy you have created at the squeegee blade. Slide the blade through the slot in your grunge cup to clean the worm off the squeegee. Continue doing this for the whole surface of the boat.

On the inside this process will almost assuredly raise some bridges. To minimize this, use a fairly light touch so you are not dragging against the cloth too much. You can also start at the top edge and work down toward the middle. In boats with a distinct chine that is creating a lot of bridges, work on the bottom from chine to centerline and then work from the top edge down to the chine.

Do not use the epoxy in the grunge cup for wetting out more cloth. This epoxy will be full

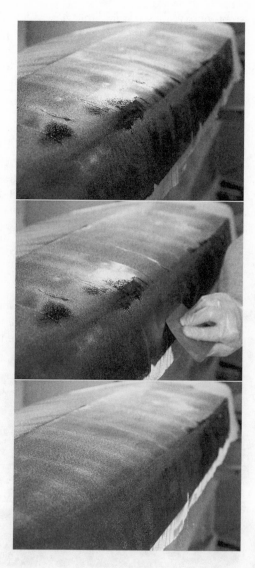

Figure 9-20. *Remove excess epoxy on your squeegee with a grunge cup. Cut a slit at the top edge of the cup. Drag the squeegee through the slot to scrape off the resin. A paper cup works better than plastic because it does not rip as easily. I cut the slit through the doubled-up area of the paper where it is a little stronger. Don't use the gunk you scrape into the cup for anything; just let it harden and discard it.*

Figure 9-19. *After wetting out the glass there are bound to be areas with excess resin as well as some with too little. Starting at the centerline, hold the squeegee at about a 45-degree angle. Pull the squeegee toward the edge, maintaining approximately the same angle as you roll down the side. Clean the epoxy off the squeegee by sliding the edge through a slot in a paper cup.*

Figure 9-21. *After squeegeeing off the excess epoxy, the surface of the fabric should not be shiny. The weave texture should be clearly visible, but the fabric should be completely translucent, without white or gray spots.*

of tiny air bubbles that will tend to stay trapped in the resin, causing a cloudy finish.

Once again, when you are finished, go back and inspect your work. Look for unsaturated cloth that is white. Look at a low angle, with your eye down near boat level to look for dull, starved or shiny, overfilled areas. If you need to dab on a little bit more epoxy, do so, but don't start fussing. If the surface looks good, with a nice even matte finish that shows the weave texture pattern and the occasional shiny spot, step away from the boat. You have probably reached the point where further fussing and fretting will only make things worse.

With exotic fabrics, it will take a little more care to be sure the fabric is fully saturated. Since you don't have the obvious feedback of turning from white to clear, you will need to do a careful inspection under good light. Look for slight changes in color and variations in gloss. Saturated cloth will usually appear somewhat darker, but in some light starved, unsaturated cloth will not reflect as much light and will appear darker.

It is worthwhile to come back in an hour and inspect the layup. The wood may soak up

some epoxy, thus starving the glass a little bit. If necessary add a little epoxy where the glass looks a little gray. You may see some starved spots at staple holes. You may be able to fill these up with a little epoxy now, although later fill coats should also do the job.

After glassing the outside you can remove the boat from the forms and start fairing the inside. Depending on my working pace, I will often apply one fill coat to the outside before starting the inside. This keeps crud from getting ground into the weave texture. The additional coat of epoxy provides some protection from workshop hazards as well.

Additional Layers

Several options are available if you want to use more than one layer of fabric. You can lay down all your layers while dry and wet them all

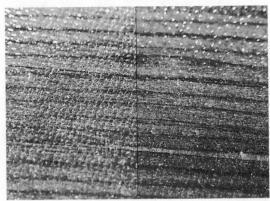

Figure 9-23. The gaps between the yarns in the fiberglass cloth may trap tiny air bubbles as you work the epoxy. You can make these bubble rise up through the cloth and pop by carefully heating the area with a hair dryer or heat gun. This works particularly well when the boat is already sealed, either with an epoxy seal coat or a prior layer of cloth. On unsealed wood it can force air out of the wood, only making your problem worse. On the left, you can see the white spots around the weave. On the right, the weave is more transparent after heating with a heat gun.

Figure 9-22. I use some V-blocks made of foam to hold the boat after I flip it over to work on the inside. You could also cover some blocks of wood with carpet scraps or make slings to support the boat.

at once; you can wet out one layer at a time, adding new layers while the prior layers are still wet; or you can lay down each layer, wet it out, and let it cure before adding the next. Each method has its own benefits and disadvantages. Obviously, laying all the layers at once is the quickest; you don't ever need to wait on the epoxy, just add enough to saturate the cloth and you are good to go. With heavy cloth it can take a lot of epoxy to soak all the way through, and getting the fabric completely wet out can take some time. With opaque cloths like Kevlar or carbon fiber that are hard to determine if they are completely saturated, this could be a real problem. It would be very easy to have it look wet out on the surface only to find that it is not bonded to the wood at all. With fiberglass you can always see when you have completely saturated the cloth, but it is likely that there will be some small, persistent bubbles that are difficult to eliminate. The texture of the cloth creates some pockets between the layers where tiny bubble get trapped. Low-viscosity resin and warm but falling temperatures can minimize the issue, but it is hard to eliminate all the bubbles.

Wetting out one layer at a time may reduce how much air is trapped between the layers, but it still allows some bubbles to remain. If you are laying up large areas, you need to be careful draping the cloth down over the existing sticky resin. The cloth can stick where you don't want it. There really isn't much benefit to sequentially wetting out large expanses of cloth unless you are using a really heavyweight cloth that is hard to wet out, but for small reinforcement patches, it is typically the most practical technique. The small bubbles left in an otherwise good layup will not have a huge structural impact. Pinhead-size points of air trapped in the weave does not mean your boat is going to fall apart the first time you hit a rock. The main impact is cosmetic. The bubbles will make the layup a little less transparent, adding a slight fog to the finish. Even this is minor, especially over light-colored wood.

The best way to assure you don't have any trapped air between layers is to do each layer individually, and let it cure before applying the next layer. However, doing this is no guarantee of a perfect layup. It is still possible to have deep pits in the wet-out fabric that will be reluctant to fill up with resin. The best solution is to apply a light fill coat, enough to fill up the pits, and let it cure before adding the next layer.

If you let the initial layers cure long enough, you have the opportunity to use masking tape and a utility knife to get a clean, smooth edge on a subsequent, smaller layer of cloth.

If you are working quickly you should not need to do anything to prep the initial layers of cloth prior to adding an additional layer. As long as the epoxy is still "green" before adding a new layer, the layers should bond well. Try pressing your thumb into the epoxy. If you can make a noticeable dent, the epoxy is green and not fully cured and the next layer will chemically bond to it. You usually have a window of 24 to 72 hours depending on the formulation of epoxy and the temperature. If the epoxy is fully cured you should sand the surface to get a mechanical bond. A mechanical bond is not as strong as a chemical bond, but it is still very strong.

A light sanding with 80-grit sandpaper and then a good scrub with a green abrasive kitchen pad such as Scotch-Brite to remove any remaining glossy areas should be enough. If you have a greasy/waxy film of amine blush, use the abrasive pad with water to remove the blush and dull the surface at the same time. Wipe the wet surface dry with a clean rag.

Trimming Edges

Any extra cloth that extends beyond the edge of the boat can usually be trimmed off with a utility knife. The longer you wait after the epoxy has cured, the harder it will be to cut, but even quite hard resin may still allow you to cut the cloth. Hold the cutting edge of the blade right up against the edge of the boat so the cloth does not bend away from the blade. Use a smooth continuous motion to slice off the cloth. Avoid sawing at the cloth with your knife. If you feel

Figure 9-24. Run the edge of a utility knife right up against the edge of the wood to get a very close trim. Cutting off a small amount of wood only means you are getting a smooth, flush trim.

Figure 9-25. You may get a bubble in the glass. This will most likely be along the gunwale/sheer. Usually you can just shave off the lifted glass by holding a knife tight against the surface. Try to get it as flush as possible, then sand the edge so it doesn't jut up. If the gap is under a gunwale or will get another layer of glass later on, wait until then and just cover it with the gunwale or lay the new layer of glass directly over the area. If this is not an option you may patch over it with an oversized scrap.

you have to do this to make the cut, your blade is probably dull or you are not cutting close enough to the edge of the boat.

If you end up with air bubbles along the edge (which is often due to the weight of the excess glass sticking up beyond the edge) you can trim them off with a knife. Try to trim as flush to the surface as you can get. The area will often be covered with a gunwale on open boats or some seam tape on decked boats, so small gaps in the glass should not matter. Large gaps might require a patch of additional fiberglass.

These bubbles near the gunwale on the inside can happen because the weight of the excess cloth extending above the gunwales sags the cloth down a bit, lifting some of the cloth off the boat. You can reduce the chance of this happening by trimming the cloth off close (1 inch) to the gunwale after it has been fully wet out, then going back and inspecting to be sure everything is smoothed down.

Whenever you have a piece of cloth that ends somewhere on the boat surface, you are going to have to deal with the inevitably ragged, unraveled edge that results from working the cloth. Some cloth will have a selvaged edge, which allows for a fairly clean border, but even this will create a large bump. To avoid this issue, you can take advantage of the fact that epoxy takes a while to set up to full hardness. You can cut into the soft epoxy and glass without damaging the harder epoxy and glass below.

Start by outlining the area you want to glass with masking tape, placing the tape just outside the area of concern. Press the tape down securely along the inside edge so epoxy does not wick under. Wet out your glass normally, overlapping the tape slightly. Allow the epoxy to start setting up, then use a utility knife with a brand-new sharp blade. Lightly cut through the epoxy and glass, pressing lightly against the surface below. Cut just inside of the tape. As you cut, peel up the tape, removing the excess fabric. You will be left with a smooth, clean edge with no loose strands of glass hanging out.

Figure 9-26. After the main body of the deck or hull has been covered with glass, you can come back and cover bits that were hard to deal with on the first go-round, such as transoms and stems. With this transom, I first applied a fill coat to the body of the hull, let that cure, then masked off the stern area before applying a layer of fiberglass to the transom.

The longer you wait, the more pressure you will need to apply to the knife. If you allow the epoxy to set up fully, you may need to press quite hard, creating the potential that you scratch the surface below, leaving a permanent light line. If you start cutting too early, you will just distort the glass without cutting efficiently. Wait a while longer and try again. You may occasionally miss a fiber, which will pull at the glass a bit as you remove the excess. Just go back and cut the fiber with your knife. The pulled glass will usually heal itself, but you may need to press it down a bit with a gloved finger.

This technique is hard to do if the underlying fabric retains its full texture after squeegeeing off excess resin. You will generally want to apply at least one light fill coat so that there are no deep pits where fibers of the fabric can sink, making them hard to cut.

Fill Coats

You went through some effort to minimize how much epoxy you applied to the cloth, thus leaving the surface with the rough texture of the cloth. Since you don't want the finished boat to have this finish, you will want to fill the weave with more epoxy.

This can be done at various times after fiberglassing the boat. I like to start the process fairly soon after applying glass. The texture of the fabric can pick up dirt that is very hard to clean out, so generally I will apply one fill coat as soon as I can after glassing. You want the glassing coat of epoxy to at least be very sticky so the new coat does not reverse all the hard work you put in getting it firmly attached to the wood.

Figure 9-27. The fill coat fills up the fabric texture (right) to create a smooth finish (left). There are several methods for doing this: some are quicker but open you up to making a mess; others are more controlled but time consuming. I brush on the epoxy using the same crisscross technique I use to apply varnish.

As long as the epoxy is still green you should be able to apply the fill coat without sanding. The epoxy is green if you can make a mark in it with your thumbnail. Your time frame here is starting several hours after glassing to 72 hours. These times will depend on the epoxy you use and the temperature in your shop. If you end up going longer, you should scrub the surface with a kitchen pad to provide some mechanical bonding surface for the new coat of epoxy. This is only marginally effective given the texture of the fabric, so try to get the first fill coat on quickly. I will often apply a fill coat the next morning after glassing to be sure the epoxy is still green.

There are a variety of methods for applying a fill coat. Some are fast, but could be messy; some are neat but may take quite a bit of time. Which you use depends on your building style and

temperament. You may also find that a system that works well for a slow-curing, low-viscosity resin is not as good for higher-viscosity, fast-curing epoxy.

I typically paint on a somewhat heavy coat of epoxy with a chip brush, using a crisscross brushing pattern. Working on about a 1-foot-wide area at a time, spread out a heavy brush load of epoxy on the surface using horizontal strokes (i.e., lengthwise on the boat). Next, even this out with vertical (athwartship) strokes, using moderate brush pressure. Finally, tip off the area with light horizontal strokes again, moving from dry toward the wet area. If you are careful to apply an even coat of uniform thickness you will not have drips or sags. Sags occur when there is an area of heavier liquid that attempts to level out. If the thickness is consistent it will tend to flow evenly, draining off the edge of the boat.

Figure 9-28. Chip brushes are good because they are cheap; that, of course, means they tend to shed bristles. This is usually not a big deal when wetting out the fiberglass because you remove any shed bristles when you squeegee excess resin off the glass, and the bristles become nearly invisible in the epoxy, so any remaining are not offensive. But when you do the fill coats the shed bristles cause drips, sags, and other surface irregularities that are better to avoid. A little CA glue along the top of the ferrule will glue in most of the loose bristles.

Figure 9-29. Most of the bristles that are still loose after gluing can be removed by vigorously wiping the brush against tape wrapped around your hand with the sticky side out. You may find an occasional stray hair as you paint epoxy on the boat that you can lift off with the tip of your brush.

For decked boats you will want to address the top and bottom of the boat in separate operations, masking between the deck and the hull as you do each. A line of masking tape just below the sheerline with the bottom edge folded up to shed drips will keep the other half smooth and clean until the epoxy sets up enough not to drool. Peel away the tape while the epoxy is still soft.

A more rushed method that could potentially turn into a real mess, but which works well for small boats, is the hot-coat method used by surfboard makers. This method involves dumping the epoxy in a big puddle on the bottom of the boat and then quickly spreading it around with a brush. As long as you spread it out evenly and don't mind some large drips on the floor, this technique can be a quick way to apply a fill coat.

This brush method takes some practice. Using a roller is more controlled. Roll on a thin, even coat, let it start to set up, and roll on a couple more coats. A short-nap roller will help push resin down into any pits or pinholes. Some people have good success squeegeeing on a thin coat—just enough to fill the low spots of the weave texture—then coming back and applying more using the brush or roller method.

The eventual goal with exterior fill coats is to be able to completely sand the boat without sanding into the fiberglass so the boat is very smooth. This usually does not happen with just one fill coat, but adding more epoxy directly over the first coat is usually not the most effective approach. Instead, start sanding the first coat a little until you start seeing signs of hitting the fiberglass. This usually looks like a slightly lighter weave pattern. When you see this weave pattern, stop sanding that area and move on. If you can sand to the point where there are no shiny, unsanded spots in the area without getting down to the weave, stop before you do hit the glass. Because epoxy takes a while to set up

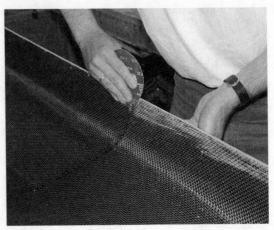

Figure 9-30. Mixing graphite powder into epoxy, creating a black paint, makes a low-friction surface that protects against scratches. Add about 10% to 15% powder by volume to the epoxy. Here I am applying it with a brush, but a roller also works well. The masking tape keeps the black stuff where I want it. Note that the finish will tend to make your clothes black if you rub against it.

Figure 9-31. Before joining the deck and hull, rough up the epoxy and fabric along the edge to assure a strong bond.

hard, you will need to wait a little while before it is ready to be sanded. How long depends on the shop temperature and epoxy formulation, but 48 to 72 hours is usually the minimum.

Because the weave texture can telegraph through several coats of resin, I will often start sanding after the first coat, just to knock off the high spots. Use coarse (60- to 80-grit) sandpaper initially, being careful not to sand into the glass. You will find more information about this process in Chapter 10.

Some people like to add a coat of graphite enhanced epoxy as a low friction, protective finish. While this finish does not provide perfect protection against scratches, it does make it a little easier for the boat to drag across rough surfaces. It is not going to make a boat any faster going through the water, but it may help to make it faster dragging the boat down a beach. The material is added just like another fill coat. Add the graphite powder to premixed epoxy (about 1 or 2 parts of powder

to 10 parts of epoxy) and mix it thoroughly. Apply the mix with a roller or brush as you would a fill coat.

Interior Fill Coat

With most boats, having a little bit of texture on the inside is not a bad thing; it will give your bottom or feet some traction so they don't slide around too much. You could go through all the effort of filling in the weave and then add some kind of nonskid surface to it, or you can take advantage of the fabric weave texture that is already there. You do want to add a little epoxy to the weave after the wet-out coat just to be sure that any remaining pinholes are filled. I will usually brush on small amounts of resin and then use a short-nap paint roller to spread it around in a thin, even coat. The nap of the roller should help get resin down into the texture.

You may decide you prefer a glassy smooth inner surface, in which case you can follow the directions for finishing the outside of the boat. If you are making a closed boat, you will need to sand the sheerline where the deck and hull will meet so there is a good surface for bonding.

Figure 9-32. Hold the deck to the hull with strips of strapping tape. The strip on the right has a wrinkle. This wrinkle will trap epoxy, creating a ripple that will require sanding. Try to avoid wrinkles.

Figure 9-33. Apply tape across the seam every 4 to 6 inches to be sure the seam does not pop while you are working on it. When the seam is aligned and secure, apply a strip of masking tape along the seam to keep the epoxy in. Burnish down the tape so there is no room for epoxy to collect.

Seam Tape

Closed boats will need the deck attached to the hull. This is done on the inside of the seam with prewoven tape and on the outside of the seam with the same fiberglass as used everywhere else on the outside. After the edges of the deck and hull have been cleaned up, finish up the bevel to provide a tight joint. Secure the deck onto the hull with packing tape, being careful to get a tight, smooth seam. Avoid wrinkles in the tape as they will create rough spots in the epoxy used to glue the seam.

Unless you know some extraordinary small people, you will need a special tool to apply tape down the inside seam. A "brush-on-a-stick" is a unique combination of a brush and a stick. The stick should be about half the length of the boat. Cut the end of the stick at a 45-degree angle, and screw a chip brush onto the end. Cut off the brush handle. At the other end, stick a finish nail through the stick so the point sticks out the other side about 1 inch. Bend the point over so it lies flat against the stick.

Tip the boat on its side and secure it in place. Try to get the seam on the bottom so gravity will be working in your favor. Measure 1- to 2-inch

Figure 9-34 Unless you have really long arms, you will need a special tools to access the far reaches of the deck/hull seam—enter "brush-on-a-stick." Screw a chip brush to the end of a 1-inch by 1-inch by about 8-foot stick, and then saw off the brush handle.

wide tape out along the outside of the boat. I usually do each seam in two halves from about 12 inches back from the bow to the middle and from the middle back to about 12 inches from the stern, with 6 inches overlap in the middle.

Lay the tape out flat on a worktable and presaturate it. Use your brush-on-a-stick to precoat the seam with epoxy.

Roll the tape up into a loose roll so you can pick it up easily, inspecting the roll to ensure it is fully saturated as you go. Starting at the middle of the boat, unroll the tape onto the seam. Keep the tape centered along the seam line. It will help to have a powerful flashlight to illuminate the interior. Some people use hiking headlamps. I use the rechargeable light that came with my cordless drill. Unroll the tape as far as you can reach with your hands, and then unroll back toward the middle for a foot or two. Then keep unrolling but going forward again. Keep unrolling back and forth until you get all the tape laid out in a neat Z-fold. You don't want any twists in the tape, just a smooth folded pile. The top layer should finish up with the loose end pointing toward the end of the boat.

Now using the nail end of the brush-on-a-stick, hold the stick with the folded end of the nail toward the deck. Spin the nail so it points up. Rotate the stick toward the deck until the nail points down. Lift the end of the tape so the nail pierces down through it about 1 inch back from the end, and then rotate the stick back up again. The tape should now be hooked on the nail on top of the stick and twisting down over the deck side of the stick.

Your goal when you extend the stick into the end of the boat is to rotate the stick toward the deck again such that the tape slips off the stick and drops on the seam. Sound tricky? Well, it really isn't that much fun, but if you mess up, just pull the tape back and try again.

Start by pushing the stick down toward the end. Keep the nail pointed up. Get some tension in the tape. If the tape starts to slide along the seam at the middle of the boat, hold onto it so you don't get too much length into the ends, making it impossible to release the tape. Get enough tension on the tape that it is lifted off the seam. Slowly lower the stick so the tape drapes gradually down the length of the seam. When the tape is aligned on the seam, rotate the stick toward the deck again so the nail points down. Look to see that the tape is not tangled on the end, and if it doesn't fall off give the stick a quick sharp push forward to release it from the nail.

Inspect your work. Check to be sure the tape is close to centered on the seam. If it favors one side or the other it is probably OK, and you may be able to tweak it a little as you brush it down later. If it is completely off to one side somewhere, you should probably pull the whole tape back and give it another go.

If it all looks good, flip your stick around and apply more resin with the brush end of the stick. By twisting the stick you can brush the tape a small distance to one side or another. Let the epoxy cure, flip the boat over, and do the other side.

After both sides are done, you can strip off the packing tape and clean up the outer seam. You can either run glass over the whole deck or hull across the seam and trim it off on the other side of the seam or mask off an inch on either side of the seam and apply bias-cut cloth across the seam.

If you are doing an open boat, be happy you don't have to do any of this, although some of these techniques may apply for installing small decks or breast hooks. When the glassing is done, you can proceed to finishing.

Chapter 10

Finishing

The finish of the boat is some form of ultraviolet protection. Epoxy is good stuff, but it does not hold up well to exposure to the sun. For most boats the finish will be some form of clear coat such as varnish with UV protective additives, but there is no reason why it couldn't be paint. This UV protection does not need to take the form of a mirror-smooth gleaming finish. You could really apply varnish at just about any time after finishing the epoxy and end up with a good protective coating that makes the boat look pretty good. How obsessive you want to get in creating a fine finish is really up to you.

The secret to a fine finish is in the preparation of the surface before applying any varnish. The more level and smooth you can make the surface, the better your finish will look. The technique to get a level surface is to sand the surface to knock down high spots and apply fill coats to raise up low spots. Once the surface is level, it is sanded with finer grits until the sanding scratches are fine enough that the varnish will fill them in.

The level to which you finish the boat may be different on the inside than the outside. A somewhat rough surface on the inside is nice for a small boat as it is less slippery. The outside is where most people will want to spend most of their effort.

Final Fill Coats

If you have not applied fill coats to start filling in the weave and it has been a while since you applied the fiberglass, you will want to clean the surface before doing so. This may be as simple as scrubbing the boat with a wet abrasive kitchen scrubby, but if it somehow got really dirty you might want to clean the surface with lacquer thinner before scrubbing with clean water.

There are lots of things that can cause issues with applying a coat of epoxy. If in doubt, the best thing to do is finish any cleaning with lots of plain water and a scrubbing pad. This is the least likely to cause problems. Sanding itself will not necessarily clean up contaminants, but instead may just spread them around more. If you somehow get oil or other gunk on the boat, you may want to use paint thinner or an appropriate solvent to clean it off, but then use some water with detergent, followed by clean water. Wipe everything off with clean rags so you aren't leaving dissolved contaminants to dry on the boat. Let the boat dry thoroughly before applying a fill coat or beginning sanding.

Sanding

The goal of sanding is to make the surface level and smooth. Supposedly when you did the previous fairing sanding, you created a smooth, even surface upon which you laid the glass. The sanding now is to reduce or eliminate any uneven spots caused by the fabric texture, edges of a glass layer, drips in the epoxy, or stray strands of fiberglass. You want to accomplish this without sanding into the fiberglass, because it is the fiberglass that provides the strength. Sanding into the fiberglass will cut the fibers, and these short fibers will not provide as much strength as long fibers. When you start cutting fibers it is time to add more epoxy.

Figure 10-1. *Epoxy takes a long time to fully cure even after it is hard to the touch. It continues to get harder as days and weeks proceed. This continued curing could cause the fabric texture to print through. To help reduce this effect and to harden the epoxy prior to sanding, I will often "cook" the boat out in the sun on a warm day. Even on a cool day, wrapping the boat in black plastic can make the boat quite warm. This accelerates the final cure.*

Figure 10-2. *A cabinet scraper does a good job of leveling small irregularities. It can be used with a lot of precision to knock down a small drip. Larger drips can be attacked with a rasp or paint scraper.*

While sanding will do most of the work of leveling the surface, big drips, nasty tangles of glass fibers, and other localized high spots are best addressed with a more aggressive tool. Rasps and scrapers make quick work of removing small high spots. Use a scraper for long ridges caused by runs and stray fibers, and a rasp for roundish hills or mountains caused by drips or tangles of fiberglass.

Run the scraper down the length of the ridge with the blade only on the ridge itself. Scrape down with several passes until the ridge is nearly level with the surrounding surface.

Be careful with the rasp, because while you are concentrating on one spot, another part of the tool may be cutting into a part of the boat you don't intend. I often wrap the end of my rasp with masking tape so it doesn't do its own thing while I'm looking elsewhere.

After you have removed the major high spots, go over the whole boat with the long-board fairing sander. I typically use quite coarse

Figure 10-3. The fairing sander is an effective tool for leveling out any irregularities introduced in the fiberglassing and fill-coat stages of building.

Figure 10-4. Systematically sand the whole surface with 60-grit sandpaper. If you start sanding into the fiberglass, stop and move on. If you are unable to eliminate all the shiny spots before sanding into the glass, apply another fill coat. When you can achieve a smooth and even surface with 60-grit sandpaper, step up to finer grades of sandpaper through 220-grit.

paper at this stage (40-grit) so the tool is very aggressive. If you are less confident, use a little bit finer grit (60 to 80), but not so fine that you get bored before you are done. Use long strokes along the length of the boat. At this point you are still just trying to knock down high spots that you didn't take care of with the rasp or scraper. You will start to notice some places where the long-board makes a lot of scratches and other places where it hardly does anything. Watch the scratched places for signs of hitting the fiberglass. You will notice lighter spots in the epoxy with a weave pattern. When you hit these spots, stop sanding that area.

If you can get fairly even scratches over the whole boat without hitting the fiberglass, you can move on to using the random orbit sander. If you are hitting glass surrounded by shiny areas, you will need to apply another fill coat. Get the surface pretty even before apply-

ing more epoxy. High spots will only cause new drips and sags. Clean off all the sanding dust, dull any remaining shiny spots with an abrasive kitchen scrubber, and clean the surface with clean water and wipe it dry.

Apply a fill coat as before, judging the thickness of the coat based on how smooth the surface is. If it is pretty smooth you won't need much thickness. After the fill coat has cured, start sanding with the long-board again as necessary.

Use the random orbit sander to create a smooth surface free of any fabric texture. Again, start with a coarse (60 to 80) sanding grit and a relatively stiff sanding pad. Hold the face of the sander flat against the surface and keep it mov-

Figure 10-5. It is extremely easy to sand through sharp edges and feature lines. Avoid touching these corners with a power sander. You would likely go through the material before you can blink. Instead, keep the pad of the sander flat on the large surfaces, leaving the corners shiny until you are done with all the power sanding, then hand sand with fine sandpaper to lightly remove the gloss.

Figure 10-6. Where you have extra layers of glass, such as around the stem, you will need to feather in the edge of the glass. This will require sanding into the glass of the thicker layer and blending it down to the surface of the surrounding glass.

ing. Be very careful around tight radius edges and feature lines. It is very easy to sand through the fiberglass on sharp corners. It is best to hand sand these areas. Work systematically down the length of the boat, working from centerline to sheerline, overlapping slightly onto previously sanded areas while moving onto new areas. Replace the sanding disks frequently. Sharp sandpaper does not require as much pressure, so it will more readily cut the tops off high spots without lowering already low spots.

The goal with the random orbit sander is to get an evenly sanded surface with no remaining shiny spots (again without sanding into the glass). The hardest shiny spots will be pits or divots down into the weave of the fiberglass. Sanding alone may not eliminate these pockmarks. When there are just a few remaining, a drop of epoxy or CA glue in the low spot will fill the hole. If there are extensive areas with little shiny spots and you can't sand anymore without removing glass, you will need to apply another fill coat.

Once you achieve a smooth surface, evenly sanded, without any shiny spots, you can start stepping up through finer sandpaper grits. Sand the surface until the scratches from the previous grit have been eliminated. If you end up sanding down to the fiberglass, roll on another light coat of epoxy. When you have reached about 180-grit sandpaper you are ready to proceed to varnishing. Finer sandpaper will make your first coat of varnish look better, but since you will be applying several coats and sanding between them, the appearance of the first coat is not that critical.

Varnishing and Painting

The traditional finish for boats is spar varnish. This was developed for boat spars that will be out in the weather as a coating to protect the wood from the weather. Typically, spar varnishes are a concoction of alkyd-modified tung oil and phenolic resins and solvents. When exposed to the air the solvents evaporate and the resins react with the oxygen in the air to form a hard protective surface.

As I mentioned earlier, the finish is used to provide UV protection. While it does make the boat look nice, that is not really the reason for taking the time and effort to do it. You can make the bare epoxy look just like a quality coat of varnish, but after a year in the sun it would start to deteriorate, and after a few years the epoxy and fiberglass would start falling off. You can use the boat for a while before varnishing if you are really eager to try it out, but you will want to get some sort of UV protection on it eventually.

The UV protection need not be varnish; paint actually provides more protection than varnish, and if you paint the boat you can be a lot less careful on the woodwork, but it does require a smoother surface to appear blemish free. Paint can be applied in much the same way as varnish. Much of the UV protection of varnish is provided by the glossy surface simply reflecting the UV rays. While a matte or satin finish looks good and does provide some UV protection, it is not quite as effective. The downside of very high gloss is that it tends to highlight flaws in the surface. For surfaces where you don't want to put as much effort into getting a flawless finish, matte and satin finishes help camouflage minor drips and other textures.

In preparation for applying a finish you will need to get the surface clean. Vacuum off the sanding dust, then rinse it off with clean water, wiping off the excess water. I will often further clean the surface by wiping it down with paint thinner or mineral spirits, again wiping it dry afterward with a clean rag.

Most boats will require you to apply the varnish or paint in stages. There will always be some places where you can't reach. With a kayak or closed boat you will probably need to work on the deck and hull in separate operations; likewise, with a canoe or open boat, the inside and outside will need to be finished at different times. Because varnish and paint like to drip, it is worthwhile masking off the edge between the deck and hull or the gunwales.

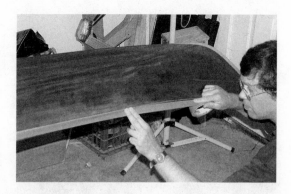

Figure 10-7. Mask off the lower edge of any area to be varnished to control any drips that may accumulate. Fold up the bottom edge of the tape to create a drip edge. Varnish the hull about 1 foot at a time, switching sides every 2 feet so you maintain a wet edge along the centerline. Remove the tape a minute or so after you have finished varnishing. Let the varnish dry, and then flip the boat over and repeat for the deck.

Apply masking tape along a strip seam or along a gunwale where the slight ripple of the edge will be hard to see.

Dust will get in the finish. Learn to accept this. Unless you can afford a space dedicated to finishing that you can keep dust free, you will end up with some dust in the finish. People have been known to strip naked so as to avoid tracking contaminants into their varnishing space. I find this a little obsessive. If you are going to use the boat, it is going to get scratched; a few specks of dust should not be a worry. Remember that the varnish or paint is for UV protection and it will still do just fine at that with a little dust in the finish.

But since we are entitled our obsessions, we might as well try to minimize how much dust is in the finish. If you have the space, do your finish work somewhere other than where you do all your sanding. If you don't have this option, clean up as much of the dust in your workspace as you can and then let the air settle for a day or two. Some people wet the floor to keep the dust down.

Before starting to apply your finish, wipe the surface down with a tack rag. This is a piece of lint-free cloth impregnated with some sticky stuff that picks up those little bits of whatever

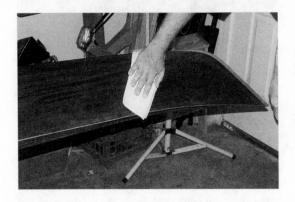

Figure 10-8. Remove dust from the surface of the boat before varnishing by vacuuming, rinsing it with water, and then wiping with a tack cloth.

it is that settles on your boat. A well-washed T-shirt wetted with mineral spirits does a pretty good job as well.

Good light is the key to being sure you don't miss a spot. Bright lights should be set down low at each end of the boat so that when you put your eyes down near the surface and look toward the light you can easily see missed spots and the ripples of a sag or drip.

You want to pour your varnish into a separate container from the can it came in. Quart-size plastic food containers such as yogurt containers work well; just make sure they are clean. These containers let you pour a bit in the bottom of the container and have enough depth that you won't spill the varnish easily. You can also get excess finish off the brush by whapping it against the inside.

A smooth coat of finish is a function of getting the liquid onto the boat in an even layer. This means it needs to be laid down evenly but

1. **Apply:**
Horizontal Strokes,
Onto the Wet,
Good Pressure

2. **Spread:**
Stroke Vertically,
Center to Sheer,
Moderate Pressure

3. **Level:**
Horizontally,
Almost No Pressure

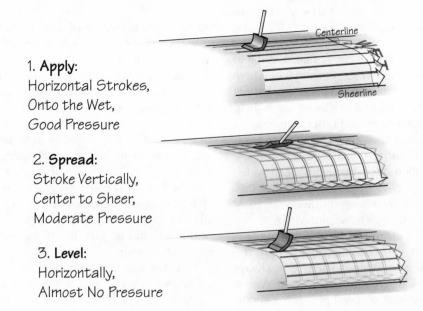

Figure 10-9. A smooth finish starts with an even coat of varnish or epoxy. Work in small sections. Fill the brush with a somewhat heavy load of finish and apply it to the boat with heavy, horizontal strokes working from the centerline down to the gunwale or sheerline. Without getting more finish, spread out that layer evenly with moderate pressure and vertical strokes. Finally, level off the finish with very light, horizontal strokes. Inspect your work before moving to the next section.

also quickly enough so that it has time to level out. If you move too slowly, the finish will be drying as you go, and any effort to apply more finish to an area that has had even 45 seconds to dry will result in a visible ripple. Experienced painters talk about a *wet edge*, which refers to the transition areas between where you have applied varnish and where you have not. At this transition, you want the finish to stay wet so that as you apply more finish it can blend in with the already coated area. Keeping this transition wet is called maintaining a wet edge.

The trick is to work fast enough that you maintain the wet edge, yet carefully enough that you apply a uniformly thick film of finish over the whole surface. Any spots with added thickness will tend to drip, run, or sag. It is possible to apply a relatively thick coat without any kind of drooling if you can maintain a consistent thickness—at the same time that you keep that wet edge. If that doesn't sound tricky enough, you also need to do it on both sides of the boat simultaneously to avoid a rough transition down the centerline. This requires that you be systematic. Don't just randomly slap the finish on everywhere until the boat is covered. You need to divide the boat up into manageable chunks, deal with those sections in a regimented manner, and then move on, confident that your system is working.

Applying the finish can be broken down into three steps: applying, spreading, and leveling. You apply the finish over the surface, spread it out evenly, and then tip it off to get it level. Break your boat down into imaginary sections running from centerline to sheerline. These sections should be small enough to cover with one brush full of paint or varnish. This will often be an area about 12 inches wide. If you used staples to hold the strips, they make a good guide to keep you organized as you work. (You knew there was a good reason for all those staples, didn't you?)

Apply the finish systematically. Work on one section at a time. Spread finish on the section with heavy horizontal strokes, applying sufficient finish to thoroughly soak the surface.

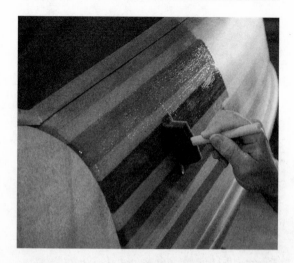

Figure 10-10. *Varnish provides UV protection for the epoxy. You want at least three coats to be sure there is enough coverage. Mask off areas where you do not want varnish. In this case I did not want to varnish over the graphite powder–epoxy bottom. The varnish will flow slightly down the side. A line of tape on the gunwale keeps this flow from creating drips along the edge. Get the upper side when you turn the boat over to varnish the inside.*

A few drips as you get the finish on the surface are OK.

Start by dipping the brush about 1 inch into your paint or varnish. Apply this in aggressive strokes moving horizontally, or back and forth along the length of the boat. Hold the brush at a 45- to 60-degree angle relative to the surface. Use enough pressure to squeeze finish out of the brush as you work over the area. If you don't quite get finish over the whole area with one brush full, dip it again, but only enough to cover the remaining area of your current section. You want the brush somewhat dry for the following steps.

After getting the material initially spread out, you want to even it out a bit. Use vertical strokes running up and down from sheer to centerline. Hold the brush at a 30- to 45-degree angle. This time use a little less pressure so you pick up excess finish where there is too much

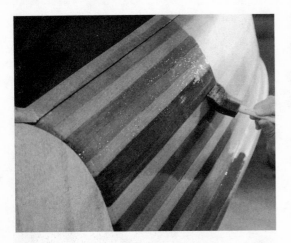

Figure 10-11. After the varnish is on the section, even out the coat with vertical strokes. Use moderate pressure to pick up varnish from thick areas and move it to sparse areas. Do not redip the brush. Look for holidays where there is no varnish by putting your eye close to the surface and looking toward the light.

Figure 10-12. Finally, lightly tip off bubbles with quick, even strokes. Brush in one direction, from the drier side to the wetter. Lift up the brush while you are moving. Double-check for holidays as you work. As soon as you finish one section, move on to the next section. This is not a time to answer the phone or go eat cookies. Do the whole boat without stopping. When you are done, peel off the tape and leave the area so you don't stir up dust.

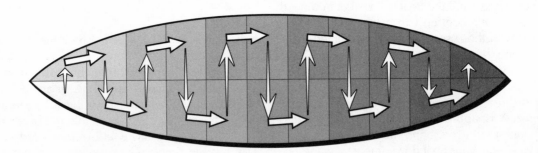

Figure 10-13. Quick-drying varnish requires a wet edge to avoid lines between varnished sections. You must move fast and not get too far ahead of the drying varnish. Work in small (1-foot-long) sections and switch sides after every second section so you are never more than one section ahead of the other side.

and lay it back down where you have missed spots. Get your eyes down near the boat so you can see the change in gloss. Look for dull spots and ripples, and brush them out as necessary.

All that working of the finish may have created some bubbles. Finally, tip off the surface with a light stroke. Hold the brush at a low angle and lightly drag it across the surface with horizontal strokes moving from the dry edge toward the wet. This will break any surface bubbles and lift up excess finish that could later drool down the side.

After another check to see that you didn't miss any spots, move to the other side of the boat and apply the finish to same band on that side. When you've finished that one section, move forward one section and repeat. Switch sides every two sections. The reason for all this running back and forth is to maintain that wet edge along the centerline. Varnish and paint start to dry the moment you brush it on the boat. When it dries enough, new coats spread on to it will not blend in well, but instead will leave brush marks on the surface. By constantly switching sides and working on relatively small areas you should be able apply a smooth coat with a minimum of visible brushstrokes.

As you move down from one 1-foot section to the next, look back to see if you have missed any spots in the previous section. Obviously, mistakes in paint will show more easily, but you need to look closely with clear varnish. You can carefully touch up this section because it should still be wet enough to blend in any new strokes, but if you go back farther to earlier mistakes, the new brushstrokes will probably fail to blend in. At this point you need to decide which is worse: a holiday without finish on it, or the ripple of a brushstroke. Honestly, I prefer a little bit uneven, but shiny surface over a dull one, so I'll touch up older holidays if I see them, but the best results will come from systematically applying a good coat on each section the first time.

When you have reached the far end of the boat, wait a minute or two and then peel off the masking tape at the bottom edge. If you peel too soon, the freshest finish may run beyond where you had the tape, making a drip. If you wait too long the finish will dry, leaving a sharp transition. Waiting a little bit can let the edge fade slightly as the finish continues to dry. Turn off the lights so you don't attract flies into the space, and leave the room until the finish is dry so you don't stir up any more dust.

In moderately warm weather most standard varnish and paints will dry in about half a day to the point where you can flip the boat over and do the other side. There are now varnishes available that allow you to apply multiple coats

Figure 10-14. Between coats of varnish you can either wet sand by hand or use fine sandpaper in a power sander. This levels the surface and helps you see your new coat of varnish by dulling the surface.

in one day without sanding between coats. With these you may apply several coats to the bottom one day, then flip the boat over and apply several on the other side.

Even with regular paint or varnish you may reapply another coat within about 72 hours without sanding. This is good if you want to build up some finish thickness but aren't too worried about a flawless finish. After this dries you can always sand it smooth before applying a final pretty coat. Painting is complete when the finish is opaque; this may be after one or two coats.

There are several reasons to sand between coats. If the finish has dried for several days it will need to be scratched up for a new coat to stick. Sanding will also remove flaws so they don't get worse with the next coat. It is a lot easier to see where you have and have not applied finish if the surface has been sanded. With it still shiny, new wet paint or varnish will look a lot like the previous dry surface.

Sanding with wet-or-dry 220-grit paper will create a smooth enough surface that the scratches generally will not show through the next coat of finish. Finer sandpaper such as 320- or 400-grit will not sand through thin coats as quickly but do not provide as much "tooth" for the next coat. If you are sanding a fairly recent coat of finish that has not reached full hardness, sanding with wet-or-dry sandpaper or fine abrasive sponges and water will help keep the abrasive from gumming up. Keep a bucket of warm water nearby and keep dipping the abrasive. You can also keep a hose or wet sponge handy to keep the surface wet. With all the water around, this is not the place to use electric power tools. Instead of your random orbit, you will want to sand by hand. Hand sanding is always a good idea around difficult contours and feature lines.

After about a week, most finishes can be sanded with dry paper, and if you have large areas to cover, a random orbit sander is a good choice. Because it is easy to burn right through the existing coats, a fine-grit paper may be a good idea, and if you have a variable-speed sander, now is the time to back off on the speed a bit. Use a soft backing pad and use a light hand on the sander.

The goal of the sanding is to just level off the surface. You want to knock off the *dust picks*, where dust has landed in the still-wet finish creating what appears to be a tiny bubble, and even out any brush marks. You do not want to sand off all the previous layers you worked so hard to apply. If the surface is already pretty smooth and all you want to do is prepare the surface for a new coat, you can use a kitchen abrasive pad to eliminate the gloss on the surface. When you are done, clean the surface and go back to the finishing step.

Repeat the sanding and varnishing process as many times as you have patience for. With paint you can stop when the finish is opaque. One coat of varnish is better than none. If it is

already halfway through the summer and you just want to get your boat in the water before the season ends, put on one coat and get your boat out and use it. Come back in the fall and complete some more coats. Three coats is a good minimum, and there is really no upper limit beyond your tolerance for tedious sanding. More coats will look better and provide more protection, but there is a point of diminishing returns somewhere around six coats.

Varnish and Varnishing Alternatives

There are a lot of alternative clear coats available. The traditional spar varnish is nice because it is relatively affordable and fairly easy to deal with. It produces a warm amber tone that nicely complements the natural colors of most woods. While it is not the most durable and long-lasting finish available, it is relatively easy to refinish.

Polyurethanes are a variety of varnish that contains constituents that react with each other after the solvents have evaporated. Many polyurethanes and varnishes are actually hybrids containing both traditional varnish components and more modern polyurethane ingredients. Polyurethanes tend to be harder, more abrasion resistant, and more durable than varnish. Early polyurethanes were highly susceptible to UV degradation, but now there are marine polyurethanes that provide good UV protection.

Most polyurethanes can be applied just like varnish, although they seem to be slightly harder to apply smoothly with a brush. Polyurethanes may be clearer than varnish, but they may also have a slightly cool, bluish tint, which may look slightly "off" on some woods. The added durability of the finish is a nice feature, but generally polyurethanes cost more than traditional spar varnish. If you are using your boat a lot, polyurethane will still get scratched up, and for practical purposes an expensive scratch-resistant coating may not last much longer in regular use than a cheaper alternative before you want to refinish the boat. Due to the harder properties of the finish, it can be a little harder to sand the surface prior to refinishing as well.

As you move up the cost spectrum you will find higher-priced polyurethane finishes that are tougher and more durable until you get into the two-part and three-part polyurethane and epoxy finishes. These finishes have a limited pot life because as soon as you mix the parts together, they start to react and are on their way to curing even before you start spreading them on the boat.

These finishes are quite appropriate for boats, and while some are formulated for brushing, spraying often provides the best results. If you are good at spraying finishes, you don't need me to tell you what is involved, and if you are not good at it, teaching spraying technique is a little beyond the scope of this book. For those who don't know how to spray finishes or don't have the equipment, you could do all the sanding on your boat and then bring it to an automotive body shop. A good automotive clear-coat that contains UV inhibitors will produce a beautiful finish on your boat.

If you go into a marine supply store, you will find a large selection of high-quality paints, most of which are suitable for applying to a strip-planked boat. Paints suitable for wood or fiberglass will adhere well to a properly prepared surface. There are primers that will help prepare the surface for a flawless finish. However, you can do well seeking out paints at the local home center. Any exterior enamel will work, and those intended for decks tend to be quite tough and will provide long-term service at a reasonable price. While they may not be as glossy as paints available from a marine supply store, you will avoid paying the premium associated with those stores.

Buffing Out the Finish

For those of us without a dust-free finishing room or access to professional paint equipment, a little dust in the finish should be a foregone conclusion. Even the guys who strip naked

Figure 10-15. You can get results almost as good as spraying by careful brushing followed by rubbing out and polishing the result. This Night Heron was sanded with 600- through 2,000-grit sandpaper and then buffed with polish.

before going into the finishing room are going to end up with some dust settling on the finish. By far the easiest solution is to accept this and not perceive it as a problem. It is only cosmetic and will not affect the performance of the boat. After a year of hard use the presence of only a little dust on the finish will be a fond memory under all the scratches.

But, I have more than once succumbed to the unreasonable perfectionism of the desire for a flawless finish. If you really want to go for it, the solution is to rub out the finish. Fine sanding to remove the dust picks and buffing compounds to restore the gloss really can provide a spectacular finish. Standard spar varnish can be buffed, as can the harder modern finishes. It takes patience, but it isn't really that complicated.

The finish needs to be very hard before proceeding. After you have finished applying all your coats of finish, let the boat sit for a minimum of at least a week. A light sanding should produce a fine dust. The first step is to level the surface, sanding off all the dust picks and small ripples. This is achieved with superfine sandpapers available through automotive supply stores. Start with as fine sandpaper as will cut down the dust spots in a reasonable time (600- to 800-grit). Finer grits will take longer, but coarser will require stepping up through more grits. Like the previous sanding, any scratches will have to be removed with successively finer grits.

Use a wet-or-dry sandpaper and some form of sanding lubricant such as paraffin oil or water. Wrap the sandpaper around a stiff sanding block such as a block of wood or a firm felt block. Apply the lubricant to the boat surface and start rubbing. This will take some elbow grease. Keep rubbing until the surface blemishes are removed. You will need a clean dry cloth to wipe off the surface so you can gauge your progress. Keep switching out your sandpaper as it gets dull, and keep applying lubricant as the surface dries. Do this to the whole surface.

When you have leveled the surface it is time to step up to the next higher grit following a progression of 600, 800, 1,000, 1,200, 1,500, 2,000. With each level you will want to completely remove the scratches made by the previous level. It should go a little quicker after the initial leveling, as you don't need to remove as much material. Remember that you do not want to remove the varnish; you are only trying to polish it. If you do go through the varnish you will need to stop, revarnish, and start all over again.

After you are done with the extra-fine sandpapers, you should have a very nice-looking surface that is smooth and even but without much gloss. This actually looks very nice and could make a beautiful-looking finish; however, since much of the UV protection is provided by simple reflection, a higher gloss is desirable. An automotive buffer and buffing compounds will bring it up to the next level.

Apply the buffing compound to a small area and start working it around with a light touch and a lamb's-wool buffing wheel, spinning at a fairly slow rate. After the compound is distributed over the area, increase the pressure to help the buffing action. As the compound dries, decrease the pressure in order to bring out the shine.

When you have finished buffing, take a step back and look at and admire the boat. Put a polarizing filter on your camera and set the boat outside somewhere to get a nice picture. The boat will never look as good again. Do yourself a favor and get the first scratch early. This will save you a lot of care and worry as you try to baby the thing. Once the first scratch has christened the boat, it will be a lot easier to get the full pleasure of owning and using a boat you built yourself.

Part III

Boats You Can Build

Chapter 11

Coot: A Pram-Bowed Dinghy

Stripping this type of boat is about as basic as it gets, and thus it makes a good strip-building 101 project for anyone new to strip-building. Because both ends are squared off, there is a minimum of tapering needed to fit against existing strips; most of the strips just hang off the ends a bit and get cut off. It should be possible for a first-time builder to completely strip this boat in a couple of days using cove-and-bead strips. Two transoms also allow a short, fat boat without radical curves. This also makes it easier to strip. Most of the strips follow a fairly straight run, bending the easy way.

I designed Coot with a long bench that runs lengthwise instead of the more typical middle seat running across the boat. This long seat lets the rower shift his or her weight forward and back easily, depending on how many people are sitting in the boat and what gear is being carried. It also encloses a large volume for positive buoyancy should the boat become flooded. On a traditionally built boat, the center crosswise seat acts as a thwart to reinforce the sides. In a strip-built boat, the fiberglass acts as a series of very small ribs. Combined with a beefy *outwale* (or gunwale on the outside), these little ribs end up creating a very stiff little boat.

Figure 11-1. *The Coot is a small dinghy or tender. The pram style with transoms at both ends makes it an easy boat to strip, and it is a suitable strip-building 101 project. A pram is a small rowing boat with squared-off ends, or transoms, at both ends. Having a transom at both ends gives you a short boat with a lot of capacity and stability, which makes it a very practical tender for a larger boat or yacht. Although I don't get into it here, it can also be easily adapted for sailing and would make a great first sailing boat for a child.*

Canoes and kayaks aside, most small boats have a stern transom, and the Coot design shows one way of dealing with this type of end. This boat also incorporates plywood seats mounted directly to the hull. This is a solid and straight-forward means of fitting out a boat.

Strongback and Forms

I wanted as simple a strongback as possible for this boat. (I actually wanted to be really lazy, so I sent Chesapeake Light Craft a file, and they sent me a package containing all the forms and the strongback, plus the plywood parts, precision-cut and ready to go.) Toward that end I used particleboard that slotted into the forms.

This system requires some careful measurement and cutting to construct, but it uses a minimum amount of material and makes the setup of the forms a breeze. All you need to do is set the stringers up on some sawhorses and then drop the forms in the slots in the proper order. This eliminates the need for any aligning; as long as the sawhorses are level and even, the forms will end up that way as well.

Because the forms are so tall, you may want to use low sawhorses so you can reach all the way to the middle of the forms while stripping. I ran into a little trouble handling this boat in a confined basement, but with a little ingenuity I was able to move it myself. Since it is wide, make sure it will fit out any doors before getting too far into the project.

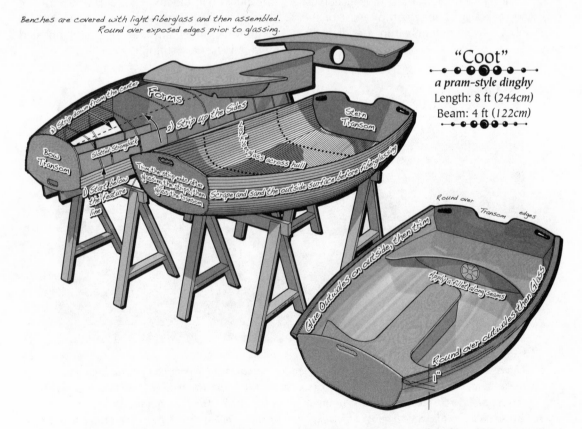

Figure 11-2. The Coot is a simple boat to strip because it has transoms at both ends and gradual curves. Simple plywood seats drop into place providing flotation. The result is a rugged little yacht tender.

Transsoms

The plywood transoms at each end of the boat also fit in place on the supporting stringers. The bow transom has tabs that help center it, and the stern is centered by the motor cutout. Some clamps secure the transoms in place.

You do not need to bevel the forms, although you could. Beveling the transoms will provide a larger gluing surface while stripping, but since the joint is filled in with a large fillet it will not significantly affect the strength in the long run.

Before installing the transoms on the strong-back it is useful to coat them with a light layer of epoxy resin. Apply it with a roller in a light coat, enough to seal the wood. This protects the plywood from glue drips and other abuse.

Stripping

Cove-and-bead strips work very well on this boat. Because of the generally gradual curvature around the forms, it is not a problem to get tight joints between the strips. However, just below the gunwale there is a little feature line where the surface of the hull is creased at a sharper edge. This feature line is designed to run parallel to the strips. Just start the first strip so that by the time you add enough strips to reach the corner on the forms, the edge of the strips will be right at the corner. The cove-and-bead design allows for a tight joint at this feature line.

Glassing

The Coot is a fat boat. Normal-width 6-ounce glass will not cover the whole girth of the out-side in one piece. Since a dinghy is often pulled up on a beach with a bit of a load aboard, it doesn't hurt to double up the glass on the bottom. Use 60-inch-wide cloth draped over one side so that it extends beyond the gunwale, and then neatly trim the other edge to follow the curvature of the strips on the side. Overlap

another layer across the bottom down onto the other side and trim it similarly.

Even though you get a clearer layup wet-ting out one layer at a time, in the interest of expediency you can just pour epoxy on the boat and wet out both layers with a squeegee. Because the upper layer has the factory edge trimmed off, it will tend to shed some loose strands of fiberglass. Keep the amount of work you do near this ragged edge to a minimum to keep it neat.

Don't glass the transoms initially. Just lay the glass on the strips and wet it out onto the ragged ends of the strips beyond the transoms. If you are careful you should not need to protect the transoms from the epoxy at this point, but you can mask them off with masking tape and waxed paper if you wish. Apply a light fill coat to the outside surface.

Inside Glass

Instead of doubling up the fiberglass on the bot-tom as on the outside, on the inside you can roll the cloth across the boat from side to side. Sixty-inch-wide cloth will reach from form 2 to form 7 to cover the middle section of the boat. The ends are then covered with triangular pieces aligned on the bias so the yarns are running at a 45-degree angle to the centerline of the boat. This makes it easier to cover from the edge of the cloth in the middle, up the sides, and onto the transom in one piece. You should be able to cut the two pieces needed to cover both ends by cutting a square piece 60 inches by 60 inches and then cutting this piece in half along the diagonal. Align the long, diagonal edge of the pieces to overlap the center section of cloth, one piece at each end. Carefully tuck the cloth down into the corner joint between the transoms and the strips. Treat the cloth gently to avoid distorting the weave unnecessarily.

Fillets. After dry-fitting the interior cloth in place, fold it back off the transoms to apply the fillets. Mix up epoxy with wood flour to make dookie schmutz and put it in a ziplock bag. Because the transom can be exposed to pretty high loads, such as an outboard motor, the joint needs a large, strong fillet. Cut off the corner of the bag to create a large hole (½ inch wide). Squeeze a large worm of schmutz into the gap. Smooth it out with a plastic spoon, using the wide part of the spoon so you don't make the fillet too small. A plastic soupspoon will work well here.

Transom. Once the fillets are applied and smooth, fold the glass back over the transoms, and start wetting out the two triangles of glass at each end. Roll back the edge of the center section of glass across the middle of the boat so you can wet out the end pieces completely first. Then fold back the wide middle piece of glass so the finished edge overlaps the end pieces, hiding the ragged trimmed edges of the end pieces.

Once the inside is fully glassed, you should apply another coat of epoxy to make sure the wood is well sealed. You may want to keep the fabric texture on the inside so it will not be too slippery. To assure there are no pinholes, roll a thin layer of epoxy onto the inside after the wet-out coat. The coat should be thin enough to maintain the texture while still thick enough to seal over any tiny holes in the fabric.

Seats. The seats and all their associated parts are cut from ½-inch-thick okoume plywood that is completely covered with 4-ounce or 6-ounce fiberglass. Notice that the bulkhead panels that support the seats are cut to the same shape as forms 2 and 7. You can use these two forms as templates. The fiberglass greatly reinforces the plywood and protects it from water and abrasion. Round over all the exposed edges of the plywood with a router and then cover both sides of all the parts with fiberglass cloth. Apply a fill coat on the upper surfaces of the seats before installation so you don't risk dripping into the boat later on. The glass is wrapped down over the rounded-over edges to assure complete protection.

The seat supports are assembled on the seats and tack-welded in place with CA glue before applying a fillet around all the joints.

Glassing the Outside of the Transoms

After completing the assembly on the inside of the boat, turn the boat over to finish up the transoms. First, trim off the strips and glass extending beyond the ends with a Japanese pull saw. Plane down any uneven spots and then sand them. Next, sand a good radius on the ends of the strips and rough up the surface of the hull back a few inches from the ends.

Use masking tape to mark off how far onto the hull you want the glass to go, about 2 inches. Using some more pieces of fiberglass cut at a 45-degree angle, glass over both transoms onto the hull.

Gunwales

Actually, the Coot just has an outwale, or the part of the gunwale on the outside of the boat. You could add an inwale on the inside if you feel your boat is going to get an unusual amount of abuse at the local dinghy dock. The outwale is an 8-foot-by-1½-inch-by-1½-inch piece of hardwood or mahogany. Cut the bottom edge at a slight angle to let the water run off easily when the boat is stored upside down. Set this strip of wood in epoxy thickened with colloidal silica, with the top of the outwale just below the top of the uppermost strip. Use clamps every 4 to 6 inches to hold it in place until the glue cures.

Finishing

After completing the fiberglassing, give everything on the outside a thorough sanding with

60-grit sandpaper, doing as much as you can before cutting into the glass. Where the edge of the second layer of cloth starts on the bottom you will have to sand a little bit into the glass to get an even surface. Then give it all a complete fill coat of epoxy.

For a boat that will likely spend a lot of time outside, it makes sense to paint most of the interior surfaces. Paint provides by far the best UV protection, so if the boat will be left upright, paint is a good finish for the inside. Leaving it bright with a varnish finish is also a viable option.

Graphite Powder

This boat will get dragged up on beaches resulting in a lot of wear and tear on the bottom. A double layer of 6-ounce glass can take a lot of abuse, but graphite powder mixed into epoxy makes a nice low-friction surface for sliding across rocks and sand.

The dimensions provided will be useful for locating the oarlocks and the various parts of the seats.

Figure 11-5 (page 177) is a drawing of the strongback boards (you will need two of these).

Materials List

Item	Material	Quantity
Strongback	1/2 in. particleboard or plywood	1/2 sheet
Forms	1/2 in. MDF, particleboard, or plywood	2 1/2 sheets
Strips	8 ft. x 1/4 in. x 3/4 in. cove-and-bead	100 pieces
Transoms	1/2 in. okoume plywood	1/2 sheet
Skeg	1/2 in. okoume plywood or 3/4 in. lumber	39 in. x 5 in.
Hull fiberglass	6 oz. 60 in. wide E-glass	16 yards
Seats	1/2 in. okoume plywood	1 sheet
Seat fiberglass	4 oz. 52 in. wide E-glass	8 yards
Resin	epoxy	2.5 gallons
Gunwales	8 ft. x 1 1/2 in. x 1 1/2 in. mahogany	2 pieces
	varnish	1 quart
	paint	1 quart
	graphite powder	< 1 quart
	colloidal silica	< 1 quart
	wood flour	1 quart
Miscellaneous	bronze oarlocks	2
	bronze oarlock sockets with mounting screws	4
	screw-in deck plates	2
	9/16 in. T-50 staples	1 box
	carpenter's glue	1 quart
	CA glue	1 4-ounce bottle

Figure 11-3. Use this table as a guide for your material needs.

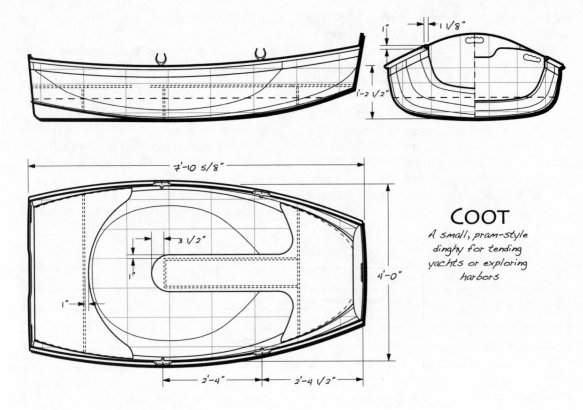

COOT

A small, pram-style dinghy for tending yachts or exploring harbors

Figure 11-4. *This three-view drawing shows, clockwise from top left, the side, or profile, view of the Coot; the end view, or body plan; and the top, or plan, view. Note that the body plan depicts the view from the front of the boat on the left, and the view from the back on the right. Over the back transom you can see the front transom sticking up as you would see it when viewing the boat from behind.*

The forms slide into the slots on these boards to hold the appropriate distance. The zero point for the slot locations is the left end of the board, with the right-hand edge of the first slot 8 inches from the end. The slots are spaced every 12 inches until form 6, which is 11½ inches from form 5. The 12-inch spacing resumes for the remainder of the forms. The transoms lean up against the angled notches at the end.

The transom offsets are used just like the form offsets. Because they are set at an angle relative to the forms, the waterline data does not actually align with the same elevations on the forms. In other words, the DWL on the bow transom is not at the DWL of the finished boat.

The gunwale rows define the point that will eventually be the top edge of the side of the boat. The feature line indicates a little crease in the shape. This is primarily an aesthetic element. When you draw the forms, make an angle here. Everywhere else, connect the points with smooth curves.

Leave the bead on the first strip. It will eventually get planed off when you install the gunwales. The Coot was designed to use 8-foot-long strips. The first strips will just barely make it, so you will want to be sure you reach both ends if you are using full 8-footers.

Work until all the pencil marks are gone (see Figure 11-17) to be sure the whole surface

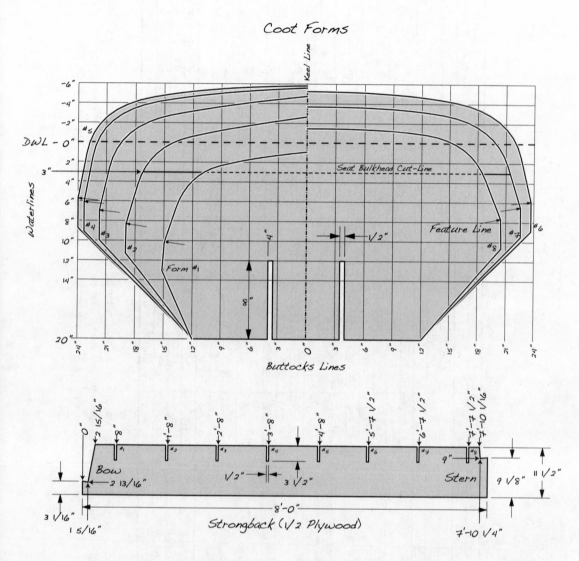

Figure 11-5. *This drawing illustrates what the forms should look like when complete. The grid corresponds to the same dimensions included in the offset table provided. The centerline is the zero point for the half-widths, and the datum waterline (DWL) is the zero point for the heights. The forms all taper down from the gunwale line toward a flat reference surface at the bottom. While 20 inches may seem like a long way from the DWL, you need this much distance so the bow transom does not extend below this surface.*

Coot Dinghy Offsets

Form:	#8	#7	#6	#5	#4	#3	#2	#1	Bow Transom	Stern Transom
Distance from Bow:	7-6	6-6	5-6	4-6	3-6	2-6	1-6	6	Transom	Transom
Elevation — Half-widths (inches from Centerline)										
Waterlines 12"			23 11/16	24	23 5/16	21 11/16	18 15/16			19 7/8
10"	20 1/2	22 9/16	23 11/16	24	23 5/16	21 1/2	18 13/16	15 1/16	13	19 7/8
8"	20 7/16	22 3/8	23 1/4	23 5/8	22 15/16	21	18 1/4	14 7/8	12 5/8	19 1/8
6"	19 13/16	21 3/4	22 3/4	23 1/4	22 9/16	20 1/2	17 11/16	14 3/16	12 1/8	18 1/8
4"	19	21 1/8	22 3/16	22 3/4	21 15/16	19 7/16	16 5/8	13 1/2	11 3/8	17 1/8
2"	17 7/8	20	20 1/2	21 1/2	20 1/2	16 3/4	13 15/16	12 1/8	9 11/16	14 5/16
DWL	15 3/8	17 1/4	16 1/4	18 3/8	16 5/16	6 9/16	4 1/2	7 9/16	0	
-2"										
-4"										
Elevations (inches above DWL)										
Half-width Keel Line	-1 7/16	-3 11/16	-5 1/4	-5 13/16	-5 9/16	-4 3/4	-2 11/16	15/16	0	-1 3/16
Buttocks 3"	-1 7/16	-3 11/16	-5 3/16	-5 3/4	-5 7/16	-4 7/16	-2 1/4	1 1/4	5/16	-1 3/16
6"	-1 3/8	-3 5/8	-5 1/8	-5 5/8	-5 1/4	-4 1/16	-1 3/4	1 11/16	3/4	-1 1/16
9"	-1 1/4	-3 7/16	-4 15/16	-5 7/16	-5	-3 11/16	-1 1/4	2 5/16	1 5/8	-15/16
12"	-15/16	-3 3/16	-4 11/16	-5 3/16	-4 11/16	-3 3/16	-5/8	3 7/8	5 9/16	-9/16
15"	-3/16	-2 3/4	-4 1/4	-4 13/16	-4 1/4	-2 5/8	9/16	10 13/16		5/16
18"	2 3/16	-1 5/8	-3 1/2	-4 1/8	-3 1/2	-1 5/16	5 1/8			3 5/16
21"		1 3/4	-1 9/16	-2 1/2	-1 1/2	4				
Gunwale Half-width	20 1/2	22 9/16	23 11/16	24	23 5/16	21 11/16	19	15 3/16	13 1/16	19 7/8
Gunwale Height	10 5/8	9 1/2	8 7/8	8 3/4	9 1/8	9 15/16	11 5/16	13 1/16	12 1/8	11
Feature Line Half-width	20 7/16	22 9/16	23 11/16	24	23 5/16	21 11/16	18 15/16	14 15/16	12 15/16	19 7/8
Feature Line Height	7 5/8	6 1/2	5 7/8	5 3/4	6 1/8	6 15/16	8 5/16	10 3/16	9 1/8	8

Figure 11-6. *The offsets are a table of numbers you can use to plot out full-size templates for all the forms and the transoms. The procedure for doing this is described in Chapter 4 where the Coot is used as the example. If you cannot find a sheet of paper large enough to draw out both sides of the boat full size, draw out half of each form and then flip over the pattern when you transfer the lines to your form material.*

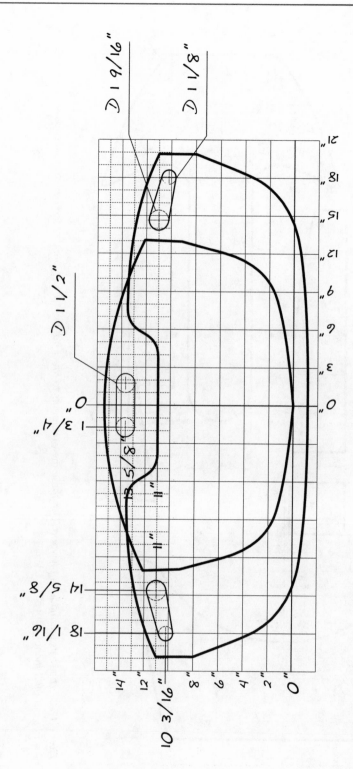

Figure 11-7. The transoms are cut from good-quality ½-inch-thick marine plywood. Use the data from the offset table to define the lower shape, and use the grid in this drawing to define the top edge. You can draw a radius of 27 ¹¹⁄₁₆ inches with a center point 12 ⁵⁄₁₆ inches below the DWL to define the top edge of the bow transom. The stem transom can be a little bit more free-form, but the edge of the cutout should be 11 inches above the DWL. These dimensions are used to reference these parts at the right elevation on the strongback. If you modify these dimensions you may need to adjust their height to make the boat fair.

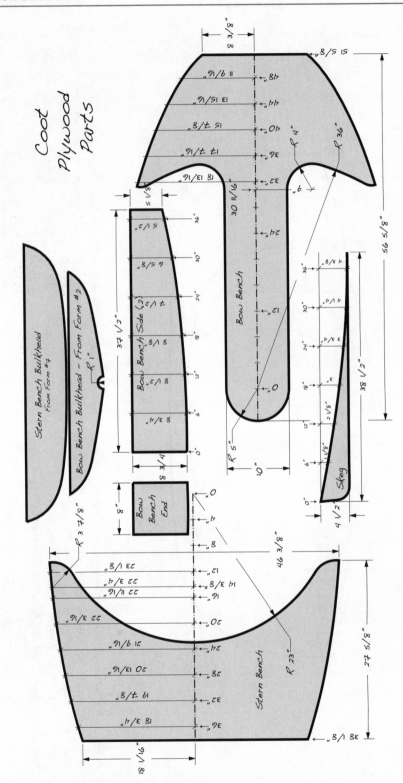

Coot Plywood Parts

Figure 11-8. *The seats are made of plywood. Use these measurements to draw out the parts. Note that the bench bulkheads are based on forms 2 and 7 cut off 3 inches above the DWL.*

Figure 11-9. *The simplest form of strongback is some plywood or, as in this case, particleboard slotted to accept the forms. This slotted beam works particularly well on a short boat where only one 8-foot length is required. Because of the size of the forms on the Coot, some large holes cut in the forms keep the weight down. Chesapeake Light Craft cut these forms for me with a CNC router, but they could be cut at home using a band saw or jigsaw. The slotted strongback has ½-inch-wide slots spaced every 12 inches.*

Figure 11-10. *The Coot has transoms (flat ends) at both ends. The transoms have been pre-coated with epoxy to protect them from glue drips and other abuse. This strongback has supports to hold the transoms in the correct position.*

Figure 11-11. *This boat has a little feature line approximately four strips down from the gunwale. To assure that it comes out even, stack up some strips, and align the top with that line so it will come out even later on. When the alignment looks right, run a staple through the strip into the form.*

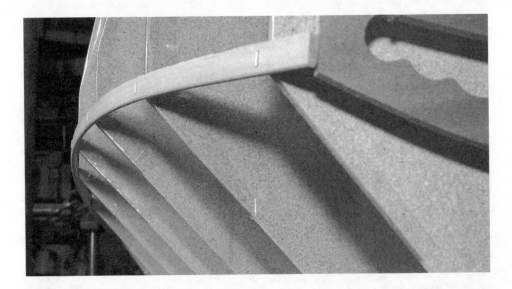

Figure 11-12. *Get your eye down near the first strip to make sure it runs in a smooth, fair curve. If you see a wiggle, pull out the staple and let the strip bend naturally. Check to see if the curve is now fair. If it is, just run a staple into the strip where it is without moving the strip. If the curve is not yet fair, try removing some more staples. If this does not work it is probably because the strip itself has a kink in it. You could just pop it off and try another strip or try restapling the strip so it is fair.*

Figure 11-13. Like the deck-hull joint of a closed boat, the centerline of many boats often requires creating a rolling bevel. Even with cove-and-bead strips you will often want to join two strips with their coves facing out. This usually requires planing the bead off, and then beveling the edges to get a tight joint. Some scrap strips clamped vertically along the centerline will provide an initial reference. See the instructions for creating a rolling bevel in Chapter 6. If you mill your own strips, you could mill yourself one strip with coves on both sides.

Figure 11-14. *Along the centerline using cove-and-bead strips you will want to have coves facing out on both sides. You can quickly clamp together two strips with a spring clamp, but you need to protect the sides of the cove. Some short pieces of strip cut down to just the bead may be fitted in the cove as a flat surface for clamping.*

Figure 11-15. *Up to this point all the strips have run beyond the edge of the transom. As you work down from the bottom of the boat you will eventually run into the strip you put on the side. You will now need to start fitting the ends of the strips against the edge of the last strip installed on the side. Plane the cove off this strip before installing it so you can fit the new strips against a flat surface.*

Figure 11-16. *Use a sharp paint scraper to remove any glue drips. Hold the scraper with two hands, with one hand near the blade to keep it from chattering. Pull with the handle low and parallel to the boat surface. Since this boat uses cove-and-bead strips the surface is already pretty even. A quick scraping should get the surface into good shape to immediately start sanding. If there are any high spots, knock them down with a block plane.*

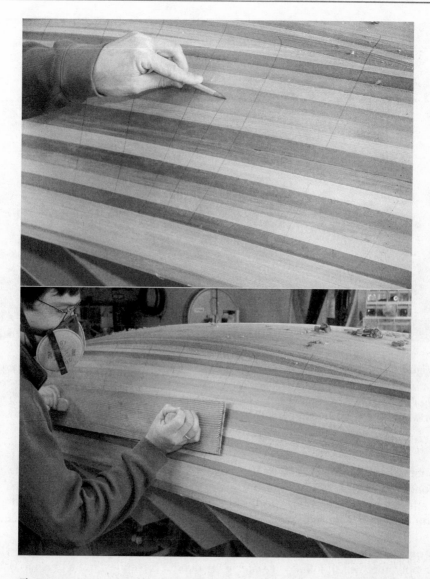

Figure 11-17. To get a fair, consistent surface you want to sand everything to approximately the same degree. You can provide sanding guides by scribbling on the surface with a soft pencil. Do not press hard, and use the side of the pencil point so you don't create grooves in the wood.

has been sanded and is quite fair. This fairing process can be done with quite coarse sandpaper, such as 40- or 60-grit. Try to sand with the grain to minimize the scratches.

After you have achieved an even surface with the fairing board, go over the whole thing with a random orbit sander. Start with 60-grit paper and sand away all the scratch marks, then start working up through finer grits to about 120-grit.

Attempting to wet out two layers of fabric simultaneously (see Figure 11-18) will invite trap-

Figure 11-18. *The Coot is too wide to span with one piece of cloth. For a light layup, you can overlap two layers along the centerline, but I wanted some added durability, so I overlapped two layers of 6-ounce cloth across the whole bottom. Trim the cloth so it follows the line of the strips. This helps hide any irregularity that may result.*

ping tiny bubbles of air in the pockets between yarns. As long as these bubbles are very small, it will not affect the strength enough to worry about. If you heat up the shop before you start glassing, and then allowing the temperature to fall, the epoxy will flow more easily and the dropping temperature will shrink any remaining trapped air. For this kind of boat, which will be dragged up on a beach, the scratches will soon overwhelm any tiny air bubbles that may result.

When I built this Coot, I only glassed the stripped part of the boat and didn't try to glass the transoms. I just left the strips and glass running off straight, and planned to come back and trim them later.

When you get down on the sides, if you need more epoxy, use a brush to dab on a little more, then squeegee it to spread it. Attempting to wet out the whole boat with just a brush will end up putting down too much epoxy, making the boat heavier than needed.

Figure 11-19. *Cover the boat with 6-ounce fiberglass. The two layers on the bottom will soak up quite a bit of resin. Pour a puddle of epoxy on the bottom and spread it around with a squeegee. Work from the middle, down the sides, and then out toward the ends.*

Figure 11-20. *The fill coat fills up the fabric texture (right) to create a smooth finish (left). Brush on the epoxy using the same crisscross technique you will eventually use to apply varnish.*

Figure 11-21. *The width of this boat makes it difficult to get off the forms. Attach a loop of tape as a handle to get a grip on the boat if you are working alone. This is one of those times that having some extra help would make your work easier.*

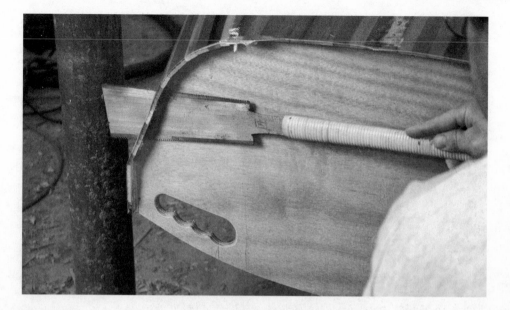

Figure 11-22. *Trim the ends of the strips even with the transom. A Japanese pull saw does a good job trimming quite flush, but it is possible to get out of alignment and scar the transom. Be careful that the blade is not scratching up the transom as you cut. Round over the corner with a block plane and sand it to prepare for fiberglassing.*

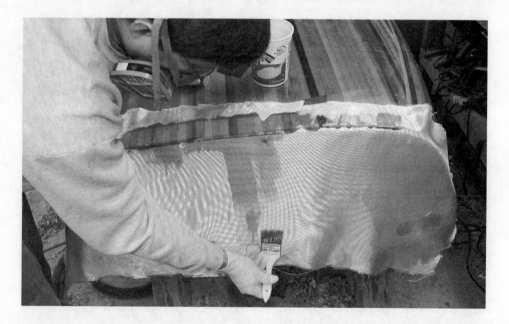

Figure 11-23. *The glass on the transom extends a couple of inches onto the strips. Note the use of blue tape to make a clean edge. The end grain of the strips absorbs a lot of resin, so either keep adding more or do a seal coat before starting the glass coat.*

Figure 11-24. After the epoxy has stiffened up a bit, but before it is really hard (1 to 2 hours after wetting out), trim off the excess glass right next to the masking tape. Use a light touch so you are not cutting into the older, harder epoxy and glass. Install a brand-new blade in the knife so it won't take much pressure to cut through the fresh glass and green epoxy. Peel off the tape as you go. If you see the tape pulling any uncut strands of cloth, cut them with the knife. The result is a smooth, clean line instead of the ragged edge.

Figure 11-25. After scraping off any glue drips with a paint scraper, use a piece of coarse sandpaper wrapped around a piece of shaped foam or wood to start smoothing the inside.

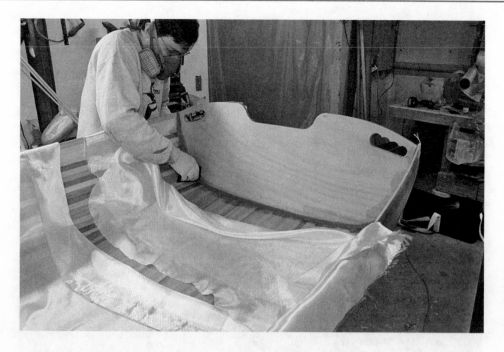

Figure 11-26. *The transoms need a fillet to help the glass conform to the shape and to add strength. Use a ziplock bag to pipe in dookie schmutz, then press it in with a spoon and clean up the excess.*

As on the outside, the glass is not wide enough to lay all the way across the inside of the boat when rolled out lengthwise. On the inside, roll one section across the boat. Try to line up the edges where the seat supports (at forms 2 and 7) will lie to reduce the visual impact of the overlapping sections. Use the lines of the staple holes as a guide. The glass for the transom is cut on a 45-degree angle, which makes it easier for the cloth to conform to the shape. Precut the cloth before doing the fillet so you don't make a mess of the cloth while working near wet epoxy. Trim the cloth a little oversize (2 to 3 inches) initially in case it shifts a little during wet-out.

After finishing the fillets on both ends, immediately fold the cloth back in place and begin wetting out the cloth, starting in the middle of the boat. Lay the finished edge of the middle piece of cloth on top of the end pieces to create a more even seam.

On the exposed edges that are not up against the hull, use a round-over bit to apply a radius to the edges. This will allow the fiberglass to wrap over the edge, providing a complete seal of the end grain.

Figure 11-27. *The seats are cut from ½-inch okoume marine plywood. I had them cut with a CNC router, but these pieces could all be cut with a band saw or jigsaw. The bottom edges of the seats need to be beveled to match the curvature of the hull. On the short, curved sides of the backseat the bevel will angle back about ¼ inch near the back corner and roll over to a bevel about ⅛ inch wide as it approaches the forward edge of the seat. The front seat needs more aggressive beveling of the curved sides, starting with a ⅛-inch-wide bevel near the horns on either side, rolling over to a nearly 1¼-inch-wide bevel at the front of the seat. A good sharp block plane makes quick and easy work of this task. Test the fit to see that the seats will sit down in the boat, with the top edge of the seat tight against the side of the boat. If you need to overdo the bevel a little to get a tight fit, that is OK. Do not remove material at the top edge as this will change the outline shape of the part. If you cannot get a tight fit around the edge, you can fill in the gap with dookie schmutz later. A rasp comes in handy for rounding off the corners where they will fit against the fillet between the strips and transom. Start with a ½-inch-diameter radius and adjust the fit as needed.*

Figure 11-28. *To protect the plywood against checking and rot, cover both the top and bottom surfaces of all the plywood parts with 4-ounce cloth. The cloth wraps down the radiused edges. When you flip over the parts to glass the other side, trim the glass flush and then overlap the edge with the new glass. Seal the end grain that will be assembled against the boat, just to be sure there is little chance for water to penetrate the plywood.*

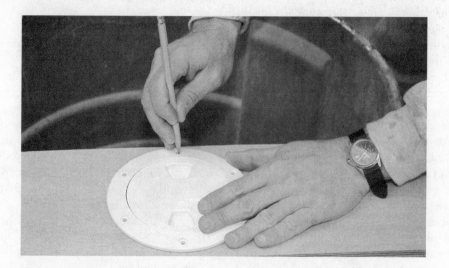

Figure 11-29. *Install access ports into all the trapped-air spaces under the seats. This allows for inspection, lets you dry out any condensation that may arise, and provides convenient dry storage. Mark the large holes with a compass, then cut them out with a jigsaw. The mounting holes can be marked using the hatch as a jig.*

Figure 11-30. *The ends of the middle-seat supports need to have 45-degree-angle mitered bevels on the inside edges to create a tight joint. Plane this with a block plane and check it with a combination square. Don't plane this down to a knife-sharp edge because you may end up changing the length of the part. Instead, watch the layers of plywood as you plane down through them and stop when you hit the bottom layer.*

Figure 11-31. *With the seat support parts laid out flat and edge to edge, tape across the joints with masking tape. When you fold the parts into position on the seat, this tape will keep the joints tight. Spot-weld all the parts in place with CA glue before removing the tape. Use a heat gun to heat up the all the joints, and then paint in some unthickened epoxy. Capillary action will suck the resin into the joint. Apply fillets of dookie schmutz along the joints between the supports and the seats, as well as the corners between the seat support parts, to create the final bond.*

The fillet joints under the middle seat do not get covered with fiberglass. Instead, just give them a quick sanding to make sure they are smooth. The outer corners on the seat supports also need to be rounded over; this can be done with a round-over bit in a router or by filing and sanding.

I could have screwed a piece of wood to the transom to support the back of the rear seat, but that would put a piece of unprotected solid wood in a trapped space where it could not be inspected or fixed if it were to start rotting. I could have protected that piece of wood with a layer of fiberglass, but that would have involved several steps. Instead I chose to reinforce the rear of the seat with a fillet, but again it is in a place that is impossible to reach. So I decided to make the fillet before installing the seat. I temporarily placed a piece of wood where the seat would go, created a fillet on it, and then removed the temporary piece. This created a

"blind" fillet in a place I could not normally reach.

Wrap a 35-inch-by-1½-inch-by-1½-inch stick with waxed paper, clamp it 8⅛ inches below the top edge of the motor cutout with some wood strips, and make a fillet beneath it as already described. When the schmutz cures, pop out the stick, leaving a nicely formed shelf that will support the back edge of the seat. A little sanding will clean it up and make it ready for the seat installation.

Don't bother with this on the front seat. This has a shorter span with very little room for a fillet, and it just doesn't need as much reinforcement.

Note the stick across the hull in Figure 11-33. This maintains the proper width of the boat. The hull may have distorted slightly at some point during construction. The seat may

Figure 11-32. The intersection of the backseat and back transom will need some reinforcement. Normally I would create a fillet underneath, but the only access to this area will be a small hole in the seat support. Therefore, I opted to make a fillet before installing the seat. You could glue and screw a cleat of wood into this position, but I like the rot resistance of a fillet in this location. A solid piece of wood as a cleat could be covered with fiberglass and epoxy to protect against rot, but this method is quicker.

Figure 11-33. Install the seat assemblies on a bead of dookie schmutz. First prepare the boat surface by sanding the mounting area. Dry-fit the seats and draw the exact locations on the hull with a pencil. Place masking tape about ½ inch away from all the mounting points to contain any squeeze-out and a later fillet.

Figure 11-34. *I installed an outwale only. Having no inwale makes it easier to drain the boat. Glue the outwales to the sides of the boat by applying a layer of epoxy thickened with colloidal silica. Spread the mayonnaise-consistency glop on both the boat and the gunwale stock. Protect the side of the boat below the gunwale with masking tape so drips won't make a mess. Install the outwale just below the top edge of the strips.*

be adjusted to fit, but bending the hull back to the right shape is often easier.

After the seat is bedded in the bead of schmutz, press it down and clamp it in place using some strips bent between the ceiling and the seat. Then squeeze in some more schmutz to create a smooth fillet along all the joints. Any larger gaps may be filled with schmutz.

Starting with just a few clamps, align the top of the gunwale slightly below the top of the strip so the bead can be planed off when the glue cures. Once you are satisfied with the alignment, place clamps every 4 to 6 inches. (You can *never* have too many clamps.) This will squeeze the epoxy mix out the bottom. Use a gloved finger to form the squeezed-out epoxy into a smooth fillet. Remember to remove the tape before the epoxy cures. Notice the rope pulling the overhanging ends together in Figure 11-34. This just draws the last bit tight against the boat.

Figure 11-35. *The edges of the outwale all start out with sharp corners. First plane down the exposed strip along the top edge so it is even with the outwale. Then use a round-over router bit to give the top edges a radius. The bottom is not at 90 degrees to the outer edge, so a standard round-over bit doesn't do the job. Instead, round it over by hand with a block plane. First create a wide chamfer, then knock the corners off the chamfer and sand it all smooth.*

Figure 11-36. *If you want to use a motor on your boat, you need to reinforce the stern. Set a piece of fiberglass-covered plywood in epoxy thickened with colloidal silica and clamp it onto the back. Clean up any squeezed-out glue, leaving a little fillet between the transom and the edge of the reinforcement.*

Figure 11-37. *Such a short boat needs a little help going straight. A short keel at the stern of the boat, sometimes called a "skeg," provides this directional stability. Cut a skeg out of some ½-inch plywood or ¾-inch solid lumber to the approximate shape. Then lay a long piece of sandpaper on the spot where the skeg will be installed and rub it back and forth to create a tight seam. Round off the exposed edges of the skeg with a ¼-inch-diameter router bit.*

Figure 11-38. *The fill coat should leave a quite smooth surface, but a good finish often requires some serious sanding. Start with 60-grit sandpaper on your random orbit sander. On the boat shown there were some rough spots along the edge where the fiberglass doubled up. The goal is to feather in these edges and level any irregularities in the surface so there are no shiny spots left on the surface. Along the edges of additional layers you will need to sand into the glass a little bit. However, if you start seeing signs of the fiberglass showing up elsewhere in the surface immediately adjacent to shiny spots, stop sanding that area. You will need to add another fill coat.*

Now cover the gunwale with a layer of fiberglass. Bias-cut strips can cover from the outside of the hull, over the top, and into the hull. See page 219 in Chapter 12 for details on this procedure.

Spot-weld the skeg in place with CA glue. Then heat the boat and skeg with a heat gun and paint on epoxy. As the parts cool they will suck epoxy into the joint. Apply a fillet right over the wet epoxy, and then glass over the whole skeg with bias-cut cloth. As an added layer of abrasion protection, run an extra layer of 9-ounce fiberglass tape down the bottom edge of the skeg.

Sand with 60-grit and recoat with further fill coats until you can get the whole surface smooth, with no shiny spots and minimal sanding into the fiberglass fabric. You can then start working up through finer sanding grits, finishing with 220.

After varnishing, install the access hatches and oarlocks. Seal the grain in the screw holes with a couple of drips of varnish. On this one, I chose to paint the interior below the seats. Paint is better UV protection than varnish, and with a boat that may spend a lot of time right-side up in the sun, the painted interior should improve the longevity.

Chapter 12

Nymph: A Solo Canoe for Double Paddle

The Nymph is a small double-paddle canoe in the tradition of the superlight-weight boats made by J. H. Rushton in the 1880s. Although it is a pocket-size little boat, the Nymph has a lot in common with other canoes. My intention with this design was to build as minimal and easy to handle a single-person boat as possible. Using ⅛-inch-thick hardwood strips, I've kept the weight down to about 15 pounds. There is not much to this boat—it is a hull with gunwales, one thwart, and a seat—but it does the trick for getting a small (less than 150 pounds) paddler out on the water. It would be easy enough to stretch the design out to 12 feet to accommodate larger paddlers by changing the form spacing to 12 inches instead of 10. The stem forms would need a little bit of adjustment, but would be pretty close as is.

Strongback and Forms

Like most canoes, this boat uses an external box beam strongback. You could use a ladder-style strongback, but a box beam is rigid and easy to assemble straight and true. For a 10-foot boat, an 8- or 9-foot strongback works well. I used a 16-foot strongback because that is what I have, so obviously you can make do with longer.

Thin strips are more flexible than thicker strips, so it pays to have the forms closer together. This provides more support, so it is less likely that the strips will bend under the pressure of sanding the boat. This pressure can create a ripple in the surface of the boat where the support of the forms causes a slight thinning of the strips. Although this slight thinning usually is not a structural problem, it can create

a small visual disruption in the smooth flow of reflections off the surface of the boat. The forms are 10 inches apart, and this seems to work well with the ⅛-inch-thick strips used, but since this boat is short and fat, its shape has a lot of curvature, which provides significant stiffness. A longer, narrower boat might need closer spacing for such thin strips.

Stems

Canoes typically have bentwood stems. With the Nymph, both the inner and outer stems are laminated from ⅛-inch-thick strips. The inner stem is made from laminations of cedar to minimize the weight, and the outer stem is laminated from cherry for strength. These stems could be made of solid ash or oak, steamed, and bent around the same forms.

Stripping

Strips this thin don't benefit much from cove-and-bead. You can just leave the edges square as they come off the saw. You may notice some places in the photos where the strips appear a little uneven. This is due to a mistake in the milling. I would have been well served by assuring the strips were more uniform in thickness. The thin strips do not allow much room for error. Minimizing errors early on will allow you some leeway for errors later.

Short, wide boats can actually be harder to strip than long, narrow boats because the strips need to do a lot of bending in a short distance. With a lot of curvature and often a lot of twisting happening in a short space, the strips

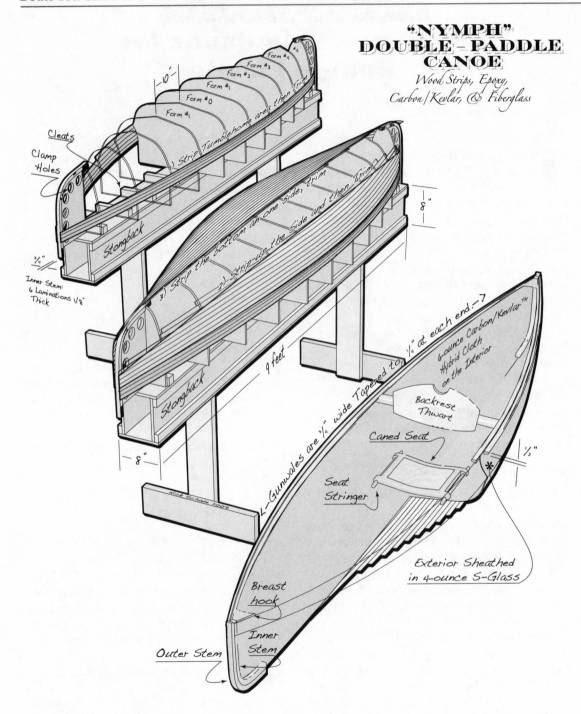

Cleats

Clamp Holes

Form #1
Form #0
Form #1
Form #2
Form #3
Form #4
Form #5

10"

1) Strip Tumblehome area, then Trim

Stongback

8"

3/4"

Inner Stem: 6 Laminations 1/8" Thick

3) Strip the bottom on one side, trim

2) Strip up the Side and then Trim

Stongback

9 feet

8"

Gunwales are 3/4" wide Tapered to 1/4" at each end 7

6-ounce Carbon/Kevlar™ Hybrid Cloth on the Interior

Backrest Thwart

Caned Seat

1/2"

*

Seat Stringer

Exterior Sheathed in 4-ounce S-Glass

Breast hook

Inner Stem

Outer Stem

Nick Schade 2003

"NYMPH" DOUBLE – PADDLE CANOE

Wood Strips, Epoxy, Carbon/Kevlar, & Fiberglass

Figure 12-1. *The Nymph follows in the tradition of George Washington Sears's vessel* Sairy Gamp *as a super-lightweight double-paddle canoe. Thin strips and minimal outfitting keep the weight down, but otherwise the construction is typical of larger strip-planked canoes.*

required a lot of stress to conform to the shape. This stress can accumulate to the point that it becomes impossible to maintain.

You can relieve this stress on the Nymph by stripping as far as you can until the strips start to get twisted and do not lie smoothly. Then mark a smooth trim line by bending another strip over these so that it follows a smooth natural curve. Trim the existing strips to this line, thus establishing a new curve that is easier for the strips to follow. Finish the bottom with the straight-line bottom stripping pattern, where you strip one side of the bottom, and then trim these strips along the keel line before fitting strips in on the other side.

Glassing

Because the strips are so thin, the fabric reinforcement is even more important than with thicker strips. S glass works well on the outside due to its greater strength compared to standard glass. Although its weave is slightly more visible than E-glass, you really need to get your nose in close to notice the difference. The carbon-Kevlar hybrid cloth on the inside adds stiffness and toughness, and makes a nice visual contrast with the wood on the exterior. Another benefit of the opaque cloth is that the interior finish work on the strips is a little less critical. If you prefer, you could get away with 6-ounce E-glass inside and out with a double layer of fabric on the bottom without a big weight penalty.

Gunwales, Seat, and Backrest

The gunwales can add quite a bit of weight. To keep the weight down, I used light basswood. But since basswood is soft like other lightweight woods, I added a layer of fiberglass to protect it. This keeps the weight down but maintains the strength.

I got lazy and used a premanufactured canoe seat, which I adapted to this boat. I mounted it to the bottom of the boat by screwing it into a stringer glued to the bottom and covered with fiberglass cloth. You could use this same technique to mount a seat to the sides of a larger canoe as well.

Materials List

Item	Material	Quantity
Strongback	8 in. × 8 in. × 9 ft. external plywood box beam	
Forms	1/2 in. MDF, particle-board, or plywood	< 1 sheet
Strips	1/8 in. × 3/4 in. square-edged cedar, basswood, or walnut	450 linear feet
Inner stems	36 in. × 1 in. × 1/8 in. western red cedar	12 pieces
Outer stems	36 in. × 1 in. × 1/8 in. cherry	12 pieces
Gunwales	10 ft. × 3/4 in. × 3/4 in. hardwood	4 pieces
Breasthooks	small scraps of hardwood	2 pieces
Backrest/thwart	28 in. × 6 in. × 2 in. Sitka spruce, or other	1 piece
Seat	premade caned canoe seat	1
Seat stringers	12 in. × 1/2 in. × 1/2 in. hardwood	2 pieces
Interior reinforcement	6 oz. carbon-Kevlar hybrid cloth	4 yards
Exterior reinforcement	4 oz. S glass	4 yards
Resin	epoxy	1.5 gallons
	varnish	1 quart
	colloidal silica	< 1 quart
Miscellaneous	carpenter's glue	< 1 quart
	9/16 in. T-50 staples	1 box
	CA glue	1 4-ounce bottle

Figure 12-2. *Use this table as a guide for your material needs.*

The backrest also serves as a thwart that maintains the width of the boat. Without a thwart, the boat could fold closed, trapping you like a pea in a pod (actually this is not likely, but it is a fun image). The solid, carved wood backrest shown here could be simplified to save time and weight, but made with a lightweight wood reinforced and protected with fiberglass it is lightweight and strong.

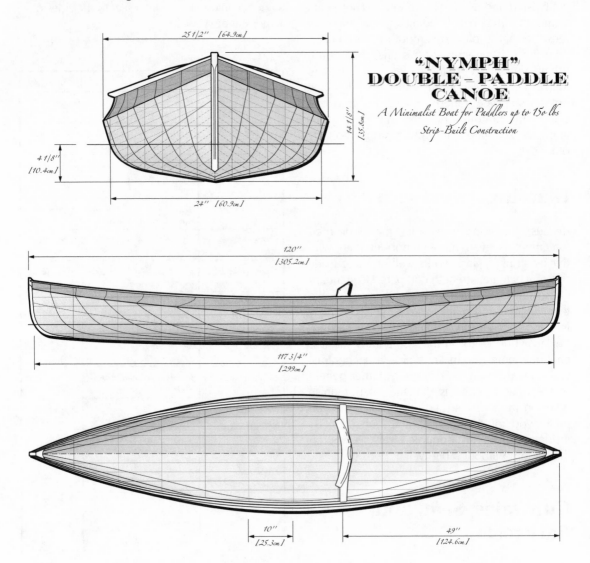

"NYMPH" DOUBLE-PADDLE CANOE

A Minimalist Boat for Paddlers up to 150 lbs
Strip-Built Construction

Figure 12-3. *The Nymph is a small boat intended for small paddlers, but it can be extended to 12 feet for larger paddlers by increasing the form spacing. Even larger people could scale up the offsets for a wider boat.*

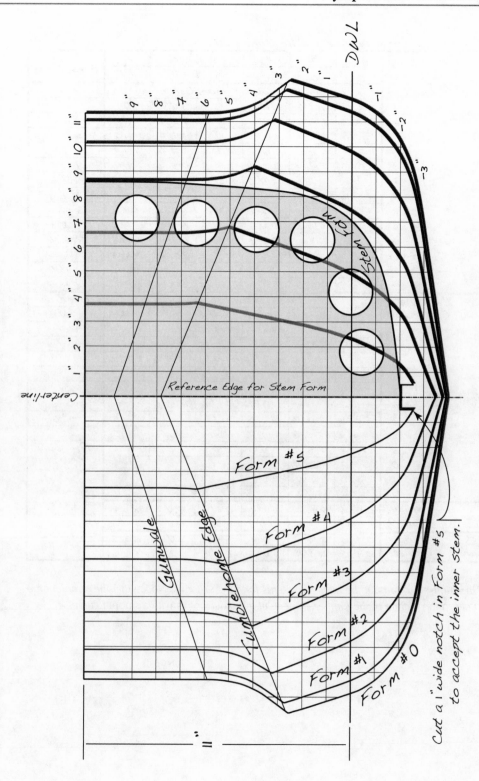

Figure 12-4. *The forms are based on the offset table. The grid shown here corresponds to the same grid used in the offsets. These forms will be mounted on the strongback flipped over from the depiction here. Because the boat is symmetrical around form 0, make two of every form except form 0.*

Nymph Double Paddle Canoe Offsets

	Form: #0	#1	#2	#3	#4	#5	Stem Form
Distance from Center:	0"	10"	20"	30"	40"	50"	
Elevation	Half-Widths (inches from Centerline)						Length
Waterlines: −3"	6 5/8	6 1/16	4 7/16	2 5/8	1 1/8	0	
−2"	10 3/16	9 5/8	7 7/8	5 1/2	3 5/16	1 1/4	3/8
−1"	11 5/16	10 3/4	9 1/16	6 11/16	4 1/4	1 7/8	5 11/16
DWL	11 7/8	11 3/8	9 3/4	7 3/8	4 7/8	2 1/4	7
1"	12 3/16	11 11/16	10 3/16	7 7/8	5 5/16	2 9/16	7 11/16
2"	12 1/2	12	10 9/16	8 5/16	5 11/16	2 13/16	8 1/16
3"	12 5/16	12 1/16	10 15/16	8 3/4	6	3	8 1/4
4"	11 11/16	11 3/8	10 5/8	9 3/16	6 3/8	3 1/4	8 5/16
5"	11 3/8	11 1/16	10 1/4	8 13/16	6 3/4	3 7/16	8 3/8
6"			10 1/8	8 5/8	6 9/16	3 5/8	8 7/16
7"					6 1/2	3 11/16	8 1/2
8"						3 11/16	8 9/16
9"							8 9/16
Half-Width	Elevations (inches above DWL)						Elevation
Buttock Lines: Center Line	−4	−3 15/16	−3 15/16	−3 3/4	−3 1/2	−2 7/8	−2 1/16
1"	−3 13/16	−3 13/16	−3 11/16	−3 7/16	−3 1/16	−2 1/4	−1 15/16
2"	−3 11/16	−3 10/16	−3 4/8	−3 3/16	−2 5/8	−3/4	−1 13/16
3"	−3 9/16	−3 4/8	−3 5/16	−2 7/8	−2 3/16	2 13/16	−1 11/16
4"	−3 3/8	−3 5/16	−3 1/16	−2 5/8	−1 5/16		−1 1/2
5"	−3 1/4	−3 3/16	−2 7/8	−2 5/16	1/4		−1 1/4
6"	−3 1/8	−3	−2 11/16	−1 11/16	2 15/16		−13/16
7"	−2 15/16	−2 13/16	−2 3/8	−5/8			−1/16
8"	−2 3/4	−2 5/8	−1 15/16	1 1/4			2
9"	−2 1/2	−2 5/16	−1 1/16	3 5/8			*The above stem form measurements are referenced from the inner edge of the form or the face of form #5*
10"	−2 1/8	−1 3/4	1/2				
11"	−1 3/8	−11/16	3 1/8				
12"	7/16	1 15/16					
Gunwales Height	5 13/16	5 15/16	6 1/4	6 3/4	7 1/2	8 1/2	
Width	11 5/16	11	10 1/8	8 5/8	6 1/2	3 11/16	
Tumblehome Edge Height	2 9/16	2 11/16	3 1/4	4	5 1/16	6 3/8	
Diagonal Width	12 5/8	12 1/4	11 1/16	9 3/16	6 3/4	3 11/16	

Figure 12-5. *Use these offsets to loft out the full-size patterns for all your forms. Notice that the tumblehome edge is a sharp corner in the outline of the forms. Connect all the other points with a smooth curve.*

Figure 12-6. *Each form is drawn out full size. These patterns are laid out on MDF, glued down with spray adhesive, and then roughly cut out with a jigsaw.*

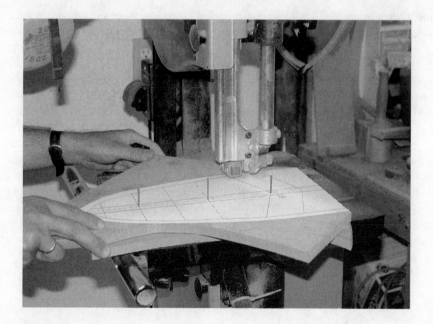

Figure 12-7. *Since the bow and stern are symmetrical on this canoe, you can nail them together and then cut them out simultaneously. If you have a steady hand on the band saw, cut right to the line. Or you can cut just proud of the line and bring it down to the line with a disk or belt sander mounted on a table.*

Figure 12-8. *Canoes and other open boats typically use an external strongback. This can be a plywood box beam, as shown, or any rigid structure made of solid lumber.*

This strongback is made of ½-inch plywood that is formed into an 8-inch-by-8-inch box beam. My strongback is about 16 feet long, but for the Nymph an 8- or 9-foot version would do fine.

Mount the forms on 10-inch centers. Screw 1½-inch-by-1½-inch cleats in section to the strongback, and then screw the forms to the cleats.

I am laminating only the inner stem in Figure 12-9, but you could do the outer stem at the same time, placing tape in between so they don't get glued together.

On an open boat, the inner stem will be visible, so aesthetics matter. It will be very hard to finish off the inner stem once it is installed with the strips attached. By doing some finish work on it now, before you install it, you can make your work easier later. A round-over bit makes quick work of easing the inner edge of the stem. A good radius also makes it easier to cover with fiberglass.

Figure 12-9. *Clean up the inner stem before securing it to the forms. It will be hard to reach when the boat is complete. After a quick cleanup with a scraper, run the stem laminations through a planer to achieve a uniform ¾-inch width.*

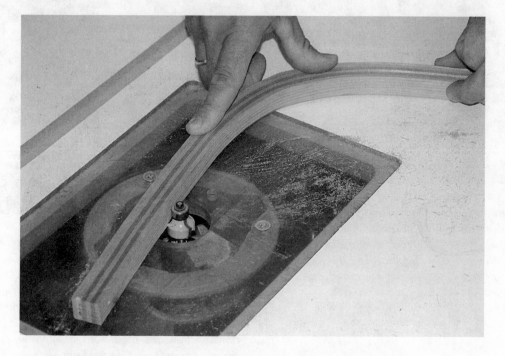

Figure 12-10. *Here I am rounding over the inner edge with a round-over bit on a router table.*

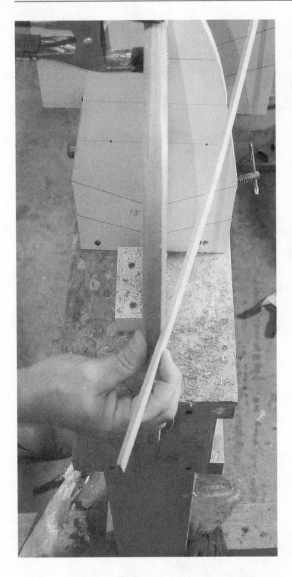

Figure 12-12. *Use a rasp or plane to bevel the edge of the inner stem. Aim the rasp toward the edge of the next form as a guide to getting the angle right.*

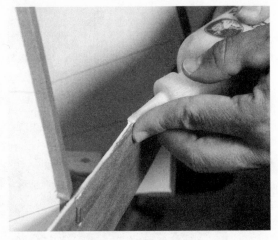

Figure 12-11. *You need to bevel the inner stem. Hold a strip against the forms; it should land flush against the bevel and bend in a fair curve. The outer edge of the stem (i.e., the forward edge of the forward stem, and the aft edge of the aft stem) should be about ½ inch wide.*

Figure 12-13. *It doesn't take a lot of glue to secure the ⅛-inch-thick strips in place, but it can be hard to direct it onto the narrow edge. It pays to have a fairly small hole in your glue dispenser so you don't get big drips coming out everywhere. With cove-and-bead strips it is quite easy to run the tip of the glue bottle down in the cove, but if you are applying glue to the bead or on a square-edged strip, you may find it helps to hold the bottle with your finger against the tip as a guide to run along the side of the strip.*

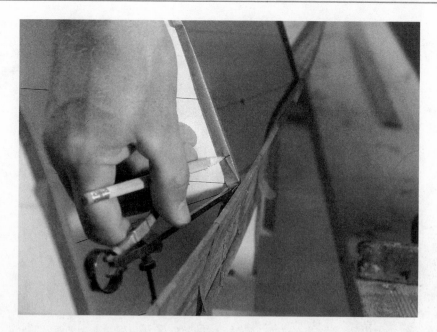

Figure 12-14. *When preparing to mark the edge of the tumblehome area, make a mark a uniform distance from the tumblehome diagonal with a compass.*

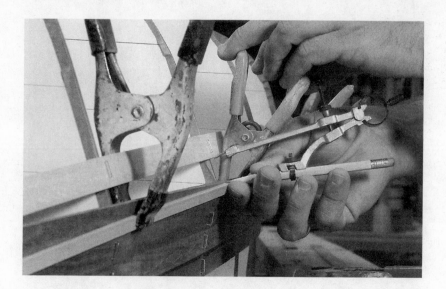

Figure 12-15. *Staple a strip on the mark you just made and check that it is fair. Then use your compass again to adjust the location of another strip clamped to the installed strips. When this strip is smooth and fair, mark a pencil line along the top edge of this strip. This indicates where you will trim the excess off the existing strips. A Japanese pull saw does a good job cutting off the excess. Cut a little above the line.*

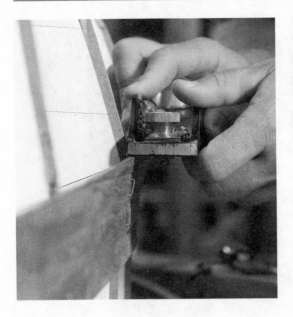

Figure 12-16. *Clean up the edge with a rabbet plane. Try for a smooth, fair curve with a consistent angle on the bevel.*

Figure 12-17. *Using a similar method as you used for the tumblehome edge, mark the centerline of the strip, cut off the excess, and plane it straight.*

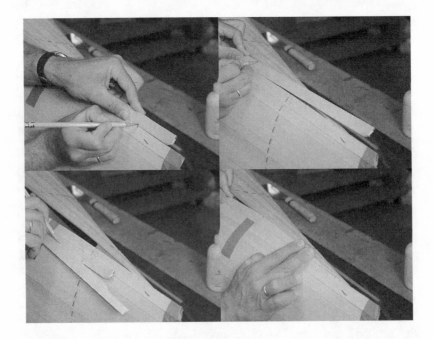

Figure 12-18. *Now it is time to close up the bottom. Fit strips into the bottom gap by marking both the length and where the upper edge of the strip crosses the gap. Connect these two points and then trim to that line.*

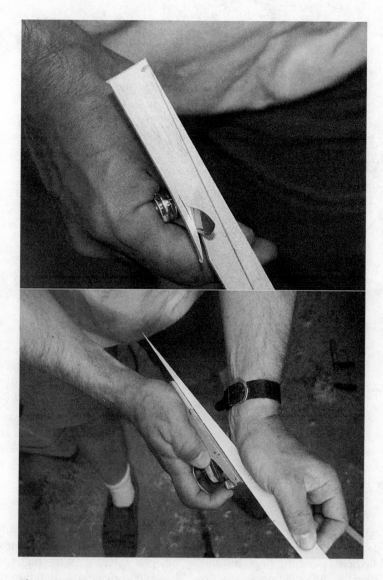

Figure 12-19. Use a jackknife to roughly remove the excess material on the strip end.

Figure 12-20. *Eventually there will be a last strip. Make the edges of the second to last strip, and maybe the third to last strip, square so that you don't need to try to fit the ends down into long holes created by a cove. Place a strip over the hole and reach in underneath to trace the shape of the hole on the underside. Without moving the strip, also mark the location of the ends of the gap on the strip. Bend a scrap strip over the marks you made to indicate the approximate shape of the hole. Either whittle away most of the excess wood or cut it off with a band saw.*

Start tapering the strip at one end. Here a piece of scrap protects the boat while allowing me to work right where I need the strip. Test the fit at this end, planing farther along as the tip starts to fit well. Try not to go beyond the previously made marks as this will indicate you are losing some of your margin of error for fitting the other end.

As you get toward the middle of the last strip, start fitting the other end. Make some alignment marks so you know where things should line up when it all fits together. As you work back toward the middle again, start working on get-

ting the length right. By carefully checking the fit, noticing where the strip binds up, and gradually planing away at the high spots, you should be able to make a snug-fitting strip. By pushing up on the existing strip from underneath you can open up the gap a bit while you press the new strip in place. Check the fit with the strip dry, and then add glue. Use strips of strapping tape stretched across the boat to pull the seam tightly together.

After scraping and sanding the boat as explained in Chapter 7 and shown in Figures 12-21 and 12-22, you will be ready to glass

Figure 12-21. Hardwoods such as this walnut respond well to scraping. A quick scraping removes glue drips and starts smoothing the surface prior to sanding. A convex scraper does a good job in the tumblehome area.

Figure 12-22. Start with coarse sandpaper in a random orbit sander to smooth the surface. Progress up through finer-grit sandpapers, finishing with 220. With hardwoods, you will want to go to finer sandpapers than with softwoods, as they tend to show scratches more readily. Be sure to keep replacing the sandpaper as it gets dull so you aren't just burnishing the surface.

Figure 12-23. Spread the epoxy around the boat with a plastic spreader or squeegee. Mix up more epoxy when there is not enough left to spread any farther.

the boat. Work quickly, and don't spend a lot of time trying to wet out every spot perfectly. Keep moving and gradually add resin as you need it. Use a brush to add spots of epoxy and then spread those spots with a squeegee.

After the glass is completely wetted out and clear, go back and remove the excess. Hold the squeegee at about 45 degrees to the surface and pull the squeegee from the centerline toward the gunwales with moderate pressure. You should pick up a blob of epoxy on your squeegee. Run the edge of the squeegee through a slot cut in a paper cup to remove this excess.

Squeegee the whole boat, aiming to get a uniform, slightly matte finish with the weave texture of the cloth fully apparent.

When the epoxy has cured, trim off the excess fiberglass with a utility knife and then remove the screws holding the forms to the strongback.

The forms may need a tap with a hammer to break them free, but the tape around the edges should let them release fairly easily.

Figure 12-24. Surfboard shapers use the hot-coat technique to apply a fill coat to the fiberglass. This involves dumping a big puddle of epoxy and quickly spreading it around with a brush. On a small boat like this, where you can keep up with the drips, this system actually works pretty well. If you are a little timid about getting a big puddle of epoxy on your floor, you may want to use the more controlled method of painting on a fill coat. When the epoxy has cured, trim off the excess fiberglass with a utility knife and remove the screws holding the forms to the strongback.

Figure 12-25. I used a hybrid carbon-Kevlar cloth on the inside. This weave has an evident pattern that will get distorted if the cloth is handled roughly. While not the end of the world structurally, distortions will be noticeable in the finished product.

Working on the inside of the boat, use your paint scraper to clean up the surface, and then sand it. Use some folded sandpaper to get into the groove next to the stems.

When the interior is ready for glassing, carefully drape the cloth down into the boat.

Carbon-Kevlar cloth is wetted out in much the same way as fiberglass; however, it is not as easy to tell when it is completely wet out. Unlike fiberglass, which transforms from white to clear when wet, the hybrid cloth just gets a little bit darker, and even when fully wet out, small bubbles can hide under the cloth. To avoid bubbles, oversaturate the cloth slightly so that it is shiny even after being left alone for a few minutes.·

Then go back and squeegee out the excess. Look for a uniform, slightly matte color. With good light, sight down the length for raised bubbles. You may need to paint on a little extra

resin to get them to lie down, then squeegee out the excess again.

After the epoxy has set up for a few hours, use a utility knife to cut around the inner stem and remove the excess cloth.

When the epoxy has cured, put some masking tape about 1 inch away from the stem and lay a piece of bias-cut cloth around the stem. The cloth should overlap the masking tape slightly. Despite the weight of the cloth, it is surprisingly accommodating in conforming to the complex shapes. Wet out this cloth carefully with a resin-wet brush.

After the epoxy has set up for a few hours, use a utility knife to trim the excess cloth about ¾ inch from the stem. Although the Kevlar can get quite difficult to cut when the epoxy is fully hardened, if you catch it while the epoxy is still soft and green, you should have no problem cutting the tough material. If the fabric is not cutting cleanly and the weave is pulling apart, you may need to let the epoxy cure a little more.

Use a foam roller to apply a thin layer of epoxy to the whole interior. This should seal any pinholes in the fabric.

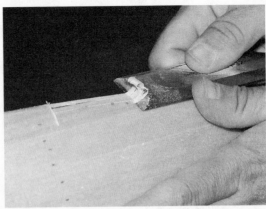

Figure 12-27. *Trim the bottom end of the outer stem to a clean edge. Hold the trimmed stem in place and use a utility knife to mark where it ends along the centerline. Use a pull saw to cut a stop line, then use a chisel to remove the wood. Make a flat surface about ¾ inch wide for mounting the outer stem.*

Figure 12-26. *A bubble roller (a grooved roller tool intended for removing bubbles from fiberglass) helps press down the cloth tight against the wood, driving any excess resin under the cloth up to the surface. While not really useful with light fiberglass, the roller can help create a lighter layup with this thicker hybrid cloth.*

Figure 12-28. *It will help if you do some preliminary shaping before installing the stem. Butter up the mounting surfaces with dookie schmutz. A screw at each end of the stem should be enough to clamp it in place. Clean off the squeeze-out before it hardens.*

The next step is to add the outer stem as shown in Figures 12-27 and 12-28. Round over the edges of the gunwales to a smooth radius so glass can be wrapped around them. Blend the gunwales and breasthook together also, as they will be glassed.

The exact shape of the backrest is not critical. The drawing in Figure 12-33 shows an

Figure 12-29. *To save weight on the gunwales I used basswood and tapered them at each end. Place both gunwales side by side and plane them both simultaneously to assure they match.*

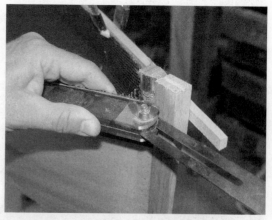

Figure 12-30. *I extended the outwales onto the stem by tapering the ends. Use a bevel gauge to transfer the angle to the outwales.*

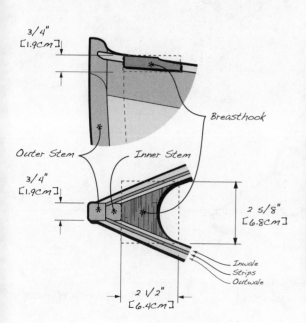

3/4"
[1.9cm]

Breasthook

Outer Stem   Inner Stem

3/4"
[1.9cm]

2 5/8"
[6.8cm]

Inwale
Strips
Outwale

2 1/2"
[6.4cm]

Figure 12-31. *The breasthook strengthens the connection between the gunwales and stem.*

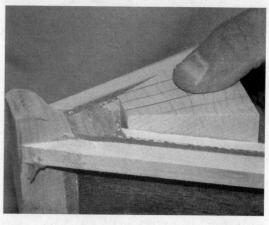

Figure 12-32. *Cut a thick chunk of wood as a breasthook and sand it to adjust the fit. Once you have a good fit you can make it thinner and sculpt it to a pleasing shape.*

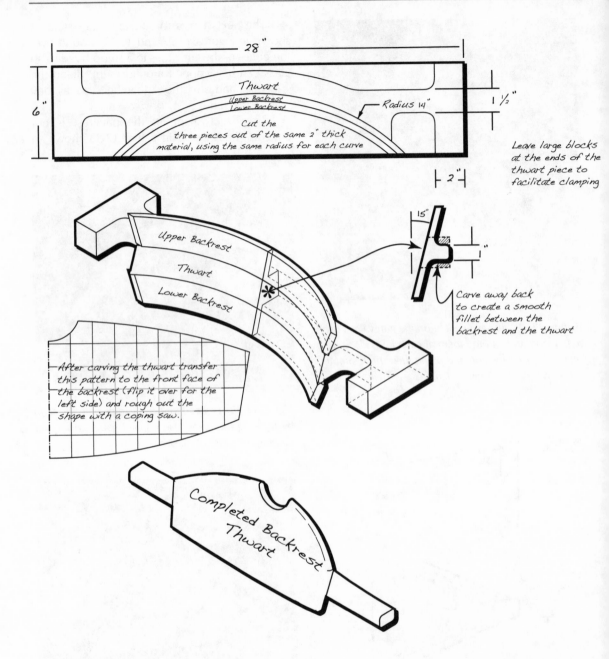

28"

6"

Thwart

Upper Backrest

Lower Backrest

Radius 14"

1 ½"

Cut the
three pieces out of the same 2" thick
material, using the same radius for each curve

2"

Leave large blocks
at the ends of the
thwart piece to
facilitate clamping

Upper Backrest

Thwart

Lower Backrest

15"

1"

*

Carve away back
to create a smooth
fillet between the
backrest and the thwart

After carving the thwart transfer
this pattern to the front face of
the backrest (flip it over for the
left side) and rough out the
shape with a coping saw.

Completed Backrest
Thwart

Figure 12-33. *The thwart serves double duty as a backrest. This wide backrest is quite comfortable. You could sculpt something from smaller stock if you want to save some weight, but by using light, strong wood and covering it with fiberglass you can keep this one very light.*

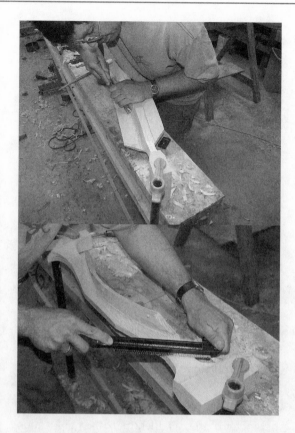

Figure 12-34. I cut the backrest from 2-inch-thick Sitka spruce. The top and bottom pieces were cut as nested pieces from the same piece of wood on a band saw with the table set at an angle. The glued up pieces were shaped with rasps and microplanes.

example superimposed on a 1-inch grid so you can transfer the shape to your own work.

A drum sander makes quick work of smoothing the front face of the backrest.

Use chisels, rasps, and planes to sculpt the backrest. I've left the ends of the center piece large and squared to facilitate clamping.

After sanding, apply glass to the backrest. Bias-cut cloth (cut diagonally to the weave) drapes nicely over the complex shape. This glass may not be needed for strength, but it does provide weather resistance.

Gently brush epoxy onto the fiberglass. Bias-cut glass distorts very easily—that is why we use it—but it means that it should be handled with a light touch. Don't drag the brush along the length of the gunwales; instead, lightly dab epoxy onto the glass until it is wet out.

After the epoxy has started to set up, use a sharp utility knife to trim the excess just above the masking tape. Don't press too hard with the knife; at this point it does not take much to cut through the glass.

After the epoxy has cured, apply another fill coat to fill in the weave. Apply masking tape about 1 inch away from the glass before brushing on the epoxy, and peel it off after about an hour.

I rounded over the exposed corners on the rail so the fiberglass will conform to it. A few spots of CA glue will hold the rail in place until

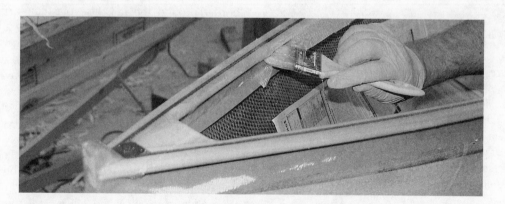

Figure 12-35. The gunwale will be covered with 3-inch-wide bias-cut strips of fiberglass. Run masking tape about ¼ inch below the bottom of the gunwale, then lay out the glass strips.

Figure 12-36. *Cover the stem with at least one layer of bias-cut fiberglass. Extend this cloth down the centerline for extra abrasion protection.*

Figure 12-37. *Many canoes and open boats need seats mounted. A standard canoe seat may be hung from the gunwales with carriage bolts, but with this boat, the seat is set on the bottom. It still needs some system to hold the seat in place. In this case I used a seat stringer, or rail, glued to the bottom and then covered with fiberglass. This same system could be used on the side of the boat for mounting the seat higher.*

it has been fiberglassed. Sand an area with a border of at least ¼ inch around the outside perimeter of the rail, then mark the rail location and mask it off with tape. Apply dots of glue to the boat, then spray the bottom side of the rail with CA accelerant. Carefully align the piece and press it in place for a few moments for the glue to set up.

Cut a piece of fiberglass with about a 1-inch border around the rail. Use bias-cut 4-ounce cloth for this. Before applying epoxy, use a heat gun or hair dryer to heat the rail and the area around it. This heat will lower the viscosity of the epoxy, and capillary action will draw the epoxy in under the rail.

Paint the rail with a good coat of epoxy while the rail is hot, before laying on the glass. Stick the cloth down on the wet epoxy and apply more epoxy to stick it down on either side of the rail onto the taped area. The end will need to be brushed down to conform with the end of the rail. If the rail is well rounded at the end, the glass should lay in with a little persuasion.

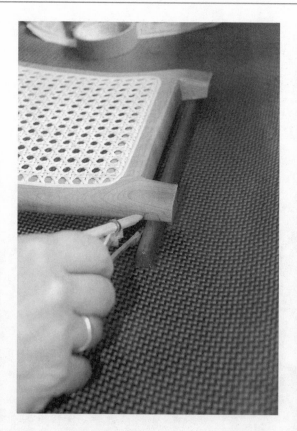

Figure 12-38. *With the seat stringer on the bottom of the boat, I wanted to get the seat as low as possible. I notched the cross arms to fit over the stringer, which let it nestle down on the bottom. For a higher-mounted seat, this would not be necessary.*

After the epoxy has set up a bit, use a utility knife to trim off the excess and peel off the masking tape.

Instead of making a seat from scratch I bought a nice, contoured, caned canoe seat and cut down the cross arms so they extend about an inch beyond the rails. The seat will fit over the rails with grooves matching the rail profile. Use a compass to mark the profile on the cross arms. Hold the compass so the pencil leg is directly above the pointer leg. Trace the pointer leg up and over the seat stringer as the pencil leg marks the contour of the stringer on the seat.

Figure 12-39. *The finished Nymph is a cute little boat suitable for exploring small lakes and ponds with a minimum of fuss. It is light enough to carry with one hand, but it is still quite rugged.*

Use a saw to cut kerfs into the groove area, and knock most of the wood out with a chisel. A sheet of coarse sandpaper wrapped around a scrap piece of rail material makes a good sanding tool and will assure a good match in the groove.

Drill mounting holes into the center of these grooves and then use the holes as guides to drill into the rail.

Chapter 13

Petrel: A Sea Kayak for Rough Waters

The Petrel is a high-performance modern sea kayak with strong traditional roots. It is sturdy enough to paddle near rough, exposed reefs and headlands while still being fun for exploring calm, sheltered bays and estuaries. Its form draws heavily from the original skin-on-frame kayaks built by the Inuits of Greenland, while adapting to needs of a modern paddler.

I gave the Petrel shown in this chapter the complete "show" boat treatment with book-matched strips and no staples. If the Coot is an example of strip-building 101, the Petrel is more of a graduate-level course. You could certainly get a beautiful, usable boat without going all out as I did on this one, but I hope it is useful to see some ways to take your work to the next level. I've no doubt that there are several levels beyond what I did here. I tried to maintain perspective on building a boat intended to be used.

Strongback and Forms

An internal strongback has the advantage that you can completely strip up the boat without ever removing the forms. This helps keep everything aligned and allows you to flip the boat over and work on both the top and the bottom while it is still in the stripped stage. It might not otherwise be strong enough to move around in this way.

I used a 2-by-4 (true dimensions) aluminum extrusion because it is dead straight, and I make enough boats that having a solid strongback is worth the cost. With a precisely straight strong-back, the setup is very straightforward as long as I cut the holes in the forms accurately.

The strongback assures the forms are lined up correctly, and L-shaped plywood spacers between the forms assure accurate spacing. The forms are locked in place by screwing down the stem forms at each end and clamping all the forms and spacers into position with a couple of wedges in the middle.

The deck and hull share the same forms and are built together, but they are not glued together until after the stripping is completed and the hull and deck have been fiberglassed separately.

These forms were cut from MDF on a band saw. Rough-cut the 2-inch-by-4-inch hole for the strongback with a handheld jigsaw, and then use a template bit in a router on a router table to follow an accurate 2-inch-by-4-inch hole template to ensure an accurate hole.

Stems

The kayak has fairly straight stems at both ends. You do not need to laminate or steam a piece to minimize the grain run-out, and you can use solid wood here. I use solid wood for the inner stem and laminate the outer stem.

Stripping

I wanted to make this boat a "show" boat, giving it a very clean, finely finished look. I used a book-matched pattern with all the strips on the deck cut from one board and installed in the

PETREL A HIGH-PERFORMANCE SEA KAYAK IN THE GREENLAND TRADITION

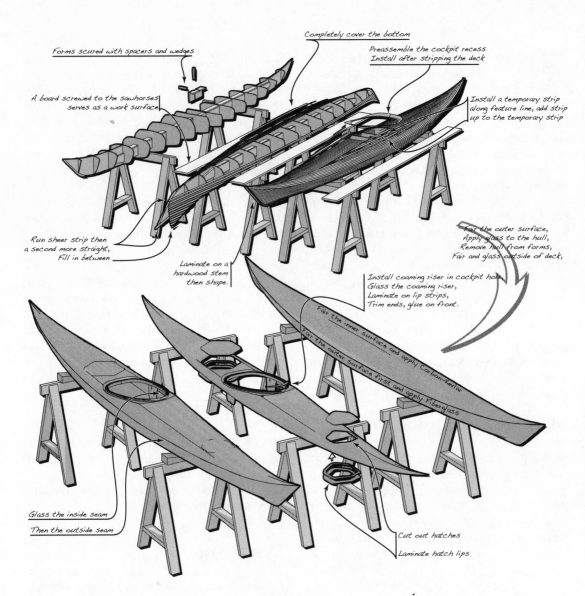

Forms scured with spacers and wedges

Completely cover the bottom

Preassemble the cockpit recess
Install after stripping the deck

A board screwed to the sawhorses
serves as a work surface

Install a temporary strip
along feature line, add strip
up to the temporary strip

Run sheer strip then
a second more straight,
Fill in between

Laminate on a
hardwood stem
then shape.

Fair the outer surface,
Apply glass to the hull,
Remove hull from forms,
Fair and glass outside of deck,

Install coaming riser in cockpit hole,
Glass the coaming riser,
Laminate on lip strips,
Trim ends, glue on front.

Fair the inner surface and apply Carbon-Kevlar

Fair the outer surface first and apply Fiberglass

Glass the inside seam

Then the outside seam

Cut out hatches

Laminate hatch lips

Figure 13-1. *The Petrel is a complex build with a lot going on. It is hard to address everything in this one chapter, but the techniques are much the same as less complex boats. Starting from forms strung on an internal strongback the hull and deck are stripped up, the coaming is installed, the outside is fiberglassed, and then the parts are removed from the forms. The inside is glassed, the hatches are installed, and then the deck is bonded back onto the hull.*

order they were cut from the board. To further enhance the look of the boat, I built it without staples. To give it even more eye appeal I stained the boat a rich mahogany red.

Book Matching

I like the side herringbone stripping pattern for kayaks. It is not necessarily the easiest, but it highlights the long, narrow lines of sea kayaks well. I used the wood from one board to strip the whole deck. The original plank was longer than the deck, so in theory I could have stripped the deck without any butt joints. However, the wood I had did not have a lot of character, and if I were to keep the strips strictly aligned side by side, the deck would have looked like it was made out of one solid piece of wood. This can look great, but it was not the look I desired. If I was going to all the effort of stripping the boat, I wanted people to get a sense of what I had done. To that end I staggered the ends of strips back with the herringbone pattern.

When I brought the ends of the strips back with the pattern, I needed to take length out of the middle of the strips, and this required making butt joints near the middle. Because I'm not taking a lot of wood out of the middle, the color of the strips matches well and the joint is not very noticeable. The result of this is to highlight the zigzag pattern of the herringbone joint, which nicely accents the boat shape. To further highlight the zigzag I used the first strips I cut off the board for the outer strips starting at the sheerline and the last strips off the board at the centerline. I made sure I had enough strips so that, where the final strips of the herringbone pattern met, they were adjacent strips out of the board.

The hull is a little less visible than the deck, and it is hard to see both sides at the same time, so maintaining a mirror-image pattern on either side of the boat seems a little self-indulgent, but why not? Again to highlight the strips I played around with the stripping order

a bit. I flipped over every other strip to create a series of V-shaped grain patterns on the bow.

Feature Lines and Chines

The design incorporates several feature lines that required some tricks to strip successfully. On the deck I wanted to incorporate an accent strip along the feature line, but I needed a way to maintain the contrasting color despite staining the whole boat. The hull also has a chine line that complicates stripping a bit.

Fiberglassing

Fiberglassing of the Petrel runs a similar course to the other two boats. On this example, the outside of the hull was covered with 4-ounce S glass. The whole hull was covered with one complete layer. I applied a light fill coat to this layer before flipping the boat over and glassing the deck. Because S glass does not disappear as completely as E-glass, I opted for the 4-ounce E-glass on the deck where it receives less abuse but gets looked at more. This too received a light fill coat before I removed the deck from the forms and then removed the forms from the hull.

The inside of the hull received a layer of 6-ounce carbon-Kevlar hybrid cloth throughout. I rolled out the pieces across the hull instead of down the length. This uses the cloth more efficiently. I aligned the first piece so one edge was just behind the cockpit; in this way no seams are obvious from the outside.

The deck received 4-ounce S glass on the inside. The deck does not get the abuse of the hull, and the glass is lighter than hybrid fabric. This also allows the inside of the hatch covers to remain a natural wood color. Around the cockpit area I added a layer of carbon fiber fabric to beef up an area that can receive large loads when the boat is lifted and the paddler gets in and out.

Cockpit Recess

The Petrel's cockpit is recessed to give it a lower profile, which makes Eskimo rolls easier. The recess is a separate assembly that needs to be fitted into a deck cutout. The easiest material to use for this assembly is 3 mm Baltic birch plywood, but I wanted wood that matched the

Materials List

Item	Materials	Quantity
Strongback	15 ft. × 2 in. × 4 in. plywood box beam, engineered lumber 2 × 4, or aluminum extrusion	
Forms	2 in. MDF, particleboard, or plywood	1 sheet
Strips	3/16 in. × 5/8 in. square-edged western red cedar	≈1,000 linear feet of strips, approximately 35 board feet of lumber
Accent strips	3/16 in. × 1/16 in. maple	≈50 linear feet
Internal stems	22 in. × 4 in. × 1/2 in. western red cedar or other softwood	1 piece
External stems	36 in. × 3/4 in. × 1/8 in. maple or other hardwood	12 pieces
Coaming lip	80 in. × 1/4 in. × 1/16 in. assorted hard- and softwoods	12 pieces
Coaming recess and hatch lips	3 mm hardwood plywood	48 in. × 48 in.
Interior reinforcement	5.6 oz. 50 in. wide carbon-Kevlar hybrid cloth	12 yards
Exterior hull reinforcement	4 oz. 60 in. wide S glass	12 yards
Exterior deck reinforcement	4 oz. 50 in. wide E-glass	6 yards
Deck-hull interior joint tape	2 in. wide 9 oz. fiberglass or Kevlar tape	34 feet
Resin	epoxy	< 2 gallons
	stain	< 1 quart
	varnish	1 quart
	colloidal silica	< 1 quart
	wood flour	< 1 quart
Miscellaneous	carpenter's glue	< 1 quart
	hot-melt glue	< 1 pound
	CA Glue	1 4-ounce bottle
	Minicel foam seat	1
	backrest	1
	foot braces	1 pair
	weather stripping material	6 feet
	shock cord	3 feet

Figure 13-2. *Use this table as a guide for your material needs.*

strips. I made this assembly from cedar veneer reinforced with fiberglass and assembled it using a method similar to the stitch-and-glue technique used to make some plywood boats.

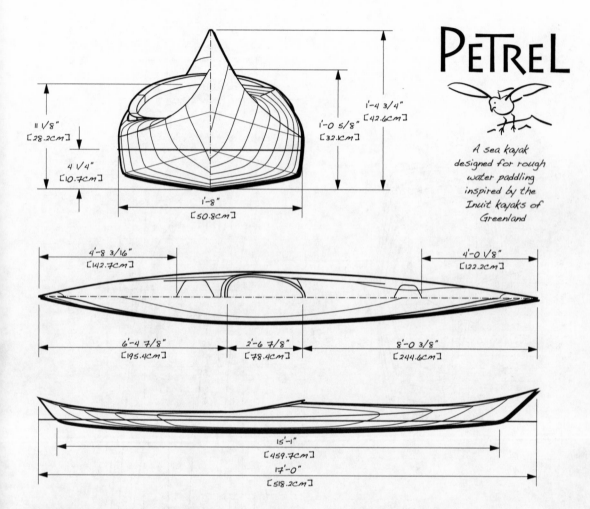

PETREL

A sea kayak designed for rough water paddling inspired by the Inuit kayaks of Greenland

Figure 13-3. *The Petrel is a full-blown sea kayak that is a lot of fun to paddle. Designed for rough water paddling, it is also suitable for exploring lakes or calm rivers. It makes a good touring boat for smaller paddlers or a day tripping boat for larger paddlers.*

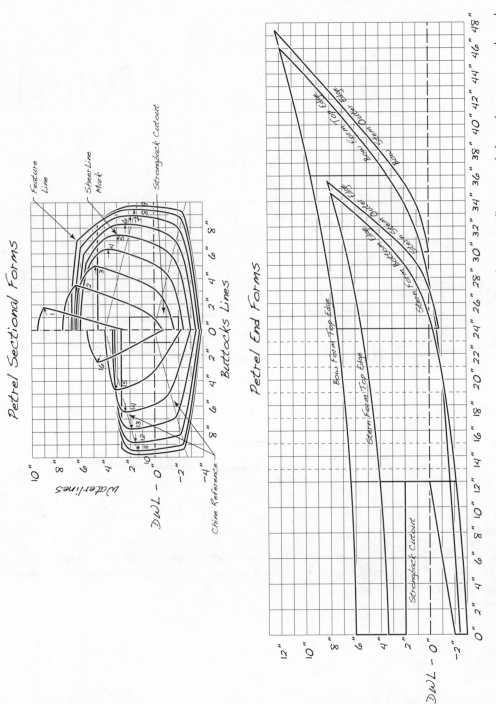

Petrel Sectional Forms

Feature Line

Sheer Line Mark

Strongback Cutout

Buttocks Lines

10"

8"

6"

4"

2"

DWL – 0"

-2"

-4"

Waterlines

Chine Reference

8" 6" 4" 2" 0" 2" 4" 6" 8"

Petrel End Forms

Bow Form Top Edge

Top Edge

Bow Form Outer Edge

Bow Stem Outer Edge

Stern Form Bottom Edge

Stern Form Outer Edge

Stern Form Outer Edge

Stem Edge

Bow Form Bottom Edge

Stern Form Top Edge

Stern Form Top Edge

Strongback Cutout

12"

10"

8"

6"

4"

2"

DWL – 0"

-2"

0" 2" 4" 6" 8" 10" 12" 14" 16" 18" 20" 22" 24" 26" 28" 30" 32" 34" 36" 38" 40" 42" 44" 46" 48"

Figure 13-4. *Loft out the forms full size. Here they are shown all stacked together, but you will want each form drawn separately and with both sides showing.*

Petrel Sea Kayak Offsets

Form:	#1	#2	#3	#4	#5	#6	#7	#8	#9	#10	#11	#12	#13	#14	#15	#16
Distance from Bow	-12"	-24"	-36"	-48"	-60"	-72"	-84"	-96"	-108"	-120"	-132"	-144"	-156"	-168"	-180"	-192"

Half-widths (inches from Centerline)

Elevation — Waterlines (deck & hull)

	#1	#2	#3	#4	#5	#6	#7	#8	#9	#10	#11	#12	#13	#14	#15	#16
9"	1 3/4															
8"	1 1/2															
7"	1 1/4															
6"	1	2 11/16	3 5/8	1 1/4	1 11/16	3 13/16	6 1/2	7 1/4								
5"	11/16	3 3/8	4 15/16	5 9/16	8/?	4 3/8	6 1/2	8	8 1/8						3/4	15/16
4"	7/16	3 3/4	4 13/16	5 5/16	8/?	4 3/4	5 5/16	8 3/4	4 1/4	4 9/16	8/?	6 3/4	6 1/4	5 5/8	4	2 5/16
3"	3/8	2 3/4	4 13/16	6 1/4	7 1/16	3 3/4	8	9 1/4	4 7/16	4 3/8	8/?	4 3/8	4 7/16	3/8	4	4 7/16
2"		2	4	5 15/16	4 7/16	4 1/8	8 3/16	9 7/16	4 11/16	4 11/16	8/?	8	4 11/16	3 3/16	4	8/?
DWL		8/?	4 13/16	5 5/16	4 5/16	8 15/16	8 15/16	9	6	4 3/16	8/?	8 3/16	4 13/16	3 3/16		8/?
-1"		9/16	4 7/16	8/?	6	4 1/8	5 15/16	6	4 11/16	4 3/16	8/?	6	4 1/2	3		8/?
-2"			3	8 1/8	8/?	6 15/16	8	3 5/16	8 3/8	8 5/8	8/?	6 5/16	4 5/16	8 3/8	3	
-3"			2	2 3/16	4 15/16	8 5/8	4 11/16	4	8 3/8	6 3/4	8/?	4 9/16	2 1/4	8 1/2	6/?	

Elevations (inches above DWL)

Half-width

	#1	#2	#3	#4	#5	#6	#7	#8	#9	#10	#11	#12	#13	#14	#15	#16
9"								3 1/2			2 3/8	2 7/8				
8"								5 1/8			2 13/16	2 5/8	2 3/4	2 7/8		
7"			3 5/8	4 9/16	5 3/16	8/?	4 7/16	6	4 15/16		3 1/16	2 15/16	3	3		
6"			3 13/16	5 5/16	5 9/16	8 1/4	5 1/2	6 1/2	4 13/16		3 1/16	3 1/16	3 1/16	3 1/16		
5"		6 13/16	3 13/16	8/?	5 3/4	8 3/8	5 3/16	3 3/8	4 3/16		3	8/?	8 3/16	4 1/16	3 1/16	
4"		6 13/16	3	8 5/8	5 9/16	6	4 1/16	3 5/8	4 11/16		3 3/16	8/?	8 3/16	3	3 3/4	
3"		4 11/16	3 3/8	6	6	6	4 1/2	3 3/4	4 11/16		3 3/16	8 3/16	4 3/16	8 5/8	3 1/4	8/?
2"		4 1/4	8 1/8	6	6 9/16	4 1/2	2	4 3/4	4 11/16		3 3/16	8 3/16	4 3/4	8 3/8	4 3/4	8/?
1"		8/?	8 1/8	4 7/16	3	4 1/4	2 1/2	4 15/16	4 15/16	3 13/16	3 5/8	4 7/8	4 11/16	3 7/8	1	3 3/16
Centerline	8 3/8	4 1/4	8 3/8	6	8/?	4 1/2	2	2	3	3	3 7/16	4 7/8	4 3/8	3 3/8	3 3/8	3 5/16
Keel	9 1/2	8/?	8/?	4 1/4	3	3/4	2 1/4	3/4	4 15/16	8 15/16	8 5/8	4 7/8	4 3/8	3	1 1/4	1 1/4

Deck Buttocks

Hull Buttocks

	#1	#2	#3	#4	#5	#6	#7	#8	#9	#10	#11	#12	#13	#14	#15	#16
	7 1/16	3 1/2	8 5/8	2 9/16	2 7/8	3 3/8	3 1/16	3/4	4 15/16	8 15/16	8 5/8	4 7/8	4 3/8	3	1 1/4	1 1/4
		2	8 1/2	4 3/4	2 2	4 1/4	2	3	4 7/16	4 3/16	3 1/16	8 3/16	8 5/8	4 1/16	3 3/16	3 3/16
		4 3/4	1 1/4	4 9/16	3 3/4	4 1/16	2 1/4	5 3/16	4 7/16	3 9/16	3 1/16	8 3/16	8 5/8	4 1/16		
				4	2 1/2	4 1/2	2 13/16	3	4 7/16	4 1/4	3/4	4 5/16	2 13/16	3 3/16		
					3 9/16	4	2 1/2	4 3/16	4 3/16	3	3 1/16	8 3/16	2	3 3/16		
						1/4	3 3/4	6 13/16	3	8 15/16	8 5/8	4 9/16				
								7	4	8 5/8	4 3/4	8 3/8				
								6 5/16			8 1/2	8 1/2				

	#1	#2	#3	#4	#5	#6	#7	#8	#9	#10	#11	#12	#13	#14	#15	#16
Sheet ½ Width	1 13/16	3 1/2	5	4 5/16	4 7/16	5 15/16	8 15/16	3/4	4 15/16	4 3/16	8 5/8	2 15/16	4 7/16	4 7/16	4 11/16	2 1/2
Sheet Height	9 5/8	6 5/8	4 7/8	3 3/16	4 7/8	3 3/4	2 1/16	4 13/16	3 3/16	4 3/16	3 3/4	6 1/16	4 7/8	2 7/16	4 3/4	4 3/4
Combing Edge ½ Width			8 3/4				15/16	15/16	3		3/4	2				
Combing Edge Height												7 1/8				
Deck Feature ½ Width						5 15/16	6 3/16	7	4 15/16		4 3/4	15/16				
Deck Feature Height						5 3/4	6 1/4	6 5/16			4	8 1/2				

Figure 13-5. The offsets for a kayak are the same as for other boats, but since the boat has a deck the table includes two sets of buttocks lines: one set for the deck and the other for the hull. The sheerline data define the seam between the deck and hull, where you will start stripping. This design has feature lines on the deck where there is a chine-like corner. Everywhere else the data points should be connected with a smooth, fair line. The cockpit edge indicates the location of the recess area.

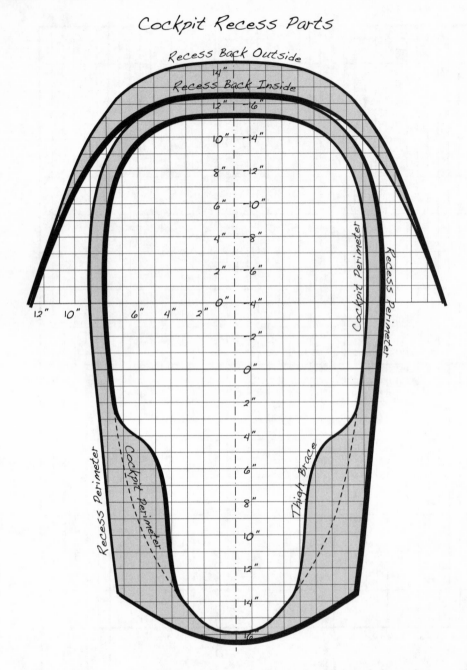

Cockpit Recess Parts

Figure 13-6. *The cockpit recess is made of two pieces assembled using stitch-and-glue techniques. The recess back lowers the cockpit below the level of the deck so the top of the coaming is about even with the back deck. The grid lines in this illustration correspond to the two offset tables, but the zero point is different on each part, thus the two sets of numbers going up the middle. The numbers on the left correspond to the recess back; the numbers on the right are for the larger recess part.*

Cockpit Recess

Longitudinal Position	Half-Widths		
	Recess Perimeter	Cockpit Perimeter	Thigh Brace
-16 3/8	0		
-16	4 5/16		
-15 3/8		0	
-15	6 3/16	3 9/16	
-14	7 3/16	5 3/8	
-13	7 13/16	6 1/4	
-12	8 1/4	6 13/16	
-11	8 9/16	7 3/16	
-10	8 3/4	7 7/16	
-9	8 15/16	7 5/8	
-8	9	7 3/4	
-7	9 1/16	7 13/16	
-6	9 1/8	7 13/16	
-5	9 1/8	7 13/16	
-4	9 1/8	7 13/16	
-3	9 1/16	7 3/4	
-2	9	7 11/16	
-1	8 7/8	7 5/8	
0	8 13/16	7 1/2	
1	8 11/16	7 3/8	
2	8 5/8	7 1/4	
3	8 1/2	7 1/16	7 1/4
4	8 7/16	6 15/16	6 1/4
5	8 5/16	6 3/4	5 1/4
6	8 3/16	6 9/16	4 13/16
7	8 1/8	6 5/16	4 9/16
8	8	6 1/16	4 7/16
9	7 15/16	5 3/4	4 3/8
10	7 13/16	5 5/16	4 5/16
11	7 11/16	4 7/8	4 3/16
12	7 9/16	4 5/16	4 1/16
13	7 7/16	3 5/8	3 13/16
13 1/2	7 3/8	<-Corner	
14	6 9/16	2 7/8	
15	4 13/16	2	
15 7/8		0	
16	2 1/2		
16 3/8	0		

Cockpit Recess Back

Distance from Centerline (inches)	Height above Baseline	
	Inside	Outside
0	12 5/8	14 1/2
1	12 5/8	14 1/2
2	12 9/16	14 7/16
3	12 1/2	14 3/8
4	12 5/16	14 1/8
5	12	13 13/16
6	11 1/2	13 5/16
7	10 13/16	12 5/8
8	9 7/8	11 1/2
9	8 5/8	10 1/16
10	6 15/16	8 1/8
11	4 15/16	5 9/16
12	2 5/8	2 7/8
13	0	0

Figures 13-7 and 13-8. *These two tables of offsets correspond to Figure 13-6. The large part includes the outer perimeter, the inner perimeter and the optional thigh brace area. The piece at the back of the recess which gets the cockpit down below the rear deck level has its own set of offsets.*

Petrel Stern Form

Length	(Height above DWL – Inches)		
	Top Edge	Bottom Edge	Stem Outer Edge
0	3 3/8	-3	
2	3 7/16	-2 7/8	
4	3 9/16	-2 13/16	
6	3 5/8	-2 5/8	
8	3 3/4	-2 1/2	
10	3 7/8	-2 5/16	
12	4 1/16	-2 1/8	
13	4 1/8	-2 1/16	
14	4 3/16	-1 15/16	
15	4 5/16	-1 13/16	
16	4 7/16	-1 11/16	
17	4 9/16	-1 9/16	
18	4 5/8	-1 7/16	
19	4 3/4	-1 1/4	
20	4 7/8	-1 1/8	
21	5 1/16	-15/16	
22	5 3/16	-3/4	
23	5 3/8	-1/2	
24	5 1/2	-1/4	-13/16
25	5 11/16	0	-9/16
26	5 7/8	3/8	-3/8
27	6 1/16	3/4	-1/16
28	6 1/4	1 5/16	3/8
29	6 7/16	1 15/16	15/16
30	6 11/16	2 13/16	1 11/16
31	6 15/16	3 3/4	2 11/16
32	7 3/16	4 13/16	3 7/8
33	7 7/16	5 15/16	5 1/16
34	7 3/4	7 1/8	6 1/4
34 5/8	7 15/16	7 15/16	
35 9/16			8 3/16

Petrel Bow Form

Length	(Height above DWL – Inches)		
	Top Edge	Bottom Edge	Stem Outer Edge
0	6 1/16	-2 7/16	
2	6 1/16	-2 5/16	
4	6 1/8	-2 3/16	
6	6 1/8	-2 1/16	
8	6 3/16	-1 15/16	
10	6 5/16	-1 13/16	
12	6 3/8	-1 5/8	
14	6 1/2	-1 1/2	
16	6 11/16	-1 3/8	
18	6 13/16	-1 3/16	
20	7 1/16	-1 1/16	
22	7 1/4	-7/8	
24	7 1/2	-5/8	
25	7 5/8	-7/16	
26	7 3/4	-5/16	
27	7 7/8	-1/8	
28	8 1/16	1/16	
29	8 3/16	1/4	
30	8 3/8	1/2	0
31	8 9/16	13/16	3/16
32	8 3/4	1 1/8	7/16
33	8 15/16	1 9/16	3/4
34	9 1/8	2 1/16	1 1/8
35	9 5/16	2 11/16	1 11/16
36	9 1/2	3 5/16	2 3/8
37	9 3/4	4 1/16	3 1/8
38	9 15/16	4 13/16	3 15/16
39	10 3/16	5 5/8	4 13/16
40	10 3/8	6 1/2	5 11/16
41	10 5/8	7 5/16	6 9/16
42	10 7/8	8 3/16	7 7/16
43	11 1/8	9 1/8	8 3/8
44	11 7/16	10	9 1/4
45	11 11/16	10 15/16	10 1/8
46	11 15/16	11 15/16	11
47			11 15/16
47 7/16			12 5/16

Figures 13-9 and 13-10. *The offsets for the bow and stern forms are both in the same format with four columns. The first column gives a location along the length of the form, starting from the interior end and proceeding out toward the tips of the boat. The second column defines the top edge of the form, and the third column the bottom edge. These two lines meet at the tip of the form. The final column indicates the outer edge of the interior stem. The interior stems will take up the space between this line and the bottom edge of the form.*

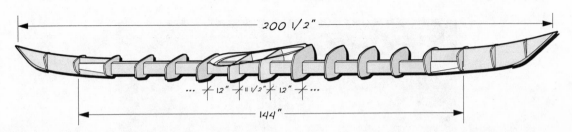

Petrel Strongback Setup

Figure 13-11. *The strongback is set up with the forms 12 inches apart except for the middle two forms where the spacing is 11½ inches. This way the strips are always touching the forms right on the outer edge of the form. This illustration shows the cockpit recess assembly where it will eventually go; you don't need to mount it at this time.*

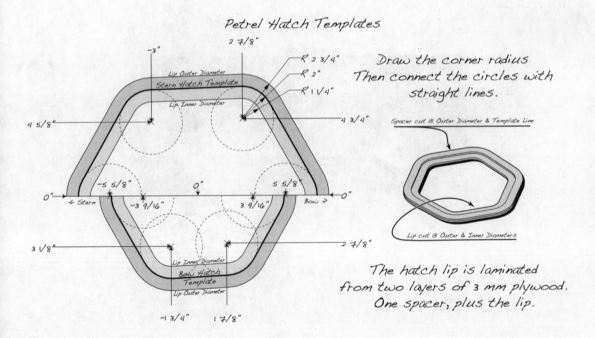

Petrel Hatch Templates

Draw the corner radius
Then connect the circles with
straight lines.

The hatch lip is laminated
from two layers of 3 mm plywood.
One spacer, plus the lip.

Figure 13-12. *The hatches are defined by drawing six 2-inch-radius circles that are connected by straight lines. The hatch cover is the part cut out of the deck along these lines. The cover is supported by a lip that is glued under the deck, and space for the gasket is provided by a spacer. The lip has an inner diameter that is ¾ inch smaller than the hatch and extends ¾ inch under the deck. The spacer inner diameter is the same as the hatch and also extends ¾ inch under the deck. See Figure 13-3 on page 227 for the location of the hatches on the deck. There is no magic in the shape of these hatches or their location. If you think you have a better idea, feel free to improvise.*

Figure 13-13. Cut out the forms with a band saw. Since this boat
will be built on an internal strongback, cut a hole in the middle. Drill
starter holes in two opposite corners, then cut the rectangle with a
jigsaw.

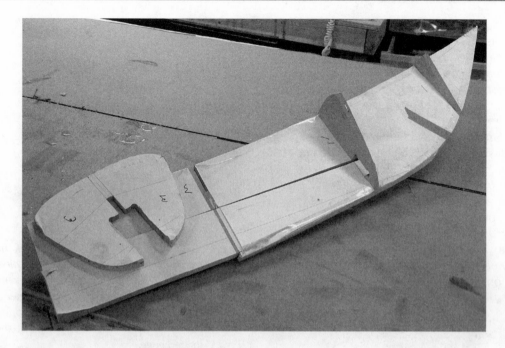

Figure 13-14. *Since I use a hollow aluminum extrusion for the strongback, I cut the end forms to slide inside the tube. The form will be centered in the tube with spacers planed for a snug fit on either side. The forms have been cut to interlock with the end forms, which saves a little glue.*

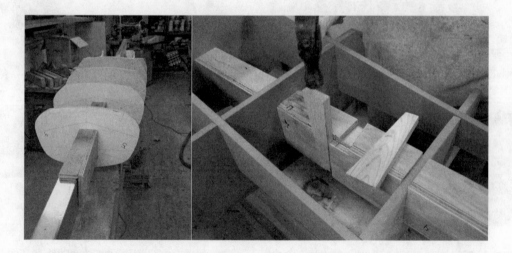

Figure 13-15. *If the holes on the forms are cut accurately, they will fit snugly over the strong-back, assuring accurate alignment. The only remaining requirement for an accurate setup is getting the spacing right. This is accomplished with L-shaped spacers. The form spacing for this boat is 12 inches, and the form thickness is ½ inch, so the spacers need to be 11½ inches long. I glued up the spacers in long pieces and cut them to length on the table saw.*

Place the forms on the strongback with spacers in between. Install the end forms in the ends and secure them in place with screws so the spacers are all snug. Then remove the middle spacer and replace it with a spacer cut to accept wedges. These wedges secure the forms tightly in place.

Use the bow and stern form offsets to create a full-size pattern of the bottom edge and stem outer edge end forms. Trace these lines onto your ½-inch-thick cedar. Cut along the stem outer edge line, then use this as a guide to trace the bottom edge line on the other side of the board. Mark a centerline along the stem outer edge. The bevel is defined by a straight line between the centerline and the bottom edge line on both sides of the board.

Figure 13-16. The inner stem of the kayak has a gradual curve that can be cut out of a solid piece of wood. Here the stem pattern is traced on western red cedar planed to ½ inch thickness. Cut the outer edge on a band saw and then plane both sides to form a bevel back to the back edge line. The result should be a V-shaped edge.

Figure 13-17. When the bevel is complete, cut the V-shaped stem off the board following the line for the back edge.

Figure 13-18. A closed boat like a kayak may have a constantly changing bevel between the deck and hull. This rolling bevel is indicated by temporarily clamping scrap strips at the sheerline so that they bisect the angle between the deck and hull. Use these scraps as guidance for planing the bevel on the first sheer strip, that is, the topmost strip on the sides of the hull.

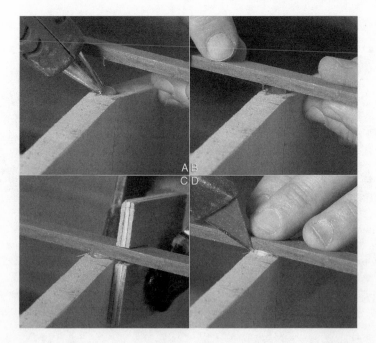

Figure 13-19. *Hot-melt glue is a substitute for staples. A small dot (A) holds the strip in place until you hit the forms with a hammer. Aim for a dot of glue about ⅛ to ¼ inch in diameter. Press the strip firmly onto the form (B). A U-jig helps hold the strip in place until the glue cools (C). Too much glue makes it harder to break off the forms, and any squeeze-out needs to be cut away (D).*

Figure 13-20. *The first strip follows the sheerline (bottom strip), and the second follows a more straight line. This second strip actually follows a diagonal line that is parallel to the run of the chine. In this way, by the time you strip up as far as the chine, the strips will approximately follow the chine so the joint with the next strip will be easier than it would be if it went in some other obscure direction.*

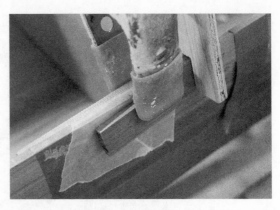

Figure 13-21. *If you need to make a lot of butt joints, a little miter box will provide accuracy and consistency. I just took a block of pine a little wider than the strips, glued scrap plywood to the sides, and then cut a slot. Angle the cut across the box and also vertically. The specific angle is not very important as long as you use the same slot every time.*

Figure 13-22. *Butt together the strips cut with the miter box in place on the boat while stripping. Use waxed paper so the scrap strip used to help align the joint does not stick to the boat. Put masking tape on either side of the joint to hold the strips in place relative to the strip below.*

Figure 13-23. *Usually you only need to bevel a new strip to match the angle of a strip already installed. However, when you have a sharp angle between subsequent strips, you will get a stronger joint by beveling both adjacent strips. It is easier to bevel the first strip before it is installed, but you could use a rabbet plane to bevel after installation.*

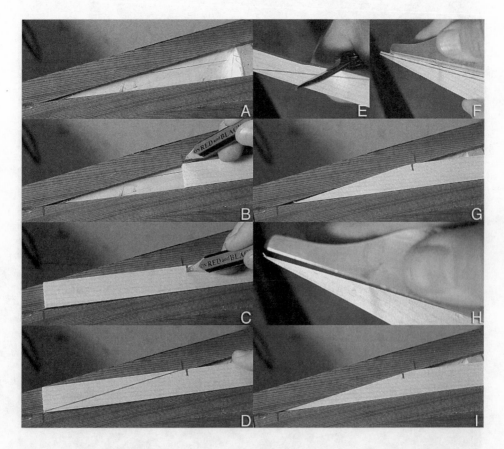

Figure 13-24. *The skill of strip-building comes in with tapering the ends of a strip to fit in with prior strips (A). Start by marking where the new strip hits the end strip (B). With the tip of the new strip aligned with the end of the gap (C), mark the length of the necessary taper. Use a straightedge to mark the taper (D). Cut off most of the scrap with a jackknife (E). Use a plane to come down close to the line (F). Check the fit (G). In this case the strip touches at the heel, leaving a gap at the toe. Hold your plane to match the visible gap (H). Plane away until you have a sharp point. Try the fit again (I) before applying glue. Notice by the location of the mark on the light strip that a good fit required planing more off this strip than originally estimated.*

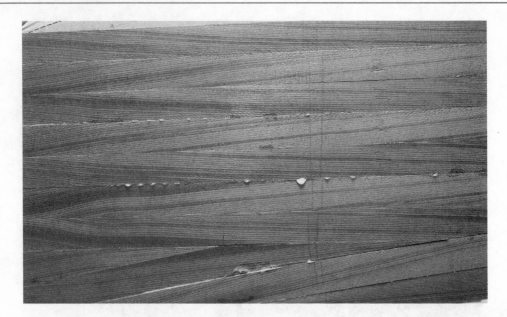

Figure 13-25. When book-matching strips you may want the grain to align across the whole face of the surface. The double line in this image was drawn across all the strips while they were aligned side by side on a workbench. Then they were fit together on the boat using these lines as alignment marks. This example uses an alternating book-matching scheme.

Figure 13-26. With long tapers you will likely need some support for the strip as you plane to assure an accurate joint. Here I am using the plank work surface mounted adjacent to the forms. A scrap strip supports the strip I am working on so I don't run into the table as I thin down the tip.

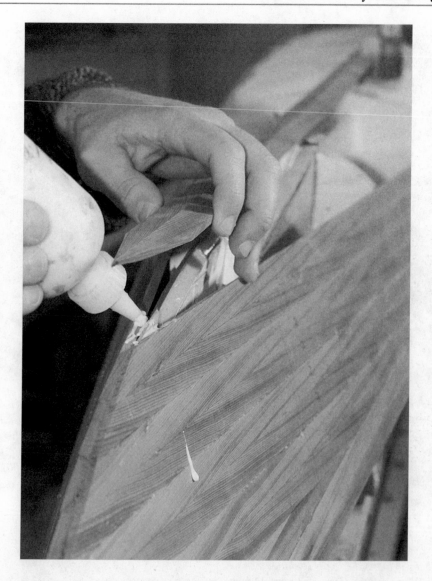

Figure 13-27. *The change from strips running parallel to the side to strips running parallel to the centerline is always a little tricky. Here I have two strips running down either side of the centerline. These strips both need to be beveled to form a tight joint. At the ends the bevel will be quite severe because the strips will twist to meet the strips on the sides. After the bevel has been fine-tuned, the ends need to be tapered to fit against the existing strips. The two strips are held tightly together with masking tape. I put the tape in place while the strips were lying flat relative to each other. When I bend the ends of the strips down to install them in place, the tape will pull them together even tighter. These strips will have a lot of stress in them, so you will need to clamp them in place after gluing them down.*

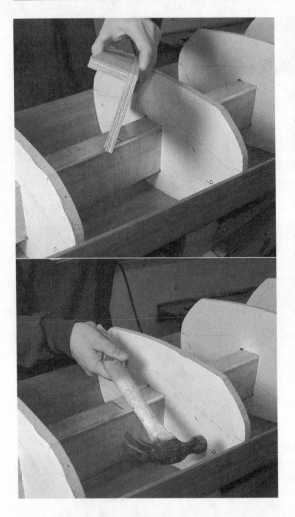

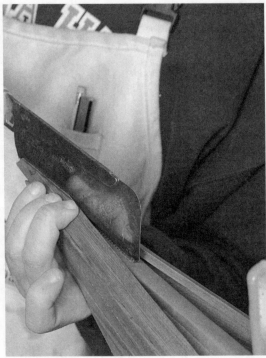

Figure 13-29. *You start the deck much like the hull. This time match your rolling bevel to the bevel on the top strip of the hull. The ends of this design meet in a V-shape that requires a matching taper on the strips approaching from both sides. Rough this out with a plane and then fine-tune it by dragging a saw through the seam.*

Figure 13-28. *When the hull is completely stripped, you can flip over the boat onto some foam cradles or slings. Since it will be harder to do after the deck has been installed, I knock the forms free now. Remove the wedges from the middle spacer and lift out the other spacers. Hit the forms with a hammer to break the hot-melt glue holding on the strips. Make sure you break free the end forms as well. When they are all free (so you will eventually be able to remove the hull), insert the spacers back in place.*

Of course, you could avoid much of this work by using the same bottom pattern as the Nymph, but I like the look of this better.

The sheer strips on the deck are not glued to the sheer strip on the hull. You will need to get the forms out somehow, and this will allow you to lift the deck off later. Just hot-melt-glue the strips to the forms. To help keep the strips in place across the sheer joint, I run some strips of masking tape along the joint between the deck and hull. This will be cut with a utility knife later.

Figure 13-30. The deck has a feature line, or crease, near the cockpit. I wanted the strips to look like they go straight across this crease, but I also wanted to put a light-colored accent strip at the crease. I installed a temporary strip below the feature line to support the ends of the strips above the feature line. I also cut a very thin strip of maple. Here I am temporarily taping this thin strip of wood to the temporary support strip. This will create a light-colored strip in the finished boat. As I fill in the strips above the feature line, I will glue their ends to this maple piece, removing the tape as it gets in the way. After I have finished filling in above the feature line I will remove the temporary support strip and fill in below. The thin maple strip will remain in place.

Figure 13-32. *With careful marking, cutting, and fitting I was able to make the strips on either side of the line continue with minimal interruption of the grain.*

Figure 13-31. *To make it appear that the strips continue across the feature line, I needed to cut the strip in half along the taper line as close as possible so almost no wood was lost. I marked the taper, cut it with a saw, then adjusted the fit with a plane. I kept the other half in a safe place until I had removed the temporary support strip, then fit the taper in as an apparent continuation of the strip above the feature line. Some wood was lost in the cutting and planing process, but it is close enough to achieve the appearance of one piece of wood.*

Figure 13-33. *The area around the cockpit is recessed by making a thin wood insert. In this case I used stained western red cedar veneer with fiberglass cloth on the underside as reinforcement. I have also used 3 mm aircraft-style plywood in similar applications on other boats.*

I glued the cockpit recess pattern to the material with spray adhesive. Since I wanted the grain to be symmetrical on either side, I folded the pattern in half, adhered one side, and then folded over the other side. The notches in the fold helped me determine it was correct after I was done.

The recess is in two pieces. I glued each pattern to the material, in-line and close together to help the grain match as well as possible. Then I cut out the parts (use a band saw or jigsaw), and cleaned up the edges with a block plane and sanding.

You want at least one layer of fiberglass going from the deck onto the coaming riser both inside and out. You also want a layer of fiberglass going all the way around the lip. This is a great place to see what bias-cut strips of fiberglass are capable of.

Figure 13-34. Bend the parts of the cockpit recess and tape them together. Then spot-weld the pieces together with CA glue.

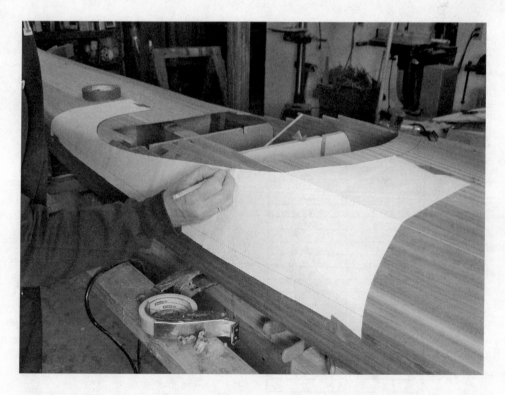

Figure 13-35. The cockpit fits into the deck in a specific location, following a specific curve. The location and curve are provided by a pattern. Mark the curve with a pencil.

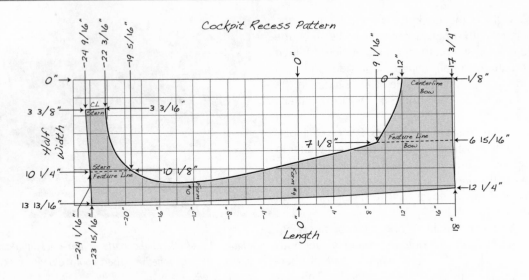

Figure 13-36. Use this template to trim the shape where the cockpit recess will be cut after stripping up the deck. Use the locations of forms 9 and 10 to determine where to place the pattern.

Petrel Cockpit Cutting Template

	Length	Half-Width
Center line Stern	-22 3/16	3 3/8
	-22 3/16	4
	-22	5 7/16
	-21 15/16	6
	-21 3/16	8
	-20	9 9/16
	-19 1/2	10
Feature Line Stern	-19 5/16	10 1/8
	-18	10 13/16
	-16	11 3/8
	-14	11 9/16
Form #10	-12	11 7/16
	-10	11 1/4
	-8	10 15/16
	-6	10 9/16
	-4	10 1/8
	-3 1/4	10
	-2	9 3/4
Form #9	0	9 1/4
	2	8 13/16
	4	8 3/8
	5 3/4	8
	6	7 15/16
	8	7 7/16
Feature Line Bow	9 1/16	7 1/8
	9 3/4	6
	10	5 5/8
	10 7/8	4
	11 11/16	2
Center line Bow	12	0

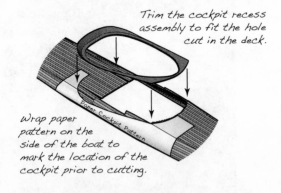

Trim the cockpit recess assembly to fit the hole cut in the deck.

Wrap paper pattern on the side of the boat to mark the location of the cockpit prior to cutting.

Figures 13-37 and 13-38. Align the index lines for form 9, form 10, centerline bow, and centerline stern with their respective features on the boat. Use the template to trace the cockpit outline on the deck. It is important that the corner at the bow feature line fall on that feature. Aligning the stern feature line is less critical.

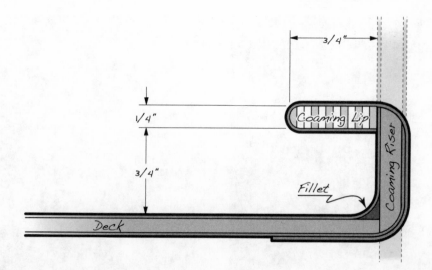

3/4"

1/4"

3/4"

Coaming Lip

Coaming Riser

Fillet

Deck

Figure 13-39. *Fabricating the cockpit coaming takes several steps. Some of these steps may be moved around. For example, I cut the cockpit hole first and put the coaming lip on later. You may find that the timing of when you are ready to do things differs. In this example, the coming riser would have been installed before any glassing was done. The lip was installed after glassing the outside, and then a layer of glass was applied from the underside of the deck up and over the lip.*

Figure 13-40. *You can use a jigsaw to cut out the cockpit area, but it tends to cut a rough line. A Japanese saw makes a cleaner cut, but it does have a little trouble cutting a curve. I used the flexible tip of a Japanese "beading" saw to make the cut. Approach the feature line from both sides and avoid cutting too far.*

Figure 13-41. *After using a saw to rough out the cockpit area, trim it to fit the recess assembly using chisels, planes, rasps, and/or sandpaper. Start with the hole a little undersized and work around the edges until a tight fit is created.*

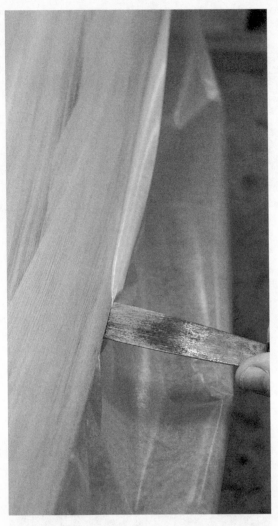

Figure 13-42. *Apply glue to the edge of the recess assembly and secure it in place with strapping tape.*

Figure 13-43. *Slide a sheet of waxed paper in between the deck and hull to protect the other half as you stain and epoxy. The seam may be quite tight—I find that a putty knife helps coax the paper into the sheer seam.*

After installing the recess, you can fair the deck and hull with a scraper, planing and sanding as needed. You will need to flip the boat over a few times. Be sure to get a smooth transition across the deck-hull joint. The deck and hull are being held together with a little bit of masking tape on the inside. This is not that secure a connection, so you need to be careful along the seam. Sand up through 120-grit sandpaper. Slip a utility knife into the sheer joint to cut the tape on the inside. Insert waxed paper between the deck and hull to protect the lower piece while you apply stain or epoxy.

Figure 13-44. Non-oil-based stains are often very quick drying. To get a smooth, even color you need make your rag quite wet with stain. If your rag becomes dry it will not fill up the grain and the stain will become blotchy. Move quickly, continuously rewetting your rag. You may be able to even out the color by wiping it all down with a rag soaked in a suitable solvent. Two coats of stain will result in more even coverage, but will be darker. Let the stain dry thoroughly before flipping the boat over to stain the other side. Here I am staining right over the accent stripe. I will clean the stain off in the next figure.

Figure 13-45. It is very hard to create a crisp edge with stain because it soaks under masking tape very easily. You can stain right over any transition, then scrape off the stain. Here I stained the whole boat and then scraped the stain off the maple feature line with a modified utility knife blade.

Figure 13-46. After the epoxy has begun to cure, you can trim off excess glass. It is best to do this trimming while the epoxy is still green, or a little soft. How soon after applying the resin this is depends on the epoxy you are using and the temperature in your shop. I usually check a couple of hours after finishing the fiberglassing.

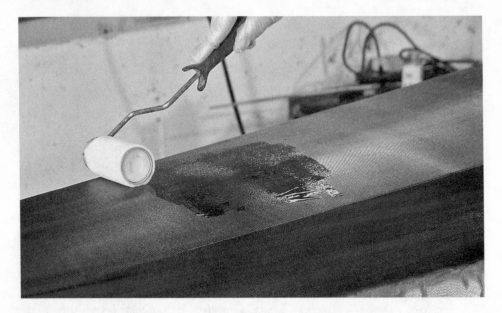

Figure 13-47. You can build up the fill coat slowly using a roller to add multiple, thin coats. On this boat I am going to apply another complete layer of glass across the hull and up onto the deck, after joining them together. Because of this I do not want to apply a fill coat that completely fills up the weave texture. This would result in a thick layer of epoxy between the layers, which would add weight but not much strength. I do, however, want to fill up the weave enough at this time so that it does not trap crud before I'm ready to apply the second layer of glass. Rolling on a moderately light coat will get the job done for now.

Figure 13-48. I installed a feature strip of light-colored contrasting wood along the top edge of the hull after the rest of the outside had been stained and fiberglassed. I glued it down and secured it with tape. After installation you can glass the inside. The outside will be reinforced when the deck is attached and the seam is glassed.

Figure 13-49. *To help ease the corner in the hard chine of the hull, pipe some epoxy thickened with wood flour into the area and then press it in with a plastic spoon. Lay the interior reinforcing fabric over this while it is still wet. Obviously, with fiberglass this would show, but it doesn't with carbon-Kevlar hybrid cloth. Mix the dookie schmutz for the fillet to a peanut-butter-like consistency, then place it in a 1 gallon ziplock plastic bag. Cut off one corner and use it like a cake decorator to place a bead of schmutz into the chine. This is a good practice wherever you have a sharp inside corner that will be hard to get the fabric to conform to.*

Figure 13-50. *The cockpit has a coaming around the hole. Start at the front and back of the coaming and glue a series of strips vertically into the hole to create the vertical part, or riser. Proceed down each side. You can't glue the strips to the edge of the hole in the thigh brace area, so instead glue their ends and stand them up in place. While this is not strong at the moment, once it is all fiberglassed, it will be plenty tough. At the transition at the end of the thigh brace, the strips change from being end-glued on top of the deck to being side-glued to the edge of the hole. Use a utility knife to carve the end. Proceed around the full circumference of the cockpit. Use hot-melt glue to hold everything in place until the fiberglass and epoxy are applied. Use a wedge-shaped strip to close up the final gap.*

Figure 13-51. *Clean up the hot-melt glue that squeezed out between the riser strips with a scraper. There will often be a small bead of glue at the bottom of each strip. This can be cut off with a utility knife. Smooth out the outside of the riser with a rasp and then sandpaper. Since the outside will be partially hidden by the lip, you don't need a perfect surface here. If you want to stain this area, do so after sanding, then paint the outside with epoxy, pipe in dookie schmutz to make a fillet, and apply a couple of layers of bias-cut fiberglass.*

Figure 13-52. When you turn over the deck you can trim off the bottom ends of the coaming riser strips. First clean out any hot-melt glue squeeze-out. The glue will quickly gum up any sandpaper or rasp. I use a high-speed right-angle grinder to bring the strips down even with the deck interior. A 36-grit disk makes quick work of the task even if it does send dust everywhere. You need to be careful, as it will grind through anything without a second thought. The disk may also be handheld to round over the edge after it has been trimmed.

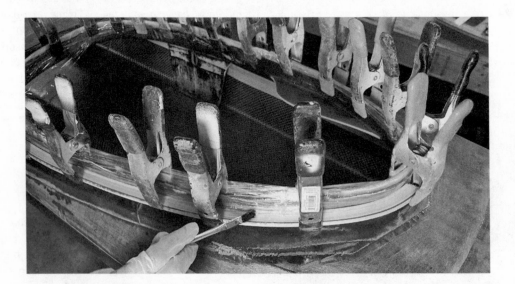

Figure 13-53. I usually finish the coaming at this time, but you could do these steps anytime after installing the riser. I use the coaming riser as a form to laminate the coaming lip. The strips should be about ³⁄₁₆ to ¼ inch wide and about ¹⁄₁₆ to ⅛ inch thick to make the bends. You will need enough strips to make a lip ¾ to 1 inch wide. Wrap the coaming riser with tape or stretch wrap (either plastic food wrap or binding wrap available at office supply or woodworking stores) so the laminations do not end up glued in place yet. The strip length should be just short of long enough to go all the way around the cockpit.

Figure 13-54. *Since the laminations are not completely around the front of the cockpit, you need to finish off the front. Trim the ends of the lamination at a tangential angle with the coaming riser, creating a smooth curve across the front. Cut a piece of 3/16-inch-thick curly maple to fit across (you could also laminate pieces instead).*

Figure 13-55. *After the coaming lip is installed, trim off the excess riser above the lip with a coping saw, grind and sand the top smooth, and round over all the corners. The inside surface of the coaming riser is not glassed over yet, but you could have. Here I wrapped one piece of bias-cut 4-ounce cloth from under the deck, up the riser, over the top of the lip, and then down under the bottom side of the lip onto the outside of the coaming riser.*

Figure 13-56. *Since the inside corner between the coaming riser and the thigh brace will be visible, I did not want to put in a messy dookie schmutz fillet. Instead I milled a piece of wood and bent it in place, securing it with CA glue. I used a cove bit to hollow out the edge of a board, then cut the small piece of molding off the board on a table saw. If desired, stain everything before installation. The piece was then trimmed and fiberglassed over.*

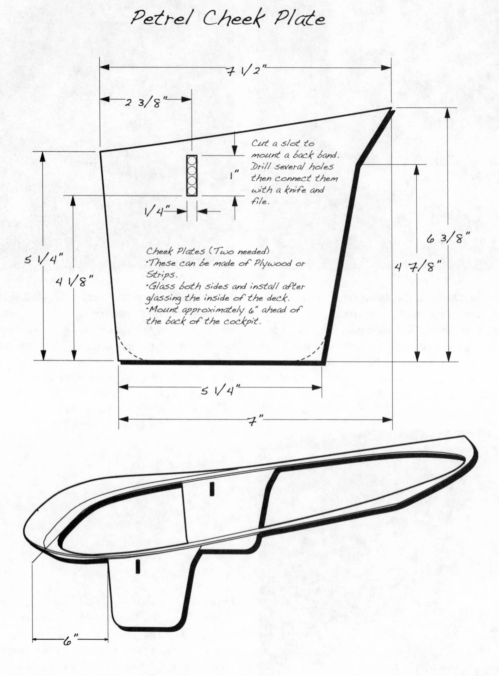

Petrel Cheek Plate

7 1/2"

2 3/8"

Cut a slot to
mount a back band.
Drill several holes
then connect them
with a knife and
file.

1"

1/4"

5 1/4"

4 1/8"

6 3/8"

4 7/8"

Cheek Plates (Two needed)
•These can be made of Plywood or
Strips.
•Glass both sides and install after
glassing the inside of the deck.
•Mount approximately 6" ahead of
the back of the cockpit.

5 1/4"

7"

6"

Figure 13-57. *The cheek plates help keep you seated in the center of the boat and provide a mounting point for a backrest. They are made from plywood or a flat panel built out of strips. The actual shape can vary, but the height and the angle of the top should stay approximately the same. These plates are mounted about 6 inches from the back of the cockpit.*

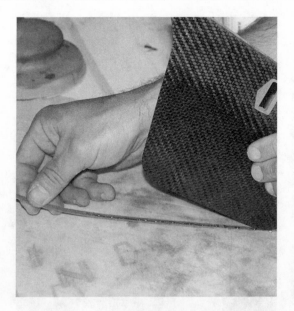

Figure 13-58. Bend a thin strip of mahogany around the edge of the cheek plate to cover any edge grain that was not sealed by epoxy. Dots of CA glue hold the edging to the cheek plate, which should be pre-sprayed with accelerant. Press the edge down against the worktable as you work around the edge to help keep the thin strip from breaking.

Figure 13-59. The backrest will eventually need a support to hold it up in back. This wooden pad eye is shaped to fit the deck, then glued in place with epoxy mixed with chopped fiberglass. It is then fiber-glassed over.

Lay all the coaming strips next to each other on a waxed-paper-covered workbench. Mix up a batch of epoxy with enough colloidal silica to make a mayonnaise-like consistency. Spread this mix in an even layer over all the laminations, then stack up the laminations as they will go on the boat.

It can take 20 to 30 clamps to hold the laminations in place. Starting centered at the back of the coaming, ease the laminations around the cockpit, bringing them around to the front. If they overlap at the front, clip them a little shorter with diagonal wire cutters.

After the glue cures, remove the clamps and the laminated lip. Scrape off the excess glue, and plane or sand the piece to a consistent thickness of about ³/₁₆ inch thick. Then glue the lip back onto the coaming riser. There should be about

³/₄ inch between the deck and the underside of the coaming lip.

It seems hard to believe that one piece of glass will wrap all that way while still conforming around the lengthwise curves of the coaming, but with thin bias-cut cloth and care, it can be done. Make the surfaces sticky by painting epoxy on everything before starting to apply glass. Then carefully lay on the strips of bias-cut cloth. Lightly dab the cloth in place and avoid tugging on it. I put on two complete layers of cloth, which makes the lip strong enough to lift the whole boat while fully loaded.

Tack the cheek plates in place beside the cockpit with CA glue, then fillet and glass them. Paint everything with more epoxy to seal any gaps between the edging and the wood underneath.

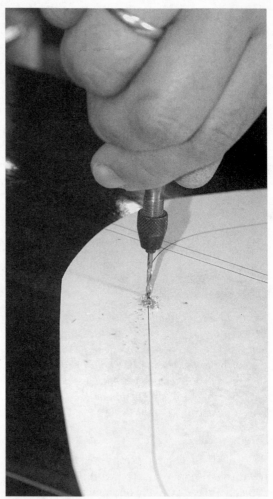

Figure 13-60. *I installed a retractable skeg on this boat. This involves installing a skeg box in the bottom of the boat. The skeg is offset to one side to reduce the chance of pebbles jamming it when dragging the boat up a beach. Install the skeg box by cutting a slot in the bottom of the boat. Here it is offset from the centerline to reduce the chance of a pebble getting jammed into it. As shown, the jigsaw is set at an angle to cut an approximately vertical hole. Insert the skeg box through the hole and tack it in with CA glue and fillet, then fiberglass it on the inside and trim it flush on the outside. After trimming, ease the corners and glass over the end grain on the outside.*

Figure 13-61. *Cut the hatches into the deck after it has been glassed on both sides. Start by spray-gluing on the pattern. Use a pin vise or similar tool to drill a series of small holes through the deck along the cut line, then open up this slot with a utility knife. Use a fine-bladed jigsaw to cut along the line.*

Figure 13-62. *The hatches need a spacer between the lip and the deck to allow for a gasket. The spacer is set in epoxy thickened with colloidal silica to make a mayonnaise-like glue. Try to clean up any squeeze-out while the glue is still wet. After the glue has set, clean up the inside edge of the hole.*

Cut the hatch lip with an inner diameter about ¾ inch smaller than the hole and with the same outer shape as the spacer. Glue the lip in place. After the glue has set, apply a fillet of dookie schmutz around the outer perimeter and glass the underside of the hatch.

Figure 13-63. *Tape around the outside of the hatch and apply a layer of 2-ounce bias-cut glass over everything. Use a utility knife to trim off next to the tape.*

257

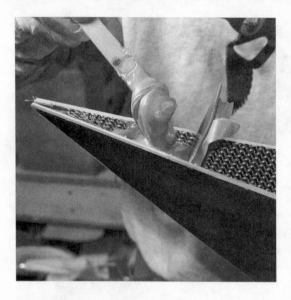

Figure 13-64. Make a dam to contain an end-pour. Strips of tape would do the job, but here I cut a piece of an old squeegee. Add as many microballoons to the epoxy as it can contain and still move a bit. Fill in behind the dam until the epoxy is even with the top of the sheer. Clean up the top surface with a rasp after the epoxy has cured. If you prefer, you can install a piece of wood instead of the epoxy; just be sure that all the grain is very well sealed so it doesn't absorb water and rot.

Figure 13-65. Sea kayaks typically have deck lines of shock cord to hold items such as water bottles on deck. For this boat, I ran the shock cord up through holes in the deck. To protect the end grain of the strips exposed by these holes, I created feed-through fittings. I made a pile of these feed-through fittings with a plunge router, a template, and router inlay bushing. I cut the outer shape with the sleeve off the inlay bushing, drilled a hole through the middle, and then cut the part of the board, leaving a ledge on the bottom. After cleaning these up on the sander, I taped the template securely to the deck, put the sleeve on the bushing, and cut a hole in the deck. The parts are pushed through from the inside, glued in place, sanded smooth, and then glassed over.

Figure 13-66. All epoxied surfaces should eventually get a coat of varnish or other UV-protective coating. For closed boats you may want to apply this finish to the inside before joining the deck and hull. A satin or matte finish looks good if you leave the fabric texture because it tends to tone down the appearance of the texture whereas a gloss finish highlights the texture.

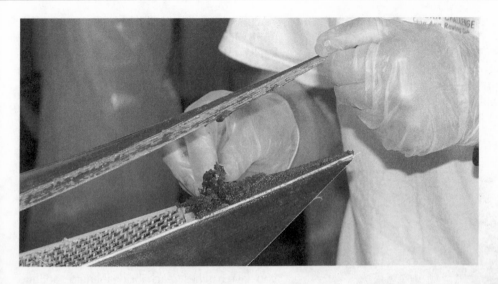

Figure 13-67. With a premade end-pour you need to secure the deck to the pour when you first start joining the deck to the hull. Spread enough thickened epoxy on the pour to securely glue down the deck. Carefully align the deck before taping it down with strapping tape.

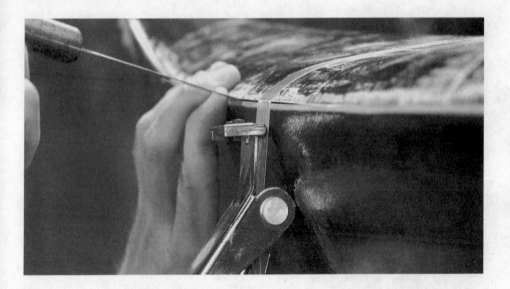

Figure 13-68. Align the rest of the deck-hull seam dry without any adhesive. Then hold it in place with strapping tape. (Fold over the free end of the tape on the roll so that when you peel off the tape you have something to grab.) If the deck does not align perfectly you can usually use hand pressure to push it into place; otherwise, slide a putty knife into the seam to lever it into alignment. Friction between the deck and hull keeps them in place; getting a lot of tension on the tape creates this friction. A tape dispenser with a cutter on the end will help you achieve this tension. Pull down hard on the packing tape as you align the seam, and press it down onto the hull securely before cutting it off the roll.

Use enough tape across the seam to assure that it does not spring loose as you work on it—about every 4 to 6 inches. Try to avoid making any wrinkles in the tape as this will allow epoxy to drip through. Run a strip of masking tape down the length of the seam, again avoiding wrinkles. Rub in the tape well to assure it sticks.

Figure 13-69. *Bonding the deck-hull seam is no fun, but it is over quickly, and it is really the best, strongest, lightest solution. As described in Chapter 9, you must run a length of prewoven tape down the inside seam. Here I am using a 1½-inch wide Kevlar tape. I'll roll it by hand as far down the seam as I can reach, then break out the brush-on-a-stick.*

Bond the deck-hull seam with woven tape on the inside. In this case I used 1½-inch-wide Kevlar tape, but fiberglass would be fine. In preparation, attach a chip brush to the end of a stick long enough to reach the end of the seam inside the boat from the cockpit (about 8 or 9 feet). Push a finishing nail through the other end of your brush-on-a-stick so the nail sticks out about 1 inch. Then presaturate the tape with epoxy by rolling it out on a worktable covered with waxed paper. Brush a liberal amount of epoxy on the tape so it is fully saturated. Brush a bit of epoxy on the seam with the brush-on-a-stick. Roll up the presaturated tape into a small, tight roll. Starting at the cockpit area, roll out the cloth as far down the seam as you can reach. If you have hatches, reach inside them to continue unrolling the tape.

When you get about to the end of your reach, lift the roll and unroll it back toward you. Undo the roll and carefully lay out and fold the tape on top of the seam in smooth, Z-folded layers without any twists. With the nail pointed up, get the stick inside the boat and hook the end of the tape onto the nail so that when you rotate the nail down, the tape can slide off. Slide the stick up into the end. Use enough tension on the tape to lift it up over the seam before gently laying the tape down onto the seam. Rotate the stick and unhook the nail.

If you don't get the tape aligned right away, it is usually easiest to pull the end back to where you can hook it on your stick and try again. You can use the brush end to move the tape a little bit; try to center the tape on the seam as best you can. When it is in place to your satisfaction, brush some more epoxy onto the tape.

Repeat this process for the other end. Let one side cure before flipping the boat over and working on the other side. When the epoxy has cured, peel off the strapping and masking tape and clean up the edge.

Reinforce the outside seam on this boat with another full layer of glass over the whole bottom of the boat, extending 1 inch onto the deck to secure the outside seam. You can also use lengths of bias-cut tape over the seam.

In this boat I used curly maple outer stem laminates, sequentially cut and glued up in order so they would look like one piece, but you can also accent the laminations by alternating types of wood.

After the glue cures, remove the tape. Grind, plane, or sand the laminations even with the hull surface. Avoid sanding into the existing glass. Round over the leading or trailing edge (depending on whether it's the bow or stern stem) to make a nice radius before laying several layers of bias-cut fiberglass over everything.

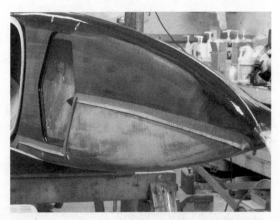

Figure 13-71. Low-viscosity epoxy runs off the boat quickly. This makes it hard to get a full fill coat on the sides. Here I have turned the boat on edge to help get the sides of the kayak filled up. Note that the bottom edge of the tape has been bent up to act as a drip edge, keeping drips from just running straight across the tape.

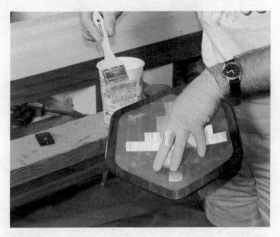

Figure 13-70. Next you need to laminate the outer stem in place on the ends. Prepare the ends by planing a flat chamfer about ½ to ¾ inch wide, fading away to nothing at the keel. Cut hardwood strips thin enough to make the bend (about ⅛ inch) that will build to a stack about as tall as the chamfer is wide. Glue these laminates together with epoxy; also apply glue to the chamfered end of the boat. Use strapping tape to bend and hold the stack tightly against the boat.

Figure 13-72. The edges of the hatch covers are covered with 2-ounce fiberglass cloth and then a couple of layers of epoxy. Making a handle out of tape makes it easier to hold onto the piece as you work.

Care and Feeding of Your Finished Boat

Compared with most wooden boats, strip-built boats don't need much maintenance. I typically do no more than put on a new coat of varnish before each season. Well, that's what I tell myself I will do. In actuality I don't usually get to it every year.

Everyday Treatment

The boat will last a long time with minimum maintenance. It is not indestructible but with some care and respect should last generations.

- Store the boat out of the sun when not in use.
- If the boat must be stored outside, it is best to keep it covered between uses.
- Do not leave the boat in the water for days at a time.
- Do not sit or stand in the boat while on dry ground or on sharp objects.
- Do not put a loaded boat down on sharp objects.
- Whenever possible, get in and out of the boat while in the water.
- Avoid dragging the boat across the ground.
- Avoid running into submerged objects.
- The boat will last the longest if stored indoors, away from extremes in temperature. Extreme heat will do more damage than cold.
- Empty and sponge out any standing water before storing. Store with the hatches open to let the bulkhead areas dry out. Salt water is not a problem, but it does dull the finish faster than fresh water, so rinsing the boat out with fresh water is a good idea.

Storage

The worst thing you can do to your boat is to put it out in the sunlight. Sunburn due to ultraviolet radiation breaks down epoxy and even paint and varnish eventually. Obviously, boats aren't as much fun to use inside as they are out on the water, so some sun exposure is desirable and pretty much mandatory. However, if at all possible, it is best to store your boats out of the sun and weather when not in use. Kick your car out of the garage—you're getting a new one of them in a few years anyway—and use the space to store your boat instead. If the rest of your family does not see the logic in this and you don't have enough room in the basement, you should try to throw a tarp over the boat and/or keep it in the shade. Rinsing the boat after use will help preserve the gloss finish. Sponge out any water in the bottom of the boat so it doesn't have an opportunity to find pinholes in the epoxy and fiberglass or freeze and open up any cracks.

I try to inspect the boat fairly frequently, looking for major scratches that may have reached the glass. If I hear a loud noise when I'm paddling over rocks, I'll take a look to make sure there was no damage that reached the wood.

Yearly Wear and Tear

Abrasion from pulling the boat up the beach will eventually sand off all the finish. It should be renewed about once a year. Wash the boat off and sand the area to be varnished. Paint on the replacement finish normally. Don't worry about getting a perfect finish on the bottom. If you're like me, the bottom will be scratched up again before you know it, so why bother trying for perfection?

The deck is another matter, though. Eventually, the inevitable mistakes are going to take their toll on the finish of the deck, which may signal that it's time to give the boat a complete refinishing. Here's how:

Remove all the hardware and lines mounted on the deck, and sand the boat until the gloss is gone everywhere. You will notice a change in tone along the surface as you sand through the varnish into the epoxy, and this is useful because you should avoid sanding too far into the epoxy. There is no need to remove all the varnish. Refinish as if you were working on a new boat. The results will probably look like new.

Bad Scratches

Some of the worst scratches will gouge through the varnish into the epoxy and fiberglass, but they're not of immediate concern. As long as they don't let water get to the wood, they don't need immediate attention. When you get a chance, you can paint some varnish onto the scratch to protect the epoxy. Rinse off the boat and scrub the scratch clean before varnishing. If it looks as though the fibers of the glass are separated from the epoxy, you may need to clean a little deeper. Wet down the scratch with a solvent such as lacquer thinner or acetone and scrub it clean, then varnish.

Dealing with Bruises

These boats are strong and will survive a lot of abuse with nothing more than cosmetic damage, but worse things happen sometimes. For example, you misjudge the timing of a wave as you pass over a rock and so, instead of passing over it, you're left teetering on the rock. If this is enough to cause a bruise that goes into the

wood, you should do a little extra work to prevent water damage.

A quick fix is to slap some varnish over the bruise to keep the water out for a while. Eventually you will need to do something more permanent.

Start by removing the damaged glass. Sand the damaged region and remove any loose glass. Feather the edges of the fiberglass so there is no sudden change in thickness. If the wood got wet, let it dry. If it got wet with salt water, rinse it off with fresh water first.

Cut out a piece of fiberglass the size of the sanded area and another slightly bigger than the area of exposed wood. If the area had more than one layer of glass on it, cut out another patch of intermediate size. Spread epoxy on the damaged area and lay on the patches starting with the largest and progressing to the smallest. Wet out each layer as you apply it. After the patch has cured, sand it smooth and revarnish it.

Patching Holes

You really did it this time. You misjudged a wave and got dropped on top of a sharp rock, and now you have a hole in the boat. This will take more effort to fix, but it's possible. Luckily this is most likely to happen near the center of mass of the boat. The reason this is lucky is that you need to be able to reach inside.

Start by cutting out all the damaged wood. You could just fit strips into the resulting hole, but your repair will be pretty obvious. If, however, you give the hole a ragged edge by cutting back every other strip a few inches, it won't show as much.

Use a razor saw to cut along the joints between strips and cut the ends off at different angles. Now you can fit and glue strips into these gaps.

After the glue dries, sand the patch smooth and fair. Now sand the glass off the original wood surrounding the patch, and fiberglass it in the manner I recommended for the bruise patch, laying down the pieces of fiberglass in order, largest to smallest.

You now need to glass the inside. Do your best to sand and fair out the new strips, and sand the glass surrounding the patch as well to prepare it for fiberglassing. Lay glass over the patch.

If you still have some of the original wood you used to build the boat, you should be able to make a good match. With a little care, you will be the only one able to see the damage.

Safety

There are a variety of risks attached to building and paddling a boat. Dust and fumes can cause long-term damage to your health, tools can remove your appendages, and the sea can drown you in your finished boat. Your safety depends on your good judgment. Recognize the risks, and act within your abilities. It is impossible to anticipate all the dangers, but with proper care the risks can be minimized.

Dangers in the Shop

Wood Dust

Wood dust caused by sawing may seem pretty benign because it's a natural product, but you need to be careful. Trees have had millions of years of evolution devoted to keeping bugs out of their hearts. In that time, they've developed some rather potent toxins. You should always remember to wear a dust mask while sawing and sanding.

Doing as much of the cutting and smoothing as you can outdoors will help. If you are buying new tools, look for tools with built-in dust collection.

Wearing a dust mask is often inconvenient, and some woods, such as cedar, smell very nice—but there's a good reason why cedar chests are used to store sweaters. It is not because they smell nice, nor is it because moths just don't like the smell. Cedar is toxic, and moths know to keep their distance when they smell it. Wear a dust mask.

Epoxy

Epoxy is relatively safe to work with, although as a petrochemical it can be dangerous when concentrated. Unlike polyester resin, it doesn't smell too bad, and it isn't as dangerous, but the fact that it doesn't stink doesn't mean it isn't a health hazard. Work in a well-ventilated space and wear a respirator. Read the manufacturer's material safety data sheet (MSDS). This should be available upon request from the manufacturer. The respirator should be designed to protect you from fumes. A dust mask should also be worn when sanding epoxy.

Epoxy Sensitivity. Many former users of epoxy had to give up working with the stuff because they became sensitized to it. These people are subject to severe reactions, including death, if they come in contact with uncured epoxy. You should not let uncured epoxy touch your bare skin. Wear long-sleeved shirts or a coverall such as a disposable paper "poopie suit." Use disposable gloves, and if they develop a hole, replace them. Instead of gloves you can get a barrier cream that provides some protection, but do not use it under gloves because it contains zinc oxide that combines with sweat to create a sensitizing agent. Resist testing new epoxy with your bare finger to determine whether it has cured.

Polyester Resin

Polyester resin smells really bad, and this is almost an advantage. It is hard to stand working with the stuff without a respirator; in fact, you'll find it more comfortable to work with a respirator than without.

Solvents

Powerful solvents such as acetone and toluene can be useful to have around. They can be used to thin epoxy or polyester resin. However, they are very dangerous and should be used with caution. Their highly volatile fumes should not be breathed. Never use a solvent to clean your skin. The solvents can easily enter your body through your skin, and they make it easier for the resin to enter your skin. *Never use a solvent as a hand cleaner.*

Wash your hands with soap and water or a waterless hand cleaner that is intended for cleaning up resin. Tools can be washed with white vinegar. Common white vinegar is very effective for softening and cleaning uncured epoxy. It is cheap, easy to get, and safe enough to eat. You should not use it to wash your hands, however. Unless you really need them, don't bother with any of the more powerful solvents for cleaning.

Fiberglass Dust

Fiberglass cloth is safe to work with. It is no more toxic than a soda bottle. It's when you're sanding it that problems start, although the long-term effects of breathing fiberglass dust are still uncertain. In my book (and this is my book) this means avoid it. Once again, wear a dust mask. There is certainly no harm in added protection.

The more obvious problem with sanding fiberglass is itching. The dust will cause a severe rash in some people. The rash goes away after a while with no apparent long-term effects, but until it goes away, it itches. Again, you should wear full-length clothing and work with good ventilation.

Your Uniform

A good uniform for working with epoxy and fiberglass is a Tyvek painter's suit with rubber bands holding the sleeves closed, rubber gloves on your hands, safety glasses, and a respirator or dust mask on your face. If you are putting your head anywhere near the wet epoxy (as when taping the interior seam) you should wrap your head and hair in a plastic bag. I am always a little afraid to let the neighbors see me dressed like this. I look like a science-fiction spaceman in this attire, but I stay clean and (I hope) healthy.

Hazardous Tools

Power tools have the ability to remove digits and limbs at worst, and draw blood at best. They should be treated with the utmost respect. Never put your fingers anywhere near the moving cutter. Use feather boards where possible. Move deliberately when using something that can cause such severe damage so quickly. Wear safety glasses whenever you use a tool with moving parts. Don't stand downrange from the spinning blade of your table saw where material ejected by a kickback may imbed itself in some unpleasant location.

Dangers in the Water

Hazardous Boats

Any activity involving taking a small boat out into open water is potentially deadly. There are no exceptions; it doesn't matter if you build a stable dinghy or a tippy canoe or kayak. There is no boat made that can protect you from all hazards on the water. Even the most seemingly benign conditions contain the elements to kill a boater. People have drowned in ankle-deep water, and most boating is more dangerous than that. Don't treat venturing out onto the water casually. Always wear a life jacket or personal floatation device (PFD). A PFD that is not already on your body when you enter the water will be almost impossible to put on once you are swimming. Floatation can be added to the boat to assure maximum buoyancy should the boat capsize and take on water. Learn as much about boating as you can before leaving the relative safety of the shore. It is impossible to make boating completely safe, but with proper precautions the dangers can be mitigated. Your boat can be broken, it can sink or capsize, you can fall out, and you could suffer a heart attack. Your boat can put you in a position where your life is in danger. Please take the precautions to protect yourself.

English and Metric Conversion Factors

The measurements used in this book are English units. The following conversions can be used:

- Multiply English units by the given factor to get metric units.
- Divide metric units by the given factor to get English units.

English Units	Factor	Metric Units
inches	2.54	centimeters
feet	30.48	centimeters
yards	0.9144	meters
pounds	0.454	kilograms
ounces	28.34	grams
fluid ounces	28.41	milliliters

Sources

Plans

Boat designs specifically intended for strip building have become increasingly easy to find. Although there are more plans for canoes and kayaks than for other types of boats, you can find designs for anything from rowing shells to high-performance sailboats.

- Aeneas Originals
  2401 Lower Valley Road
  Kalispell, MT 59901
  406-752-3202
  aeneasoriginals.com
  Ben Louden has plans for several sliding-seat rowing shells.

- Bear Mountain Boat Shop
  P.O. Box 191
  Peterborough, ON K9J 6Y8
  Canada
  877-392-8880; 705-740-0470
  bearmountainboats.com
  Bear Mountain is the home of Ted Moores, noted author of several books on strip-building boats. It offers traditional canoe designs as well as modern canoe and kayak designs by Steve Killing, as well as supplies, materials, and kits.

- Compumarine
  260 Camino Apolena
  Rio Rico, AZ 85648
  520-604-6700
  compumarine.com
  Compumarine offers cedar-strip designs for dinghies and a canoe.

- Glen-L
  9152 Rosecrans Avenue
  Bellflower, CA 90706
  562-630-6258
  glen-l.com
  This company offers kits and full-size plans for rowing boats and canoes.

- Green Valley Boat Works
  P.O. Box 20004, Pioneer Park Postal
    Outlet
  Kitchener, ON N2P 2B4
  Canada
  greenval.com
  Green Valley offers plans by designer John Winters for solo and tandem canoes and sea kayaks.

- Guillemot Kayaks
  54 South Rd
  Groton, CT 06340
  860-659-8847
  guillemot-kayaks.com
  My company offers full-size plans for the designs in this book as well as other canoes, rowboats, and kayaks.

- International Swift Solo
  c/o Bram Dally
  11223 136th Avenue East
  Puyallup, WA 98374
  253-848-4732
  single-handedskiffs.com
  This company offers plans and parts for
  a high-performance solo sailing skiff.

- Laughing Loon
  344 Gardiner Road
  Jefferson, ME 04348
  207-549-3531
  laughingloon.com
  Here you can find designs for solo
  canoes and sea kayaks by Rob Macks.

- Outer-Island
  7 Jeffrey Lane
  Branford, CT 06405
  outer-island.com
  This is the place for Jay Babina's Outer-
  Island sea kayak plans.

- Redfish Custom Kayak & Canoe
  Company
  153 Otto Street, Suite G
  Port Townsend, WA 98368
  360-808-5488; 360-379-1131
  redfishkayak.com
  Redfish offers plans and materials for
  several sea kayaks by Joe Greenley.

- Selway Fisher Design
  15 King Street
  Melksham, Wiltshire SN12 6HB
  United Kingdom
  44-1225-705074
  selway-fisher.com
  This company offers plans for canoes,
  kayaks, and other larger boats.

- Shearwater Boats
  83 Captain Perry Drive
  Phippsburg, ME 04562
  207-386-0129
  shearwater-boats.com
  My brother, Eric Schade, runs
  Shearwater Boats. He offers plans for sea
  kayaks and other boats.

Boat Design Software

- Free!Ship
  sourceforge.net/projects/freeship
  An open source boat design application.
  It can be used to design just about any
  kind of boat you can imagine.

- KayakFoundry
  blueheronkayaks.com/kayak/software/
      software.htm
  If you want to design your own kayak,
  this free software by Ross Leidy produces drawings of all the forms needed
  to strip-plank a kayak.

Tools and Materials

Some tools and materials are easily found at a
hardware store, but chances are good you will
have trouble tracking down some of the more
specialized items locally. If you live near the
water you may be able to find a boating supply
chandlery, but you may have to resort to mail-
order or online sources for some of the more
obscure things.

Lumber suppliers catering to custom home-
builders typically have a better selection of
wood than home centers. If they do not stock
the wood you want, they can often order it for
you.

Several companies now offer high-quality kits including all the materials to build strip-planked boats, and if you don't have all the tools to mill your own strips, you can find sources that will mill them for you. You could probably get a local cabinet shop to mill strips, but be sure you order enough on the first run, because they may not want to do it again.

- Adirondack Guideboat
  P.O. Box 144
  Charlotte, VT 05445
  866-425-3926
  adirondack-guide-boat.com
  Here you can find kits for Adirondack guideboats.

- Chesapeake Light Craft
  1805 George Avenue
  Annapolis, MD 21401
  410-267-0137
  clcboats.com
  Get kits for all the designs in this book as well as premilled strips, fiberglass, epoxy, and other boatbuilding materials.

- Essex Industries
  P.O. Box 374
  Mineville, NY 12956
  518-942-6671
  essexindustries.org
  Ash and cane canoe seats and accessories are available through Essex.

- Jamestown Distributors
  17 Peckham Drive
  Bristol, RI 02809
  800-497-0010; 401-253-3840
  jamestowndistributors.com
  This company offers a wide selection of boatbuilding tools plus fiberglass and other fabrics and epoxy.

- Newfound Woodworks
  67 Danforth Brook Road
  Bristol, NH 03222
  603-744-6872
  newfound.com
  Newfound Woodworks offers cove-and-bead strips and other building materials, as well as plans and kits for a variety of canoes, kayaks, and rowing boats.

- Shaw & Tenney
  20 Water Street
  Orono, ME 04473
  800-240-4867; 207-866-4867
  shawandtenney.com
  Oars, paddles, seats, and other outfitting hardware for canoes and rowing boats are the specialty of this company.

- Sweet Composites
  6211 Ridge Drive
  Bethesda, MD 20816
  301-229-2201
  sweetcomposites.com
  This is a mail-order source of reinforcing fabrics including fiberglass, carbon fiber, Kevlar, and hybrids. It also offers tools for working with these fabrics and epoxy.

- Woodcraft
  800-225-1153 (orders)
  www.woodcraft.com
  This is a mail-order site for woodworking tools, stains, and router bits that also has retail locations around the country.

Websites

Some well-selected keywords entered into your favorite search engine will provide a wealth of sites with worthwhile information about building boats, the strip-built method, and any other subject that you may want more background in. Many builders have posted journals and slide shows of their boatbuilding experiences, and these can be a good resource for learning alternative tricks.

- Boatdesign.net.
  This website connects boat designers and boatbuilders.

- Building-strip-planked-boats.com.
  This is the website for this book. Look here for updates and corrections to the book as well as useful information. Includes links to all the websites included in this list plus any new sites I come across as time goes on.

- Duckworksmagazine.com.
  This online magazine is dedicated to messing about in small boats.

- KayakForum.com.
  This is a discussion board hosted by the author for people interested in building kayaks but open to people building any kind of small boat.

- WoodenBoat.com/forum.
  This forum is hosted by *WoodenBoat* magazine and covers all topics related to wooden boats.

- *Wood Handbook.* fpl.fs.fed.us/documnts/fplgtr/fplgtr113/fplgtr113.htm. This publication from the USDA Forest Products Laboratory discusses wood as an engineering material. It is also available as a print publication.

Bibliography

Strip-planking has been around for quite a while now, and there are several good books available on the subject. While this book attempts to be comprehensive, you would probably be well served by exposure to alternative ideas from other books. If you are a novice woodworker, there are good books about using hand tools and keeping them sharp that go into more detail than is permitted by the scope of this book.

Brown, J. D. *Rip, Strip, & Row! A Builder's Guide to the Cosine Wherry.* Larkspur, CA: Tamal Vista Publications, 1985. Instructions for building a rowing boat.

Folsom, Randy. *Strip-Built Canoe: How to Build a Beautiful, Lightweight, Cedar-Strip Canoe.* North Charleston, SC: BookSurge, 2007. A newer book on building canoes.

Gardner, John. *Building Classic Small Craft: Complete Plans and Instructions for 47 Boats.* Camden, ME: International Marine, 2004. A tour-de-force book on small boat building from one of the saviors of skills. It never hurts to go back and see how small wooden boats were originally built.

Gerr, Dave. *The Nature of Boats.* Camden, ME: International Marine, 1995. A wide-ranging treatise on how boats work—from design through construction and use.

Gilpatrick, Gil. *Building a Strip Canoe: Plans for Eight Canoes, plus Paddles and Cane Seats.* Rev. ed. Freeport, ME: Delorme Mapping Company, 2002. The book I originally learned strip-building from. Some of the techniques are a bit out of date, but the attitude of getting a boat on the water is a good one.

Gougeon, Meade. *The Gougeon Brothers on Boat Construction: Wood and West Systems Materials.* 5th ed. Bay City, MI: Gougeon Bros., 2005. Written by the makers of West Systems epoxy with their products in mind. This a large reference with a lot of information about building boats with wood and epoxy.

Hazen, David. *Stripper's Guide to Canoe-Building: With Drawings.* Larkspur, CA: Tamal Vista Publications, 1983. An early guide to building canoes and kayaks. Includes full-size drawings of the boats.

Lee, Leonard. *The Complete Guide to Sharpening.* Newtown, CT: Taunton Press, 1995. Sharp tools work better. This book will teach you how to get your tools sharp.

Manley, Atwood. *Rushton and His Times in American Canoeing.* Syracuse, NY: Syracuse University Press, 1968. J. Henry Rushton was one of the premier builders of the golden age of canoeing in the 1880s. The book includes offsets for some boats that could be adapted to strip-plank construction.

McCarthy, Henry "Mac." *Featherweight Boat-building: A WoodenBoat Book*. Brooklin, ME: WoodenBoat Books, 1996. Plans and instructions for strip-building a Wee Lassie double-paddle canoe.

Moores, Ted. *Canoecraft: An Illustrated Guide to Fine Woodstrip Construction*. Toronto: Firefly Books, 2000. The introduction to cedar-strip and epoxy canoe building for many builders and a valuable resource. Includes offsets for several canoes.

———. *Kayakcraft: Fine Woodstrip Kayak Construction*. Brooklin, ME: WoodenBoat, 1999. A follow-up to *Canoecraft* that also describes some kayaks. Includes offsets for several kayaks.

Moores, Ted, and Greg Rössel. *Kayaks You Can Build*. Buffalo, NY: Firefly Books, 2004. A book about plywood kayak construction, but the fiberglassing skills required are the same as for strip-planking.

Olivette, Michael J., and John D. Michne. *Building an Adirondack Guideboat: Wood Strip Reproductions of the Virginia*. Utica, NY: Nicholas K. Burns Publishing, 2005. Building a traditional-looking Adirondack guideboat using modern strip-built methods.

Rössel, Greg. *The Boatbuilder's Apprentice: The Ins and Outs of Building Lapstrake, Carvel, Stitch-and-Glue, Strip-Planked, and Other Wooden Boats*. Camden, ME: International Marine, 2007. An overview of a wide variety of boatbuilding techniques.

Schade, Nick. *The Strip-Built Sea Kayak: Three Rugged, Beautiful Boats You Can Build*. Camden, ME: Ragged Mountain Press, 1998. My first book on building kayaks. Includes offsets for three kayaks.

Van Leuven, Susan. *Illustrated Guide to Wood Strip Canoe Building*. Atglen, PA: Schiffer Publishing, 1998. Color photographs of all stages of building a canoe.

———. *Woodstrip Rowing Craft: How to Build, Step by Step*. Atglen, PA: Schiffer, 2007. Color photographs of building a rowing boat.

Watson, Aldren A. *Hand Tools: Their Ways and Workings*. New York: W. W. Norton & Company, 2002. A good guide to using hand tools.

Index

Index